T3-BPL-635

Vocational and Professional Capability

Also available from Continuum

Philosophy of Education Richard Pring
Perspectives of Quality in Adult Learning Peter Boshier

Vocational and Professional Capability

An Epistemological and Ontological Study
of Occupational Expertise

Gerard Lum

continuum

Continuum International Publishing Group

The Tower Building   80 Maiden Lane, Suite 704
11 York Road   New York
London, SE1 7NX   NY 10038

www.continuumbooks.com

British Library Cataloguing-in-Publication Data
A catalogue record for this book is available from the British Library.

ISBN: 9781847061188 (hardcover)

Library of Congress Cataloging-in-Publication Data
Lum, Gerard.
  Vocational and professional capability: an epistemological and ontological study of occupational expertise/Gerard Lum.
       p. cm.
  Includes bibliographical references.
  ISBN 978-1-84706-118-8 (hardback: alk. paper)
  1. Vocational education–Great Britain. 2. Professional education–Great Britain. 3. Skilled labor–Great Britain. I. Title.

  LC1047.G7L86 2009
  370.11'30941–dc22   2009008788

Typeset by BookEns, Royston, Herts.
Printed in Great Britain by the MPG books Group, Bodmin and King's Lynn

Contents

Acknowledgements

Grateful acknowledgements are due to Wiley-Blackwell for permission to use material from the following articles: 'Where's the Competence in Competence-based Education and Training?' *Journal of Philosophy of Education* (1999) 33, (3), 'Towards a Richer Conception of Vocational Preparation' *Journal of Philosophy of Education* (2003) 37, (1) and 'On the non-discursive nature of competence' *Educational Philosophy and Theory* (2004) 36, (5). I am profoundly grateful to Professor Christopher Winch for his encouragement and discussions which have provided much enjoyable and profitable philosophical stimulus. I also wish to take this opportunity to express my indebtedness to the late Dr Peter Perkins with whom I was able to rehearse in conversation many of the arguments of this book in the early stages of its development. Most of all, thanks are due to my wife Sarah, for her unstinting patience and support, having endured and even encouraged my philosophic preoccupations.

To the memory of Bobby

Introduction

This study is concerned with vocational and professional capability, by which is meant the entirety of those skills, competences, capacities, perceptions, attitudes and forms of knowledge which a person might require in order to fulfil an occupational role. I use the term 'capability' advisedly in place of the more customary 'skill' or 'competence'.[1] As we shall see, terms such as 'skill' and 'competence' come to us replete with an accumulation of conceptual baggage. For example, to use the term 'skill' is, for some, to imply merely some kind of physical or manual dexterity; in psychology it has certain behaviourist associations; in sociology 'skilled' has connotations of working class, blue collar, etc.; when used politically the term can refer to a specific category of trade union membership. All of these uses are to be found in the literature in connection with the vocational aspects of education and yet it might be said that none of them are entirely in accord with how the term is more commonly understood when describing an occupation. For 'skilled' has long been a term of approbation to acknowledge the often considerable understanding involved in knowing how to proceed in a particular activity – skilled workers being distinguished from unskilled more by virtue of what they know than by what they do.[2] The term 'competence', brought to prominence by the growth of competence-based education and training (CBET), is likely to provoke even more diverse reactions. For some it represents the very essence of what is required for consummate performance, while for others the term is at best epistemologically ambiguous, and at worst indicative of a deeply impoverished conception of the educational enterprise. Given such diverse interpretations of these terms, it is in the hope of avoiding prejudgement of the issues that the phrase 'vocational capability' is employed. But in order to emphasize that it is not some special 'concept' that is being delineated I will use it interchangeably with 'competence', 'skill', etc., and where a specific meaning is intended I will make this clear in the text.

The study arose from a personal dissatisfaction with certain theoretical assumptions in relation to the notions of 'skill', 'training', 'competence', etc., which have persisted in the education literature throughout the latter half of the twentieth century and continue today. Many of these assumptions run counter to my own intuitions about the nature of vocational capability and seem unhelpful in providing solutions to many questions relating to recent developments in vocational and professional education, both in the UK and elsewhere, namely the tendency towards 'competence-based' 'outcomes-based' or 'skills-based' approaches, a tendency which has impacted on vocational and mainstream education alike.

A central aim of this book is to show why these kinds of approaches are fundamentally wrong-headed. This is not, of course, an empirical claim about the quality of provision in universities, training schools or further education colleges. Rather, it is to say that current official arrangements are irredeemably antithetical to true educational concerns and as such necessarily detract from the best efforts of educators and institutions to produce capable practitioners; insofar as educators do succeed in this endeavour they do so *in spite of* current arrangements rather than because of them.

But the target here is not merely that of current policy. As already intimated, underlying the arrangements which have come to predominate in education over the past two or three decades are a number of interconnected theoretical assumptions which might be summed up as follows. First, there is the assumption that skills, competences or capabilities are such as can be non-problematically related to definite ends or 'outcomes' and that they are generally amenable to being tied down to clear-cut specifications or rules. Second, there is the assumption that skills, competences, etc. are 'inert' in the sense that a person's view of the world is not transformed by undergoing training or possessing skills. And third, there is a certain kind of epistemological assumption: the idea that there are essentially two kinds of knowledge, a knowing *how* and a knowing *that*, and that it is appropriate for occupational capability to be associated predominantly, if not exclusively, with the former rather than the latter.

Now this way of thinking about the vocational is neither new nor unique; assumptions of this kind can be traced back at least as far as Aristotle and are certainly long-standing in the education literature. They might be said to represent the 'common-sense' view of the vocational and as such can be found supporting the most diverse range of causes imaginable. It is a characterization just as likely to be embraced by the industrialist for its implicit instrumentality as it is by the trade unionist who might have cause to be suspicious of the overly academic or theoretical. It goes almost without saying that these are the very assumptions espoused with almost religious fervour by those who have a stake in the 'NVQ industry'.[3] And ironically, it is precisely this characterization of the vocational which has long been propounded so vigorously by many philosophers of education in order to distance the vocational from a liberal education with the intention of protecting the latter from vocationalizing tendencies. 'Ironically' because, ultimately, this characterization has given encouragement to those who believe that by terminological sleight of hand (e.g. by referring to so-called 'thinking skills') these same characteristics can be extended to the wider educational enterprise. But most significant of all is that this conception of the vocational is on all fours with the bureaucratic imperative to standardize and impose accountability – the inevitable accompaniment to increased state involvement in vocational education and training (VET) in recent times. And this provides at least part of the explanation why these long-standing assumptions – for so long implicit in much theorizing about education and held in common by the most unlikely of bedfellows – have recently come to dominate so completely official policy on vocational provision and assessment. Suffice it to say that notwithstanding this almost universal assent, I intend to show that each and every one of these long-held assumptions about the vocational is completely and utterly mistaken.

This study is driven by two concerns, one theoretical and one practical. On the one hand a concern that prevailing accounts in the literature of what it is to be vocationally capable are inadequate and philosophically incoherent. On the other hand a concern that these shortcomings have resulted in the failure to formulate a coherent and effective critical response to recent developments in vocational and professional education. In setting out to answer the question of what it is, epistemologically and ontologically speaking, for someone to be vocationally capable I offer a threefold critique of what I argue is the prevailing view. First, I set out to reveal its conceptual incoherence; second, I demonstrate that its philosophical and methodological underpinnings are untenable; and third, I propose an alternative, theoretically more coherent account of vocational and professional capability. One overarching aim, however, is therapeutic: to explain how circumstances could have conspired to bring about a state of affairs which is profoundly and irredeemably adverse to the provision of effective vocational and professional education.

It may be useful to say a brief word about how this study developed during the writing. In the early stages I took the issue of occupational capability to be essentially an epistemological matter, assuming that the issue was one of clarifying what it is a person *knows* when he or she is competent, skilled, etc. However, my thinking on this was to be taken in another direction by two very different philosophical projects. The first was John Searle's book *The Construction of Social Reality*. In his book Searle poses the question of how is it possible for there to be 'objective' facts about the world which are entirely dependent upon human agreement. How is it possible, for example, for it be a matter of objective fact that a person is married, has won at chess, is President of the United States, and so on. His answer is to suggest that these kinds of facts refer to a constructed social reality, an ontology of spectacular complexity which *we* create. It seemed to me that much of what Searle was saying could apply equally to the 'facts' relating to vocational capability, and that they too could be said to refer to a similarly complex ontology the complexity of which goes largely unrecognized because we *learn* to see it as a simple phenomenon. It was thus that I came to the view that questions about the nature of vocational capability are first and foremost ontological questions.

At the same time I felt there were certain problems with Searle's account, certain inconsistencies relating to his attachment to philosophical realism and a correspondence notion of truth, which remained unresolved. Indeed, the second thing that influenced the direction of this study and which ultimately made it possible to ameliorate Searle's account of 'constructed social reality' was my becoming aware of the acute significance of the work of Martin Heidegger.[4] It was clear that Heidegger's 'analytic of everydayness' had profound implications for any understanding of vocational or professional capability. Having been published well over half a century earlier, not only does Heidegger's work foreshadow much of Searle's ontology of social 'reality', but it also avoids some of the difficulties faced by Searle's account. However, what remained valuable about the kind of picture suggested by Searle, was that in being generally representative of the prevailing consensus in modern Western societies – a consensus centred on the foundational status of empirical science – it seemed to provide a better purchase on many of the 'common-sense' assumptions I wished to critique. It was thus that I set out to develop an account consistent with Searle's as a default position, while at the same time proposing a philosophically more comprehensive and ultimately more coherent position based on ontological considerations suggested by Heidegger's work. Consequently, the conception of vocational and professional capability that is developed here benefits both from Searle's notion of 'constructed social reality' and from Heidegger's account of 'Being-in-the-world'.

Background to the problem

For a great many occupations the history of vocational preparation is a history of ever-increasing state or quasi-official involvement, accompanied by a similarly incremental trend towards the standardization and bureaucratization of occupational skills and training provision. It is possible to track the progress of this kind of tendency in the UK from the establishment of the Mechanics Institutes in the mid-nineteenth century (see Cotgrove, 1958), through the formation of the first industrial training quangos and then on to what, for many, is the apotheosis of vocational standardization: the highly bureaucratic 'competence-based' procedures of the National Vocational Qualification (NVQ). Importantly, since the tendency towards standardization and bureaucratization invariably involved attempts to try to make formal and explicit that which previously had tended to be passed tacitly from master to apprentice, from practitioner to trainee, we might say that an important feature of this increasing state involvement was that it caused vocational education and training (VET) provision increasingly to be linked to the capacity to articulate or specify the exact nature of skills and capabilities required. Indeed, John Dewey (1966) recognized precisely this modern 'disposition to make explicit and deliberate vocational implications previously tacit' (p. 313). But the more immediate point here arises from the fact that, given the likelihood of dissension on these matters, it was also a tendency which raised the prospect of serious consideration being given to the nature of the skills required for a given occupation. In this sense we might say that it was inevitable that increasing state involvement in VET would eventually draw attention to important questions about the precise nature of skill, competence and training.[5]

From the 1960s in the UK, with growing state involvement and a succession of controversial government VET initiatives, there was no shortage of contributions to the literature relating to VET policy. Commentators were increasingly preoccupied with questions such as whether the provision of training was such as to serve the best interests of industry (Corfield, 1991; Guy, 1991), commerce (Jarvis and Prais, 1991), unemployed youth (Ainley and Corney, 1990), adults (Edwards, 1991), women (Wickham, 1985), and so on. However, VET still received relatively little attention from British philosophers of education. Relatively little of the literature of philosophy of education of this period – a literature largely preoccupied with conceptions of liberal education and the radical responses to it – dealt specifically with matters of vocational preparation, with the notions of skill, competence or training. Perhaps this was because the vocational simply did not hold a necessary fascination for philosophers. We get an inkling of this perhaps in Richard Peters' (1977) claim that concepts such as education and politics are 'philosophically interesting in ways in which engineering is not' (p. 139). But behind this self-confessed lack of interest lay an identifiable philosophical stance towards the vocational aspects of education – certain assumptions relating to notions such as skill and training which were implicit in the way that many philosophers delineated 'the concept of education'. So widespread were these assumptions that it will be argued here that they can effectively be regarded as an 'orthodoxy'.

Although there is no evidence to suggest that this orthodoxy ever had a direct influence on VET practice, nevertheless these underlying assumptions continued to persist in the literature. There were, of course, notable exceptions to this quiet consensus: commentators who shared neither the same methodological approach to the analysis of concepts nor the same presumptions about vocational capability. Of particular importance on this score were those who drew attention to the essentially tacit nature of skills and abilities, for this seemed to point in an entirely different direction to the prevailing consensus. It is perhaps significant that the two main champions of this approach, Michael Polanyi and Donald Schön, were neither British nor connected with British philosophy of education.

It was with the introduction of competence-based education and training (CBET) that philosophical interest in the vocational first began to stir and ideas relating to skill and competence began to attract unprecedented attention. Initially, discussion centred upon concerns that the introduction of the competence-based National Vocational Qualification (NVQ) into further education threatened to damage the quality of skills provision in the UK (Hyland, 1990; 1991a; 1991b; 1991c; Hodkinson, 1991; Smithers, 1993). But as the competence approach spread downwards into schools and upwards into higher education the growing political and managerial preoccupation with 'competences' and 'skills' induced a new anxiety and a more urgent need to scrutinize those 'concepts' which had previously been of little philosophical interest. By the 1990s, a substantial literature had begun to accumulate dedicated to either expounding upon or criticizing 'the concept of competence' and it was thus that many of the assumptions which had for so long been implicit – particularly in the liberal portrayal of the academic–vocational divide – now came to the fore and came to be of practical import. It is with a consideration of these assumptions that this study begins.

Overview of the argument

I begin by observing that it is possible to discern a pattern of inter-related theoretical assumptions in the literature relating to VET, assumptions which can be traced from the period in which ordinary language techniques became predominant in philosophy of education through to the present day. I suggest that so widespread have these ideas become, that it is appropriate to think of them as constituting a kind of orthodoxy and that many of these assumptions remain prevalent in much theorizing about education today, particularly with respect to the relationship between the academic and the vocational. I also suggest that these same theoretical assumptions can be seen to have substantive practical consequences: underpinning current competence-based approaches to VET and demands for a skills-based general curriculum, while also shaping the critical response to such developments.

Examining the means by which these assumptions are justified in the literature, I show that their philosophical underpinnings can be traced back to the positivism and ordinary language techniques of Oxford philosophy. I examine this philosophical background in some detail along with the criticisms which have been directed at it. The implications of Oxford philosophy for philosophy of education generally, and for the orthodox conceptions of skill and training in particular, are then explored. I conclude that the ordinary language techniques of analysis fail to support the orthodox claims relating to concepts such as skill and training and that, under scrutiny, the putatively 'objective' and value-free analyses by which the orthodox concepts are delineated turn out to be substantively value-laden, employing spurious linguistic reasoning in order to support certain social, political and cultural prejudices.

Noting that the distinction between 'knowing how' and 'knowing that' occupies a central position in the orthodoxy, one widely acknowledged to be of epistemological import, I examine this dichotomy in the context of Gilbert Ryle's argument before turning to consider its implications for education. After examining the behaviourist implications of Ryle's argument and the sort of criticisms which might be directed at these, I challenge the assumption that 'knowing how' and 'knowing that' denote two epistemologically distinct kinds of knowledge. First, I demonstrate that there is no consensus on how they are to be distinguished and that how the distinction is interpreted is entirely dependent upon the interpreter's wider purposes. Second, I show that by Ryle's own account the distinction is really about the evidential conditions of our claims about the knowledgeable states of others – hence the idea that it represents two kinds of knowledge points to something of an inconsistency in Ryle's thesis, one caused in part by his reliance on ordinary language techniques. I go on to show how the erroneous assumption that the distinction denotes two kinds of knowledge not only has intensely divisive educational and social consequences, but also is fundamentally inimical to providing a coherent epistemological account of vocational capability. I then suggest a preliminary resolution of the 'knowing how–knowing that' dichotomy by invoking Michael Oakeshott's notion of knowledge as a 'manifold of abilities'.

Of central concern in this study is the issue of 'competence-based' education and training. In Chapter 4 I argue that one of the consequences of the continuing influence of ordinary language techniques in philosophy of education is that it has led to a radical misinterpretation of the competence issue and a failure on the part of critics to correctly isolate CBET's unique, identifying features. After examining claims on both sides of the 'competence debate' I show that the prevailing tendency to identify CBET with 'competence' is fundamentally mistaken and that the competence approach is more properly characterized by its methodological strategy of employing statements to describe 'competence' and 'outcomes'. Attention is drawn to CBET's implicit assumption that such statements can non-problematically describe human capabilities and some preliminary objections are considered. Of particular importance on this score is the fact that the demand for precise specifications causes an 'ontological shift' in the focus of the specification, something which, again, can be seen to be socially divisive in being of greater detriment to the epistemic estimation of some occupations than others. I suggest that the seemingly innocuous suggestion that such statements simply describe the 'facts' relating to competence cannot properly be evaluated until we have explored more fully what it is, ontologically speaking, to be skilled, competent or vocationally capable.

Drawing on the work of John Searle it is proposed that such facts might be thought of as referring to a 'constructed' social reality, an ontology of extraordinary complexity that I suggest has profound implications for our understanding of vocational and professional capability. After outlining some of the main features of Searle's constructivist thesis it is noted that certain aspects of his position – based upon philosophical realism and a correspondence conception of truth – are inherently problematic. I argue that Heidegger's conception of Being-in-the-world indicates a possible resolution of some of these difficulties and provides a more coherent ontological account of human engagement. However, recognizing that Searle's position is more generally representative of the prevailing consensus in modern Western societies – a consensus centred on the foundational status of empirical science – I suggest that it will also be useful to develop Searle's account as a 'default position' from which to critique the orthodox conception of vocational capability. To that end some important areas of correspondence and divergence between Searle and Heidegger are explored. It is concluded that whichever position we adopt, the inadequacies of the orthodoxy, with its empiricist/objectivist assumptions, are manifest and that a different kind of explanation and a different conception of 'objectivity' must be adopted if we are to provide a more coherent account of vocational capability.

Next, I begin to set out an alternative conception of vocational and professional capability based upon Searle's notion of constructed social reality and Heidegger's account of Being-in-the-world. I show how Searle's thesis concerning the assignment of function and his conception Background, allied with Heidegger's 'analytic of everydayness', provide valuable insights into the nature of human capabilities; capabilities which at their most fundamental constitute the means by which we are able to perceive, experience and give meaning to the world around us. I refer to Abercrombie's work on perception, in particular her claim that perception involves the application of 'schemata' and unconscious processes of interpretation and judgement, in order to develop the idea that the way we see the world is profoundly contingent and value-laden. Noting the substantial degree of congruence between these very different perspectives, I argue that the kind of primordial understandings and abilities they suggest are broadly consistent with a conception of occupational capability based upon Oakeshott's account of knowledge as a manifold of abilities. Moreover, I also suggest that such a conception serves to indicate the profound inadequacy of accounts of vocational capability couched in terms of descriptions of behaviour or propositional knowledge.

One of the most important theoretical issues for VET and yet one of the least discussed in the literature is that of 'rules'. I note the existence of two radically opposed positions on this matter. On the one hand there are those who are keen to stress the importance of such things as 'judgement' and 'reflection' and who would take the view that the highest of human achievements arise from the autonomous creativity of the individual – rather than from behaviour which is 'rule-governed'. On the other hand there are those who would argue that whenever it makes sense to say that there is a 'right' and a 'wrong' way of doing something, then it follows that that activity must necessarily be rule-governed. The philosophical merits of these two positions are considered through the work of Michael Oakeshott and Peter

Winch respectively. It is suggested that in order to extricate a more coherent conception of rule-governed behaviour it is necessary to distinguish three fundamentally different kinds of rules: regulative, explanatory and constitutive. Examining the first two of these it is suggested that while each might be seen to play some part in skilled or competent performance, there are profound difficulties with the idea that either is sufficient to provide an account of vocational capability as something which is essentially rule-governed.

Having dismissed the possibility that either regulative or explanatory rules are sufficient for rule-governed behaviour, I turn next to consider how the notion of constitutive rules might be said to relate to vocational capability. Examining them first in the context of Searle's constructivist thesis, I concur with Searle in acknowledging that people have the ability to evolve practices which are 'functionally equivalent' to explicit constitutive rules. I suggest, however, that under scrutiny there are difficulties with his account and that the phenomenon he describes is actually indicative of a more fundamental phenomenon – what I refer to as the innate constitutive structure of the Background. In contrast to Searle, whose use of the term is restricted to formal social institutions, I suggest that the notion of a constitutive rule is fundamental to any meaningful behaviour. However, I also acknowledge that this conception of rule-governed behaviour leaves us in need of an explanation of how it is possible for vocational capability to be a social phenomenon. Noting the existence in the literature of claims to the effect that skill is a 'social construct', these claims are examined before being rejected in favour of an alternative strategy. Invoking Anthony Giddens' notion of the duality of structure it is argued that vocational capability is 'socially constructed' by virtue of the capacity human beings have for the reflexive understanding of recursive practices.

Returning to consider CBET in light of all this, it is concluded that CBET's strategy of employing 'competence statements' to provide precise descriptions of competence is based upon certain untenable assumptions relating to the semantic status of such statements and the ontological and epistemological constructs to which they are intended to correspond. Considering CBET's claim to be able to *infer* competence, it is argued that CBET necessarily *precludes* the use of inference in making judgements about people's capabilities. Importantly, this shows CBET to be fundamentally at odds with the established legal understanding of worker competence and the processes employed in law to judge competence. It is concluded that such considerations are of devastating consequence for the entire project of competence-based and skills-based education and training.

The study concludes by considering various theoretical implications of the proposed alternative conception of occupational capability. The orthodoxy is re-evaluated in the light of this proposed alternative and its inadequacies more clearly identified. Finally, I consider the implications of this for the issue of the vocational–liberal divide and for the 'problem of justification' in higher education.

Notes

[1] No special connection is intended here with the notion of 'capability' as Amartya Sen and others have used it. Similarly, no special distinction is implied by my reference to the vocational and the professional – the theory developed here is common to *both*; only later will I suggest how the vocational and the professional might be differentiated in light of this theory.

[2] This distinction is brought out by considering that both might be seen to *do* things with more or less dexterity – it is the skilled worker's *understanding* of what he or she does that sets him or her apart.

[3] That is, the whole gamut of training providers and others who have a commercial interest in the provision of National Vocational Qualifications (NVQs), or in Scotland SVQs.

[4] It was Paul Standish's (1997) paper, 'Heidegger and the technology of further education', which first brought to my attention the acute significance of Martin Heidegger's work for our understanding of human involvements including, as Standish showed, those relating to vocational capability.

[5] Another development which might also be seen to have drawn attention to these questions is the 'rapid destruction and reconstruction of skills' (Harvey, 1990, p. 150); that is, changes to the occupational grouping of tasks – the 'flexibility' which has been identified as a characteristic of post-Fordist, postmodern production.

1

The Orthodox Conception of the Vocational

In the latter half of the twentieth century, the period during which modern philosophy of education effectively developed as a discipline, certain ideas relating to those concepts most closely identified with VET, those of skill and training, began to find expression in a burgeoning literature on philosophy of education. Perhaps somewhat surprisingly these ideas were not the result of any purposeful or extensive examination of the vocational enterprise, of the processes of training, or of what it is to be skilled; indeed, it might even be said that such matters tended to receive relatively scant philosophical attention. Rather, the references to skill and training which began to appear in the literature during this period tended to be subsidiary to other purposes, by-products of a very different project: that of elucidating 'the concept of education'.

It is well known that R. S. Peters was in the vanguard of such endeavours: it was he who did more than anyone else to 'put philosophy of education on the map' (Straughan and Wilson, 1987, p. 1) and who undertook what was probably the 'most rigorous and thoroughgoing analysis of the concept ever undertaken' (Hamm, 1989, p. 29). Not least among Peters' concerns – and he was certainly not alone in this – was to distance the business of education from vocational or instrumental ends: to be educated a person must 'exhibit some mastery of forms of thought and awareness which are not harnessed purely to utilitarian or vocational purposes' (Peters, 1973, p. 9). For Peters, one way of getting clearer about what education *is* was to be clear about what it is *not*. Thus it was that Peters 'led the way in establishing' (Bridges, 1996, p. 365) the distinction between 'the concept of education' and those concepts, such as training and skill, more typically associated with VET.

As Dearden (1986) notes, the arguments by which Peters made these distinctions were 'mainly linguistic' (p. 72). Adopting the strategies of Oxford philosophy Peters, together with many other philosophers of education, came to see the prime task of philosophy as one of finding the 'logically necessary conditions for the use of a word' (Hirst and Peters, 1970, p. 6): 'what we do is examine the use of words in order to see what principle or principles govern their use. If we can make these explicit we have uncovered the concept' (*ibid.*,

p. 4). On this view it is regarded to be of some import to note, for example, that 'We talk more naturally of "educating the emotions" than we do of training them' (Peters, 1980, p. 93). This preoccupation with language use was defended on the grounds that it is essential to obtain clarity in the use of terms:

> Clarification of what exactly is meant, for instance, by 'instruction' and 'training', would serve to elucidate in what specific contexts it is proper to employ these terms and on what factors precisely the use of them turns. (Hirst and Peters, 1970, p. 84)

Now it must be stressed that it was never Peters' intention to add to our understanding of the vocational enterprise, nor is there any evidence to suggest that his work at any time has had any *direct* or intended influence on arrangements for VET. Nevertheless, Peters' work is highly significant here for two reasons. First, because his approach to philosophy of education was for a time highly influential: as we shall see, a generation or more of educational theorists adopted not only his distinctive methodological approach to analysing concepts such as skill and training but often echoed, almost verbatim, his pronouncements on them. To this day Peters' influence continues to reverberate in the work of many leading educational theorists and thus continues, albeit implicitly, to influence the way in which many think and theorize about education and how they respond to questions about skill and training. The second reason why Peters' work is of relevance here is that in his use of 'ordinary language' techniques he inadvertently draws attention to many of the assumptions about skill and training which find expression in everyday speech. 'Inadvertently' because while for Peters such analyses held the promise of conceptual clarification, it will be suggested here that they might more appropriately be regarded as providing an insight into many of the questionable presuppositions which not only remain as common currency in everyday language but also, and more importantly, can be seen to inform much of the thinking behind current policy-making and practice in vocational education and training. I want to suggest that these presuppositions, these ways of thinking about skill and training, might be thought of as constituting an 'orthodoxy', and that this orthodoxy is reproduced in the work of Peters and other philosophers of education as an identifiable pattern of inter-related theoretical conceptions. It is to this orthodoxy, these conceptions of skill and training, that we now turn.

The anatomy of a mistake

One characteristic which, for Peters, clearly distinguishes the concepts of skill and training from that of education is that of 'specificity'. He suggests that while 'education' suggests a 'lack of specificity' (1973, p. 7), the term 'training' 'has application whenever anything coming up to a clear-cut specification has to be learnt', or when 'there is some specifiable type of performance that has to be mastered' (*ibid.*, p. 15); something which can be 'tied down to specifiable rules' (*ibid.*, p. 16). The idea that the notions of training or skill are distinguished by being more readily disposed to specification is one which continues to find wide acceptance, as exemplified by Richard Pring (1995) when he tells us that 'The advantage of the concept of skill for curriculum planners is that it is quite specific' (p. 153). Similarly, Barnett (1994) says 'We cannot teach "skills" as such: we have to specify the skills we have in mind' (p. 57).

Closely related to the idea of specificity is that of narrowness, the idea that the vocational somehow lends itself to being 'narrowly specified' (Barrow, 1981, p. 58) or has a narrow focus (Kleinig, 1982; Hamm, 1989). On this view, one reason why we distinguish between education and training in ordinary language is because education is in some sense a broader enterprise than training: 'We distinguish between educating people and training them because for us education is no longer compatible with any narrowly conceived enterprise' (Hirst and Peters, 1970, p. 25; see also Langford, 1973). One interpretation of this 'narrowness' is reflected in the fact that in ordinary language we talk about people being 'trained *for* jobs, *as* mechanics, and *in* science' (original emphasis; Peters, 1973, p. 7), or, conversely, in the fact that 'We do not speak of educating a man as a scientist or as an historian anymore than we speak of educating a man as a cook or a builder' (Gribble, 1969, p. 10). On this view, then, the notion of training 'always suggests confinement' (Peters, 1973, p. 7).

For some, however, the narrowness associated with training is also related to the 'simple nature of the achievement and to the paucity of rational understanding and cognitive implications required for the mastery' (Hamm, 1989, p. 37). The idea that training 'lacks the wider cognitive implications of "education"' (Peters, 1980, p. 94), or that it is characterized by a 'lack of cognitive implications' (Chambers, 1984, p. 24), or that skills 'do not have a wide-ranging cognitive content' (Peters, 1966, p. 159; see also Peters, 1980, p. 95), is a recurring one.

Another frequently made claim is that the concepts of training and education are to be distinguished by the fact that they denote two fundamentally different kinds of knowledge. Under Peters' influence, Gilbert Ryle's famous distinction between 'knowing how' and 'knowing that' became widely used in the analysis of educational concepts. The distinction is one which remains as common currency in educational theory and not infrequently adopted for the purpose of distinguishing between training and education (see, for example, Henderson, 1961; Pring, 1995). Invoking Ryle's distinction, Peters (1980) insists that while education 'involves "knowing that" as well as "knowing how"' (p. 96), with many skills there is 'very little to know ... It is largely a matter of "knowing how" rather than "knowing that", of knack rather than understanding' (*ibid.*, p. 95; see also Peters, 1966). Skills and 'know-how' are exemplified by such things as 'riding bicycles, swimming or golf' (Peters, 1980, p. 95). Indeed, Peters' association of 'know-how' with the riding of bicycles seems to have had an enduring influence (see, for example, Pring, 1995, p. 146).

In similar vein Woods and Barrow (1975) see an important distinction to be made between the 'mechanical' or 'knowing-what-to-do kind of understanding' involved in vocational or instrumental ends, and the 'superior' 'reasoned understanding' or capacity to 'understand why' which characterizes the business of education. For Woods and Barrow the distinction is brought out by considering how a failure to understand might be remedied:

> Failure to understand in the sense of not knowing what to do can be remedied by giving a simple instruction or set of instructions – 'You just stick this wire in there'. (*Ibid.*, p. 47)

On this view, while someone may thus understand *what* to do, such instructions do not enable him or her to understand *why* and it is the latter which characterizes education.

The idea that being trained is somehow characterized by the possession of limited understanding is, again, one which appears to be a common theme:

> We often say of a man that he is highly trained, but not educated. What lies behind this condemnation? It is not that the man has mastered a skill of which we disapprove. For we could say this of a doctor or even of a philosopher who had mastered certain ploys or moves in argument ... It is rather that he has a very limited conception of what he is doing. (Peters, 1980, p. 93)

Accordingly, training is distinguished from education in that 'little emphasis is placed on the underlying *rationale*' (original emphasis; Peters, 1973, p. 15). The business of teaching is to be contrasted with training or instructing because teaching 'suggests that a *rationale* is to be grasped behind the skill or body of knowledge' (original emphasis; *ibid.*, p. 19). The sentiment is echoed in Pring's claim that, as regards skill, 'The role of theory takes a back place because the skilled craftsman knows from doing; he knows *practically*; success requires no theoretical analysis of principles behind the practice.' (original emphasis; Pring, 1995, p. 153). Thus one can be successfully trained without necessarily understanding the principles involved in what one has been trained to do (Ducasse, 1958).

In much the same way that Peters regards 'rationale' as being something distinct from skill, in the sense that it either may or may not accompany skilled performance, so too with intelligence – a person may be intelligent but lack the skill, or skilled but lack the intelligence:

we can say that a person is generally intelligent in the way he always approaches situations by trying to relate what he is doing to some over-all purpose; but he may lack the skill to bring off what he is trying to do. An intelligent carpenter or golfer may be too unskilled to be a good carpenter or golfer. (Hirst and Peters, 1970, p. 55)

Another point on which, it is claimed, the concepts of education and training diverge is in the different extents to which it is appropriate to associate each with behaviourist learning principles. While stressing the cognitively rich connotations of education, the concepts of training and skill are frequently linked with the behaviourist model. Perhaps one reason for this is the fact that the very term 'skill' has long been appropriated by behaviourists: as Bleth (1965) notes, skill is the 'primary component' (p. 249) in the behaviourist model. So, while being at pains to warn against a behaviourist approach to education, Peters' (1980) account of training is explicitly behaviourist: while an 'educated man' is distinguished 'not so much by what he does' as by his understanding, by what he 'grasps' (p. 96), training, Peters tells us, 'suggests the acquisition of appropriate habits of response in a limited situation' (*ibid.*, p. 94). Again, there is considerable unanimity for the behaviourist conception of training outlined by Peters: the idea that training is essentially about 'forming models of habit and behaviour' (Thomas Greene quoted in M. Greene, 1973, p. 172), that it is related to conditioning (Greene, 1973) or that its purpose is simply to produce 'a certain kind of performance' (Bereiter, 1972, p. 391). Similarly, Bigge (1982) takes training to be 'aimed primarily at acquiring habits or modes of behaviour. It is teaching someone *to do* so and so: it is shaping behaviour' (original emphasis; p. 117). The point is reiterated by Kleinig (1982) for whom the idea of training, again, is associated with forming habits and routine responses, being 'more directly connected with behaviour or performance than with independent mastery' (p. 49).

A further important distinction drawn between the concepts of education and training is in relation to what Peters (1973) calls the 'attitudinal aspect' (p. 8) of the sort of knowledge which he sees as an essential part of what it is to be educated. He contrasts this with the 'inert' understanding which characterizes being trained: a person's outlook or general view of the world is not transformed by being trained. In being educated, people 'must come to care about what they are doing' (Gribble, 1969, p. 11) whereas training, according to Ryle (1972), for example, is essentially value neutral: 'a proficiency can always be improperly as well as properly employed' (p. 48); training in penmanship may or may not make a forger. So while in order that we can reasonably claim to be educating someone it is essential that 'something of value is passed on' (Peters, 1980, p. 87); there is no such requirement in order for us to claim that we are training someone – we might, to use Peters' example, be training someone in the art of torture. Indeed, it is possible for training to be 'anti-educative' insofar as it is designed to produce uncritical obedience or unthinking conformity: 'A trained mind may well be indoctrinated and the trained character is all too often mechanical' (Kleinig, 1982, p. 49). Hence it is education, rather than training or instruction, which is rightly connected with the idea of judgement and character (see, for example, Maskell, 1999).

By way of consolidating these accounts of 'training' and 'skill' we can say that, on this view, they are characterized as follows: first, they are seen as related to specific or definite ends, and in this sense are characterized by a sort of confinement or narrowness of focus. Not only is it possible for these ends to be clearly specified, but so too can the skills required to achieve those ends, as can the processes of training necessary to impart those skills – skilled activity, in short, is something which can be 'tied down' to clear-cut specifications and identifiable rules. These concepts are distinguished by virtue of the fact that they denote a particular kind of knowledge: a knowing *how* as opposed to a knowing *that*. It is a kind of knowing characterized predominantly by its lack of cognitive implications and by a kind of understanding which is limited, for one can be trained or skilled without necessarily knowing the rationale or the theoretical principles that lie behind practice. On this account it is appropriate to associate training with behaviourist learning principles because training is primarily about 'shaping behaviour' and forming 'appropriate habits of response'. Furthermore, the notions of training and skill are inert in the sense that a person's view of the world is not transformed by undergoing training or possessing skills; such things are essentially value-neutral and hence have little bearing on, say, a persons character or their capacity for judgement.

Here, then, we have the outlines of what we might call the orthodox account of the concepts of skill and training. Before going on to examine their philosophical validity I want to turn our attention to the matter of how we should properly understand these analyses, for it turns out that there is considerable ambiguity concerning what it is exactly that is being described.

Getting clearer about the orthodoxy

We have already noted that it would be a mistake to regard the above analyses as being explicitly intended to add to our understanding of the vocational enterprise. It would be a misrepresentation of Peters to read him as suggesting that the concepts of skill and training he describes constitute a thoroughgoing account of vocational or professional capability, or that they are intended either to describe or prescribe how the business of vocational preparation is or should be carried out. But, that said, if the concepts presented in these analyses are not intended to be descriptive of the aims or processes of vocational preparation then we might reasonably ask *how do* these concepts stand in relation to VET? It would be bizarre for such recurrent references to training and skill not to have *some* bearing on VET, or some import for our understanding of what it is to be vocationally capable.

It is not difficult to discern the broad implicative thrust of these analyses for the concept of education. In short, what all of these authors intend is that our understanding of liberal education should be sufficiently rich and that we come to conceive of education as something which is profoundly life-enhancing. It is a conception which they regard as incompatible not only with being 'harnessed purely to utilitarian or vocational purposes' (Peters, 1973, p. 9) but also with being conceived of in terms of those concepts normally associated with vocational preparation. In broad terms, then, this much is clear. But what is fundamentally at issue here, and conspicuously disregarded in these analyses, is how these concepts, *as they are elucidated here*, might be understood in relation to VET. It would seem that although we have here what are claimed to be some of the salient features of the 'concepts' of training and skill, concepts which are steadfastly contrasted with the concept of education, we remain in a state of puzzlement about what exactly it is that is being described.

The only clear consensus seems to be that it is 'concepts' that are being described. Yet, there is a degree of ambiguity in what is meant by 'concept'; indeed, one commentator (Wilson, 1979) has expressed difficulty in understanding what some have meant when they talk about 'concepts' in the context of philosophy of education. He notes that some appear to regard 'concept' as equivalent to 'word' as, for example, when they talk about the 'use' of a concept. For Wilson, 'concept' means 'the range of meaning, or rules governing the use, of the term' (*ibid.*, p. 34); an interpretation which seems in broad agreement with Hirst's and Peters' belief that concepts can be uncovered by identifying the 'principles' which govern the use of words or the 'logically necessary conditions' for their use. As we have seen, the procedure used to establish the detail of these rules, principles or conditions is that of examining the de facto use of terms in ordinary language. Later we will consider the philosophical validity of these procedures, but the more immediate problem here is that despite all this talk about 'concepts', there remains a degree of ambiguity about what it is exactly that is being described.

Since it is a point on which the literature is noticeably reticent it is left to us to weigh the various possibilities. One possibility is that we might take the concepts of education and training as outlined in these analyses as intended to be exclusively applicable to the liberal and the vocational spheres respectively, i.e. the liberal enterprise being uniquely about 'education' and vocational preparation predominantly concerned with 'training'. Although rather a crude reading, there are some indications in the literature which seem to support this interpretation, as, for example, when Peters notes that 'we talk about a person being trained as a philosopher, scientist or cook ... we do not use the phrase "educated *as* a philosopher, scientist or cook"' (original emphasis; 1980, p. 93). Here, Peters seems to be suggesting that any and all of the preparation required for any kind of vocation is necessarily a qualitatively different exercise from that of education and that the line between education and training is essentially accordant with that drawn between the liberal and the vocational. But there are two immediate difficulties with this interpretation. First, many people would acknowledge that training and the acquisition of skills, even as conceived above, have some valid and useful part to play in a liberal or general education. The second difficulty is that, given the epistemological and cognitive thinness of the concepts of training and skill delineated in these analyses, to suggest that this is *all* that VET consists of is patently unconvincing: it is difficult to see how the vocational preparation of, say, a medical doctor could be conceived of in such impoverished terms. On the above view training might equip the doctor with certain physical skills, instil appropriate habits or behaviour, provide manual dexterity or the right 'knack' in the performance of tasks. But training, thus conceived, would be a far from sufficient preparation: the doctor will also require a considerable amount of knowledge, a deep understanding and an acute capacity for judgement, and will certainly be required to grasp the rationale behind what he or she is doing and know the reason why of things. Neither would it be sufficient for such understanding to be inert, for it would be essential to adopt the values appropriate to medical practice and come to care for what he or she is doing.

One way out of this difficulty and, at first sight, a more credible reading of these analyses might be to understand them as suggesting that both the liberal and the vocational spheres of provision comprise elements of education *and* training. Accordingly, we might acknowledge on the one hand that training and the development of skill have a place in the liberal sphere and, on the other, that vocational preparation can be thought of as consisting partly of training and partly of education – we do, after all, refer to vocational education *and* training. But then another difficulty arises: we might reasonably ask what exactly is achieved by making such a distinction. For if the concepts of skill and training really are as thin as these analyses suggest, and, as Peters indicates, they are rightly associated with the kind of capabilities involved in 'riding bicycles, swimming, or golf' (*ibid.*, p. 95), then the need to distinguish them from education effectively disappears. First, because the distinction becomes prosaic: we hardly need to be persuaded that there is a world of difference between being educated and being able to ride a bicycle. Second, because the threat to Peters' conception of a liberal education comes not from the proposal that it should be directed at such things as riding bicycles, but rather from demands that it should be directed at vocational or instrumental ends. Our acknowledgement that being educated is vastly different from being able to ride a bicycle is of little consequence unless we are able to ascertain that vocational capability *is* in some sense substantially like riding bicycles and this, as we have already seen, seems to be controverted by those instances of vocational capability which cannot adequately be accounted for in such impoverished terms. So even if we accept the idea that the concepts of skill and training, as delineated here, are features of both the liberal and the vocational spheres, it is difficult to see how this furthers our understanding of how the processes of VET are to be distinguished from those of education, and yet it is supposedly for this very reason that these concepts are being delineated. Furthermore, if we were to say that 'skill' is only one aspect of vocational capability, and 'training' is only one part of what would be required by way of a complete vocational preparation, then we would appear to be in need of further concepts to describe what it is to be more fully capable or what is required by way of a more complete preparation. On this interpretation, to describe plumbers as 'skilled' would presumably be an incomplete description of their capabilities and to say that they have been 'trained' would be to acknowledge receipt of only some part of a fuller preparation, and then perhaps only a minor part.

A variation on this reading, one which might be seen to avoid some of the above objections, would be to understand these analyses as relating to VET not in any definitive or absolute sense but rather as a more general indication of what the vocational *tends* towards. For example, it might be argued that although there are some instances of vocational capability which transcend the concept of 'skill' and that the preparation required in some such instances may go beyond the concept of 'training', nevertheless, there is an overall *tendency* for the vocational to exhibit the characteristics delineated in these analyses, and it is this tendency which distinguishes the notion of training from that of education. So, rather than claiming to be universally or comprehensively descriptive of all VET, or even some identifiable portion of it, on this reading these concepts might be understood as having a far looser meaning and as being pertinent to different occupations in different degrees.

On the face of it this is a fairly weak claim, but it is by no means innocuous. Part of its appeal – and the reason why it is likely to be adopted as a default position by those who hold the orthodox view – is that its ambiguity renders it largely impervious to criticism. Whether or to what extent the orthodox account is appropriate for describing the capabilities and preparation of, say, a doctor, a plumber or a supermarket shelf-filler becomes a moot point, and one where dissent from the orthodoxy must be argued case by case. But the most crucial feature of this interpretation is its inherent divisiveness, for to adopt such an interpretation is to be encouraged to discriminate between those occupations which are deemed to be more suitably described by the orthodox conception and those which are not. For example, we might take the view that the orthodox concepts of skill and training are entirely appropriate for the purpose of describing the capabilities and preparation of, say, a plumber, but that they are less, if at all, pertinent to the practice of architecture. Perhaps in the first instance this might be justified by pointing to differences in the nature of the work, but ultimately it would inevitably become necessary to discriminate on the grounds of alleged epistemological differences between occupations. Ronald Barnett (1994) typifies this sort of position when he claims to be able to place occupations along an 'axis' according to whether they are characterized more by 'formal knowledge' or by 'physical action'. We shall consider this sort of claim in more detail in Chapter 3; the point to note here is that when the orthodox concepts of skill and training are allied with assumptions of this kind they become the grounds for discriminating, not simply between the liberal and the vocational, but between the professions and the crafts, between white collar and blue collar, and so on. Suffice it to say that the questionable epistemological validity of such judgements and their potentially divisive consequences will be a recurring theme throughout this study.

It would appear, then, that it is extremely difficult to extract from these analyses any clear and consistent theoretical stance which might be non-problematically associated with the concepts they purport to elucidate. We might already begin to suspect that this lack of cohesion is due to some fundamental difficulty with these supposed 'concepts'. This is not, however, to suggest that the orthodoxy is in any way insignificant, for, as we shall see, the assumptions articulated in these analyses can be seen to have far-reaching theoretical and practical consequences.

Consequences of the orthodoxy

For evidence that these kinds of assumptions can have substantive practical consequences for VET we need look no further than current competence-based approaches to education and training. There is a remarkable degree of correspondence between the orthodoxy and the assumptions which underpin CBET methodology. This is not to say that the competence movement has purposefully sought to develop its methods by reference to this or indeed any theoretical position; indeed, it might even be said that there is a conspicuous lack of *any* theoretical justification for CBET's methods (Hyland, 1994). Rather, it would seem that the correspondence between the orthodox position and CBET is due more to the fact that the invocation of ordinary language usage which underlies the orthodox account – its preoccupation with what we mean when we use words such as skill or training – tends to coincide with CBET's naïve attempts to ground educational practice in essentially the same aphoristic commonplaces; often ascribing to such commonplaces a kind of 'slogan status' (*ibid.*, p. 27).

We might note that the very same presumptions about specificity and narrowness of focus which characterize the orthodox conception are at the heart of CBET methodology. Fundamental to CBET is the idea that it is possible, by means of functional analysis, to identify specific ends or outcomes and then isolate and focus on the individual capabilities which will attain those ends (see, for example, Debling, 1989, p. 87; Mitchell, 1989, pp. 56–9; Mathews, 1995, pp. 247–8). Even more fundamental to the competence approach is the idea that it is possible for such capabilities to be 'tied down' to identifiable rules and precise and clear-cut specifications – or, to use the terminology of CBET, specified by means of 'competence statements' (see, for example, Jessup, 1991). CBET can also be seen to adopt the orthodox assumption that there are essentially two discrete and separately identifiable epistemic forms or 'constructs' (Wolf, 1989): the idea that being competent is about having 'skills *and* knowledge' (my emphasis; Jessup, 1991, p. 57), a knowing how *and* a knowing that – usually described as 'performance' and 'underpinning knowledge'.

Perhaps most crucial of all – again a feature which CBET has in common with the orthodoxy – is CBET's inherent behaviourism. Frequently associated with behavioural psychology (Bull, 1985; Smithers, 1993), CBET, particularly in its NVQ guise, has been widely criticized for its behaviourist approach to assessment (Ashworth and Saxton, 1990; Hodkinson, 1992; Hyland, 1992, 1993a, 1993b, 1994). It has been pointed out that the 'most prevalent construct of competence is behaviourist. It rests on a description of behaviour' (Norris, 1991, p. 332), and that CBET employs 'simplistic behavioural objectives' (Collins, 1991, p. 90) which expressly make 'overt behaviour' the 'significant variable' in assessment (Marshall, 1991, p. 61). And as Terry Hyland (1997) has argued, competence strategies are 'not just contingently but *intrinsically* behaviouristic' (original emphasis; p. 492); it is an inherent feature of the competence approach.

There is, then, a substantial degree of correspondence between the orthodox conception of skill and many of the assumptions which either implicitly or explicitly underpin current competence-based approaches to education and training. Some might be surprised by the suggestion that theoretical precedents for CBET can be found in the work of 'liberal' philosophers of education, not least because CBET might appear to be fundamentally at odds with any conception of a liberal education.[6] In order to account for this incongruity we should note that there is one crucial difference between competence strategists and those who promote the orthodoxy as a defence of liberal education: while the orthodox concepts of skill and training were originally conceived as a way of differentiating the vocational and the liberal, the competence strategist simply recognizes no such distinction. As Gilbert Jessup (1991), then Director of the National Council for Vocational Qualifications, was keen to point out, CBET's approach is appropriate 'for all learning which is considered important or that people want' (p. 130); it is thus that CBET is able effectively to 'eradicate the distinction between education and training' (*ibid.*, p. 4). We might describe CBET's position by saying that while it enthusiastically embraces the orthodoxy, it dismisses the claim that such features are characteristic of training as opposed to education or that they constitute grounds for distinguishing training and education.

But it is not only in VET that the orthodoxy can be seen to have substantive consequences. Amid increasing political interest in skills, and galvanized by the prevailing view that they are 'central to economic success' (Campbell, 2000, p. 2), the orthodox assumptions relating to skill now find application far beyond VET. Everywhere there is ' "skills talk", the tendency to call all manner of human knacks, abilities, competencies, capacities, qualities and virtues alike "skills" ' (Blake, Smith and Standish, 1998, p. 56). In the 'language of performativity, of effectiveness' (Blake, Smeyers, Smith and Standish, 1998, p. 133) it is not 'barmy theory' (*ibid.*, p. 82) that individuals or nations require in order to succeed in the world, but skills and competences: '*Competence* becomes a common noun in a kind of aggressive reification: a practical skill that gets results' (original emphasis; *ibid.*). Hence, it is no longer, say, mastery of the subject that is a mark of excellence in the teacher but such things as 'communication skills'. Importantly, those who speak this 'contemporary language of skills' (Barnett, 1994, p. 55) do so in the idiom of the orthodoxy, for, just as with competence, it is precisely those features which the orthodoxy ascribes to 'skill' which gives it its political and managerial appeal. Above all, to apply the orthodox conception of skill to educationally complex phenomena is to be allowed to perpetrate the deception of representing such phenomena as essentially simple, quantifiable and non-controversial. It allows one to talk of such things as 'communication skills', 'problem-solving skills' or 'parenting skills' in ways which belie both the complexity of the capabilities indicated by these terms and the extent of what would be required in order to attain them.

Not surprisingly, the spread of 'skills talk' from VET to other educational sectors has met with fierce criticism. It has been argued that the new vocabulary of skills and competences not only 'represents an epistemological assault on the very character of what counts as reason in the university' (*ibid.*, p. 71) but also is fundamentally inappropriate for the vocational preparation of professionals (Pring, 1995).

Now what is crucially important here is that this counter-attack has been directed not at the orthodox assumptions which underpin this 'skills talk', but rather at the notion of skill per se. Barnett (1994), for example, in attempting to distance the university from the rationale of skills, reasons as follows: 'To say of someone that he or she is skilful is to damn with faint praise. It is to imply that he or she is merely skilful, no matter how complex the skills in question. A higher education designed around skills is no higher education' (p. 61). Richard Pring similarly militates against the notion of skill:

> The disadvantage of attaching so much importance to skill is that the concept fails to do justice to the other mental qualities and cognitive achievements which are so much more than skills ... Skills which make one competent are necessary but not sufficient; teachers need to be more than good at a craft ... communication is much more than a skill. It involves

sensitive understanding of the audience and an understanding of that which is to be communicated. (Pring, 1995, pp. 153–4)

Conceived in these terms – in terms of the orthodoxy, as something lacking in 'mental qualities and cognitive achievements' and 'understanding' – it could hardly be denied that 'the concept of skill' is indeed insufficient to account for the capabilities of teachers, or to denote what it is that is involved in communication. But this kind of argument requires closer attention. The obvious corollary of acknowledging that teachers need to be 'more than good at a craft' is that there are some occupations where this would not be a requirement: a craftsman, we might presume, would simply need to be 'good at a craft'. Moreover, the clear inference, on Pring's view, is that being 'good at a craft' is synonymous with the possession of skills; this is a crucial point for it indicates that the issue here is not merely one of semantics.[7] We are thus led to deduce that the notion of skill – conceived of as something lacking in 'mental qualities and cognitive achievements' and 'understanding' – may well be appropriate for describing the capabilities of a craftsman but it is not appropriate for describing those of a teacher.

Obviously, there is an immediate difficulty here, for it might be objected – albeit counter to the orthodoxy which Pring endorses – that being 'good at a craft' also demands certain mental capacities and forms of understanding; if this is so then Pring's grounds for distinguishing between the professions and the crafts seem to evaporate, along with his reasons for debarring the skills approach from the professions. Aware of this flaw, Pring attempts to head off the objection by re-stating the orthodoxy, complaining that 'it is a particular ploy of the vocational trainers to extend the concepts of skill to cover mental and personal qualities – judgement, imagination, understanding, shrewdness – which are very different from skills' (*ibid.*, p. 154). Yet it might equally be said that the reason why 'the vocational trainers' incorporate such qualities in the notion of skill is that, for them, *that* is what being skilled is. It is a dispute which is central to the concerns of this study; suffice it to say for the moment that ultimately, *pace* Pring, we shall have cause to take seriously the contention that being skilled necessarily involves certain 'mental and personal qualities'.

The main point here is that not for the first time the strategy of defending against the encroachment of the skills approach can be seen to be essentially one of, first, depicting skill as an epistemologically and cognitively impoverished phenomenon, and then, having portrayed the concept in sufficiently negative terms, pronouncing that it is fundamentally inappropriate for liberal/higher/professional or whichever sector of education is to be safeguarded from the encroachment of the skills/competence approach. Paradoxically, therefore, the tactic is one of actually reaffirming the very assumptions which motivate the skills/competence lobby, i.e. the orthodox assumptions.

The strategy flounders for several reasons. First, because it unintentionally lends support to the skills lobby by reaffirming the orthodoxy – it would, for example, be a very different tactic to reject the skills/competence agenda on the grounds that it entails an inadequate conception of skill or competence and is thus inadequate in any context. Second, because in being seen to disparage the 'concept of skill' the strategy has the appearance of railing against prevailing economic priorities – if not common sense. Third, because the somewhat dubious distinctions made between occupations or between educational sectors appear to be motivated more by protectionistic anxieties than by the discernment of any substantive epistemological or cognitive differences.[8]

This is not to deny the possibility of there being epistemological or cognitive differences between occupations; neither is it to concede anything to those who wish to extend the 'skills agenda' into higher education or the training of professionals. It is simply to note that the orthodoxy is firmly entrenched on *both* sides of the debate about skills – promoted both by those who would advocate a skills approach, and by those who would oppose it.

What is clear is that the orthodox conceptualization of skill and training is no mere idiosyncrasy but an identifiable set of inter-related assumptions which have been and continue to be of substantive theoretical and practical import. The assumptions which constitute this orthodoxy, first formally articulated by those who sought to defend liberal education from vocationalizing tendencies, are held in common not just by those who would promote competence approaches in VET and skills-based approaches in education generally, but also, importantly, by those who would wish to resist such tendencies. The question now is whether there is any coherent *philosophical* justification for these assumptions. Even if we already suspect that the assumptions which make up the orthodoxy are utterly implausible, we nonetheless stand in need of some explanation as to how a generation of philosophers of education could get it so wrong. It is to this philosophical background that we now turn.

Notes

6   Not all commentators would regard CBET as incompatible with a liberal education; see, for example, Bridges (1996).

7   The point here is that were it not for this equating of the notion of 'skill' with the capabilities of certain occupations – an association which, as we shall see, Pring makes explicit below – the disagreement might be taken to be simply about what is meant by the term 'skill'.

8   It has not gone unnoticed, for example, that 'Middle class professions such as medicine, law and architecture are remarkably unwilling to agree that their own qualifications – like plumbing and nursing – are vocational and competence-based' (TES, 1997).

2

Philosophical Foundations of the Orthodoxy

We have noted the way in which attempts to justify the orthodox conceptions of skill and training tend to employ philosophical methods which have their roots in what has become known as 'Oxford philosophy'. The term Oxford philosophy encompasses two main phases of philosophical activity, the first being logical positivism. Originating in Vienna between the two world wars, logical positivism was introduced into Oxford by A. J. Ayer in 1936 with his highly influential book *Language, Truth and Logic*, but there were also important influences from Cambridge, particularly from Moore, Wittgenstein, Russell and Whitehead. For those who came under the sway of logical positivism the essential and indeed sole task of philosophy was to determine the criterion of demarcation between sense and non-sense; that is, to distinguish between statements which are meaningful and those which are meaningless. On this view there are only two forms of meaningful, indicative statement. First, there are analytic statements such as those in mathematics and logic which are true or false by definition. If a statement is not analytic, then it must be synthetic and, for the logical positivist, meaningful if and only if it is empirically verifiable – if its truth or falsity is capable of being ascertained by experience. For the logical positivist, synthetic statements which could not be verified by either empirical science or direct experience (i.e. common sense) were to be regarded as empty claims based on groundless presupposition or subjective opinion. This, the central tenet of logical positivism, became known as the Verification Principle. For our purposes it is of interest to note here that since the only evidence acceptable for verifying statements about mental processes or intentional states is evidence of observed behaviour, verificationism inevitably tends towards behaviourism.[9]

The reign of logical positivism turned out to be short lived not least because it had effectively been refuted before it began. Karl Popper's *Logic der Forschung* (1934; published in 1959 as *The Logic of Scientific Discovery*) reiterated the point, long since established by Hume, that since a finite number of observations could not provide a basis for unrestrictedly general statements about the world, it is not possible for *any* scientific law to be empirically verified. Accordingly, not even science could meet the criterion of the

Verification Principle and, moreover, since the Verification Principle was itself neither analytic nor empirically verifiable, it too was by its own criterion meaningless. But it was logical positivism's other, and perhaps even more fundamental mistake which was to have the most lasting consequences – its assumption that the proper role of philosophy is that of establishing a criterion of meaning. With this, logical positivism effectively changed the conception of what philosophy is.

Wittgenstein's influence in this change was instrumental; indeed, it might be said that prior to Wittgenstein's (1978) pronouncement that 'All philosophy is a "critique of language"' (p. 19) philosophers would never have accepted the idea that philosophy could be restricted to matters of language or the uses of words (Mundle, 1979). Logical positivism inherited from Wittgenstein's *Tractatus Logico-Philosophicus* the idea 'that there are no genuine philosophical problems, and that all a philosopher can do is to unmask and dissolve the linguistic puzzles which have been proposed by traditional philosophy' (Popper, 1978, p. 70). The philosophical problems of more than two millennia were thus dismissed as emanating from an abuse or misuse of language; such problems, it was assumed, would simply evaporate once the linguistic mistakes were correctly diagnosed (Gellner, 1959). The mistake, as Peter Winch (1965) was later to say, was to assume that we can make a clear distinction between the world and the language we use to describe the world and then suppose that it is out of the latter that the problems of philosophy arise. Short lived though it was, logical positivism was a turning point: 'It was at that point in its history that philosophy in the empiricist tradition stopped regarding its task as the understanding of the world and saw itself as clarifying formulations in language …' (Magee, 1998, p. 48). In short, philosophy was no longer the aim of philosophy (see Scruton, 1997).

In the 1950s logical positivism came to be superseded by the second phase of Oxford philosophy: linguistic analysis or linguistic philosophy. While abandoning logical positivism's presumptions about the primacy of science as a first-order activity, linguistic analysis, nevertheless and rather oddly, retained logical positivism's assumption that the proper role of philosophy was the second-order activity of analysing language and getting clear about the meanings of words. Philosophy thus came to be regarded as being exclusively about language – about the clarification of concepts as expressed in words. According to Geoffrey Warnock (in conversation with Bryan Magee in the latter's *Modern British Philosophy*) it was G. E. Moore who 'led many philosophers to think that philosophy is *entirely* analysis – that the philosopher does not, so to speak, assert propositions on his own account but *only* analyses propositions asserted by others' (original emphasis; Magee, 1973, p. 117). One highly influential aspect of Moore's philosophy worth mentioning briefly here was his defence of common sense (see Moore, 1925): the idea being that there is a great deal we can know about the world, matters which we can justifiably regard as certain fact, simply by means of common sense. Indeed, linguistic philosophy was effectively an extension of this view; it was, as Gellner (1959) has argued, simply the 'buttressing up of common sense' (p. 32) by an oversimplistic reading of the later Wittgenstein's (1968) claim that 'the meaning of a word is its use in the language' (p. 20), though it is doubtful that Wittgenstein ever saw the role of philosophy as one of seeking out the 'correct' uses of words (see Halliday, 1990).

That this essentially anti-philosophical position subsequently came to dominate so much British philosophy was regarded by some as an intellectual catastrophe:

> To understate the matter as politely as I can, the commonsense view of the world can be the metaphysics only of the insufficiently seriously reflective. Russell, ruder than I, described it as the metaphysics of savages. (Magee, 1998, p. 53)

As Russell himself said in *The Problems of Philosophy*:

> common sense leaves us completely in the dark as to the true intrinsic nature of physical objects, and if there were good reason to regard them as mental, we could not legitimately reject this opinion merely because it strikes us as strange. The truth about physical objects *must* be strange. (Original emphasis; Russell, 1967, p. 38)

Under Austin's influence many came to regard everyday speech as a 'repository of philosophical truths' (Lyons, 1980, p. 28).[10] Gilbert Ryle provided one of the earliest explicit declarations of an exclusively linguistic approach to philosophy when he tentatively suggested that 'to inquire and even say "what it really means to say so and so" ... this is what philosophical analysis is, and this is the sole and whole function of philosophy' (Ryle, 1971, p. 61). Ryle's *The Concept of Mind* was to become the most important and influential work of linguistic analysis to emerge from the Oxford of this period and, as we shall see, it was to be a particularly important influence on some of the leading figures in the analytical philosophy of education.

It would be difficult to overstate the extent of the influence exerted by this 'powerful modern school of language analysts' (Popper, 1978, p. 70). In his philosophical autobiography Bryan Magee (1998) gives a revealing first-hand account of his own time at Oxford when the hegemony of Oxford philosophy was at its height and when the reign of the Verification Principle meant that, with the exception of logic, the whole of philosophy was effectively outlawed. As Magee says, philosophers became reluctant to say anything unless it could meet the standards of evidence required for scientific utterances and the term 'metaphysics' became a term of contempt for anything which couldn't. Philosophy consisted of the analysis of familiar words, eventually degenerating into 'a nit-picking dissection of any and every commonplace utterance' (p. 92):

if one studied philosophy at Oxford during that period, nearly all discussions and investigations were about some piece of linguistic utterance ... '*What exactly do you mean by* ...' became the commonest opening to a challenging question, and '*Suppose we wanted to say* ...' the commonest introduction to a conjecture; and in both cases this would be followed by a discussion of the word, or forms of words ... (Original emphasis; *ibid.*, p. 79)

Like Peter Winch, Magee remonstrates that there is a clear distinction to be made between philosophy conceived as an attempt to understand the world, dealing with questions about the extent to which we can have knowledge of it, and philosophy conceived as linguistic analysis with its discussions about meaning and detailed distinctions of linguistic usage. As Magee points out, even Locke, with his famous emphasis on the importance of getting clear about concepts, nevertheless demonstrates in his own work that he never saw the main task of philosophy as being either exclusively or even chiefly about language. For Magee, linguistic analysis 'can do no more than clarify what we are already in possession of' (*ibid.*, p.114); it cannot provide solutions to philosophical problems about non-linguistic reality. On Magee's view, only those who fail to recognize that reality presents us with philosophical problems could believe linguistic clarification to be the central task of philosophy. The linguistic analysts had effectively abandoned what had since Thales been the most important task of philosophy – that of understanding the world. In the same vein, Mundle (1979) argued that linguistic analysis constitutes a rejection of philosophy; it leaves serious philosophical problems untouched and derives from a fundamental misunderstanding of the relations between grammar and philosophy. We might say that the fundamental mistake made by the linguistic analysts is that which Schopenhauer (1969) had famously warned against when, in his critique of Kant, he made the point that philosophy should properly be regarded as a science (*Wissenschaft*) *in* concepts rather than *of* concepts. As Quine (1960) points out, while clarification may help either a physicist or a philosopher, it does not follow that either physics or ontology is 'really about language'. Similarly, Popper (1959; 1978) reminds us that the successful operation of science is not at all dependent on a continual debate about the meaning of its fundamental terms and that for philosophy to be so concerned is to preclude from discussion matters of any real philosophical substance. For David Bridges (1997), who has criticized the use of linguistic techniques in education, this kind of analysis reached its 'preposterous apotheosis' with R. M. Hare's claim that 'disputes between trade unions and management could be brought to an end if only we get clarity and agreement as to the meaning of the word "fair"' (pp. 181–2).

Although it was the logical positivists who had first pressed the term 'metaphysics' into a pejorative sense, using it to denote meaninglessness (Quine, 1969), their hostility to any kind of explanatory theory was shared by the linguistic analysts, who failed to realize that the linguistic distinctions they were making had little significance except in relation to a wider explanatory framework. Richard Rorty (1980) has pointed out that the very idea of conceptual analysis, of philosophy as the explication of meanings, is one which is rooted in an erroneous view of knowledge as accurate representation of reality and of the mind mirroring or reflecting, more or less accurately, that reality. According to Rorty, without this view of knowledge the idea that philosophy could consist in conceptual analysis 'would not have made sense' (p. 12). The crucial point here is that although linguistic philosophy rarely proffered any explicit, coherent doctrine or philosophical position, the distinctions drawn by linguistic analysts were nevertheless irredeemably grounded in implicit assumptions about the world.

In the absence of any supporting explanatory theory, such assumptions could only be justified by spurious linguistic reasoning. In 1959 Ernest Gellner identified numerous fallacious procedural rules which underpinned the methodology of linguistic analysis. First, 'the argument from the paradigm case' – which is to argue from the actual use of words to some claim about the world. Second, 'the generalised version of the naturalistic fallacy'; that is, the inference of answers to evaluative questions by recourse to the actual use of words. Third, 'the contrast theory of meaning', which is to assume that a term only has meaning if it is not entirely inclusive, its meaning dependent upon distinctions. Gellner concluded that the entire movement of linguistic analysis, with its 'impressionistic lexicography' (p. 265), was profoundly mistaken.

In another thoroughgoing critique of linguistic philosophy, C. W. K. Mundle (1979) showed that Austin, Ayer, Ryle, *et al.* were guilty of gross grammatical and logical errors. Mundle demonstrated that linguistic philosophy is characterized by what he called 'legislative linguistics'; that is, the espousing in the interests of a particular theory false assertions about what we do, or cannot, or may not, say – without having established the rules of language use upon which such assumptions are based. Mundle also showed how linguistic philosophers can be seen to invent rules about the use of language and then apply those rules as though they were a priori thereby deducing what we cannot or may not say, or what we do or do not mean when we use certain words, what Mundle calls 'a priori linguistics'.

In mainstream philosophy the 'linguistic turn' was relatively short lived: by 1956 Copleston, in his survey of contemporary philosophers, was able to report that there were few who would still assimilate philosophical problems to problems of language. Certainly by the 1970s the idea that philosophical problems could be resolved by appealing to linguistic usage had fallen into general disrepute (Passmore, 1988), even to the extent that a new generation of Oxford philosophers had come to regard it as 'impoverished and fraudulent' (Platts, 1979; see also Scruton, 1982). What the linguistic analysts had failed or simply not wanted to acknowledge was the simple fact that scrutinizing the use of words will not 'reveal significant non-contingent truths about reality' (Jonathan, 1985, p. 17). Despite its decline in mainstream philosophy, the linguistic methodology continued to have a strong influence in philosophy of education and in the 1970s British philosophy of education was still 'almost exclusively associated with the school of linguistic analysis' (Bridges, 1997, p. 181). When, eventually, the use of linguistic analysis in philosophy of education did decline it was perhaps not so much because of any explicit philosophical repudiation of its tenets, but more because 'people became bored with endless analysis of terms ... perhaps also because people came to question the relevance of these analyses and to expose some of the inconsistencies' (Halliday, 1990, p. 29). It is perhaps for this reason that while there are few philosophers of education who today would overtly and unconditionally endorse linguistic techniques, nevertheless, a residue of such techniques can be seen to persist in philosophy of education.

It is significant that even those who employed linguistic techniques in philosophy of education at times expressed reservations about the validity of the methodology. For example, Hirst and Peters (1970) warned against adopting a 'crude view of the relationship between words and things' (p. 12), saying that: 'To do conceptual analysis, unless something depends on getting clearer about the structure underlying how we speak, may be a fascinating pastime, but it is not philosophy' (*ibid.*, p. 10). However, they also adopted the Oxford line that 'getting clearer' *is* the priority and that the proper role of philosophy *is* precisely to be concerned with these 'second-order' kind of questions. So while warning against the expectation of finding 'a hard and fast set of logically necessary conditions for *all* uses of a word' (original emphasis; *ibid.*, p. 12), they nevertheless maintained an affinity for the linguistic method: 'We may not always be successful in our search for logically necessary conditions for the use of a word. But sometimes we may be' (*ibid.*, p. 6).

Oxford philosophy and philosophy of education

The logical positivism of Oxford philosophy provided philosophical under-pinning for the view, one which remains common currency in modern Western societies, that all discoverable, meaningful truths about the world are discoverable by scientific method, that all true facts about the world can be assimilated to scientific facts and that our common-sense view of the world is essentially correct. This perspective is on all fours with a conception of vocational capability centred on technical or instrumental rationality: the idea that vocational practice properly consists in utilizing 'objective' empirical scientific and technical knowledge in an entirely instrumental approach to the world. As Donald Schön (1996) put it: 'Technical Rationality is the Positivist epistemology of practice' (p. 31). And John Halliday has suggested that, in the context of educational research, linguistic or analytical philosophy of education (APE) can be seen to support and reinforce what is essentially an empiricist foundationalist epistemology:

By offering the possibility of hypostatizing meaning, APE has been supposed to guarantee that the assignation of the variables could be held constant throughout the research and its application so that the researchers could proceed according to models apotheosized by a commitment to empiricist epistemology and procedure. (Halliday, 1990, p. 27)

Both, as Halliday emphasizes, are essentially objectivist: the one claiming to be able to determine objective truth through empirical method, the other claiming to ascertain the objective meaning of words by examining how they are used, thus assuming the possibility of what we might call semantic certitude. Later we will see how these same empiricist/objectivist assumptions run through the prevailing conception of skill/training, not only explicitly informing Ryle's behaviourist account of intelligent action (and indirectly influencing Peters and many other philosophers of education), but also being pragmatically reproduced in CBET's methodological strategy.

The adoption of linguistic techniques had several important consequences for the orthodoxy, not least in influencing the way in which questions of a philosophical nature were framed. In sharing Oxford philosophy's preoccupation with meaning, many philosophers of education were quite simply led to ask the wrong kind of question. Rather than asking, say, 'What is it to act skilfully?', or 'How does a person become vocationally capable?', they would ask, 'What do we mean when we use the word "skill"?', or 'What do we mean when we speak of someone being "trained"?' To frame the questions thus is not only to assume a direct correspondence between the world and the language we use to describe it; it is also to assume that objectivity of meaning can be arrived at by reference to the ordinary use of words.

But one problem for the linguistic analyst, as Halliday (1990) has pointed out, is how to decide what counts as 'ordinary' or 'normal' usage. At best, the choice will tend to be determined by the analyst's own preconceptions about education, skill, training, etc.; hence, at the very least, linguistic analysis is open to the charge that its methodology 'simply reinforces its prior commitment to certain values or norms' (*ibid.*, p. 24). At worst, 'objectivity' is realized by wilfully restricting the focus of the analysis to an exiguously narrow selection from the range of possible uses or meanings of a particular term, selecting only those which support some broader thesis. Far from being the 'objective', definitive accounts they are claimed to be, the orthodox 'concepts' of skill and training might more appropriately be regarded as having been purposefully configured from examples of ordinary usage selected according to whether or not they happen to coincide with the analyst's wider purposes.[11] In so doing they can thus be seen to employ the kind of spurious linguistic reasoning which Gellner (1959) and Mundle (1979) had shown to be characteristic of linguistic analysis: 'legislating' about what we do, or cannot, or may not, say in relation to a given concept and arguing from a particular usage of words to some claim about the world.

It was precisely by such means that Peters was able to create 'an over-simple distinction' (Bridges, 1996, p. 365) between education and training. The 'analyses' by which the orthodox conceptions of skill and training are supposedly legitimated can be seen to contain many instances of this kind of reasoning[12] and Peters is dismissive of those who might not share his particular analysis of a 'concept':

> The concept of educating people, as distinct from merely training them, has developed and is mirrored in the different words that people use who have developed this differentiated concept. The fact that there may be many people who do not have this concept, or who have it but use the words loosely, does not effect the conceptual distinction to which I am drawing attention. (Peters, 1966, p. 30)

One characteristic feature of linguistic analysis, one which can be seen to have had generally pernicious consequences for philosophy of education, particularly in relation to the orthodoxy, is its inherent tendency towards the drawing of *distinctions* between words (Gellner, 1959; Magee, 1998). Typically, the explication of a concept would entail its being contrasted with another concept, as, for example, education with training. Moreover, each concept would be elucidated by examples of ordinary usage selected with the sole purpose of highlighting the supposed antithetical relationship between the two terms – the fact that not all instances of ordinary usage support this opposition (instances, for example, where the words 'training' and 'education' are effectively synonymous (Daveney, 1973)) being purposefully disregarded in order to emphasize a dichotomous relationship between the terms. There is thus a sense in which linguistic methodology is congenitally prone towards the divisive and that rather than attempting to identify unifying themes, principles or common features, it tends to engender the very educational and philosophical dualisms which John Dewey (1966) recognized as being so 'deeply entangled . . . with the whole subject of vocational education' (p. 307). Indeed, it turns out that the linguistic techniques of Oxford philosophy provided the means by which explications of terms such as skill and training could be represented as 'objective', disinterested analyses while substantively supporting other priorities. As we shall now see, under scrutiny these analyses can be seen to form part of an identifiable, interested and value-laden account of the educational enterprise.

Two epistemologies – two cultures

In laying bare the meanings of terms in an ostensibly objective, value-free manner, linguistic analysis claimed to be detached from matters of value. Political and moral issues such as, for example, the optimum balance for education between the liberal and the vocational, or the kind of education parents should choose for their children, were claimed to be beyond the remit of analysis (Peters, 1980). However, analysis was not at all the objective, disinterested investigation it purported to be, for its analyses turn out to be intensely value-laden (Harris, 1980). As one radical critic explains, the 'second-order' activities of linguistic analysis are far from neutral and should more properly be seen as a disguised representation of certain political and class interests:

> Analysis takes language, everyday theory and common sense as given and fails to comprehend the ensemble as a product of certain practices which are historically contingent, and politically and economically ordered. (Matthews, 1980, p. 164)

Similarly, Dennis Cato (1987) has argued that the kind of analyses offered by Peters are 'not the spectatorial mapping' they are claimed to be and that Peters clearly 'imports his own values into the clarificatory activity' (p. 35).

Linguistic analysis is also value-laden in a further, far less subtle sense, for its strategy can often be seen to be one of arranging its explications of concepts in such a way as to make certain moral or political choices a foregone conclusion. Thus, in order to promote a particular conception of liberal, non-instrumental education, the tactic was to contrast the concept of 'education' – carefully elucidated as something profoundly rich and life-enhancing – with concepts such as 'training' and 'skill' depicted in such a way as to stress their epistemological and cognitive vacuity.

Another feature of linguistic analysis is its inherent conservatism. Alasdair MacIntyre (1981) has pointed out that the technique of analytical philosophy is essentially one of describing the language of the present. Richard Rorty (1980) makes a similar point when he says that traditional philosophy's search for objectivity involves a 'self-deceptive effort to eternalise the normal discourse of the day' (p. 11). But the analyses produced by Peters *et al.* are conservative in a further, though related sense, of promoting – along with their conception of liberal education – an identifiable set of values and priorities. In his attack on 'liberal' education Kevin Harris points out that analytical philosophers of education such as Hirst and Peters

> managed to 'justify' in their collected works virtually every aspect of the social and educational *status quo* that might serve the interests of those wishing to preserve the *status quo*, and to present those justifications as rational, logical, and disinterested. The end result was to serve and satisfy not only a large number of people at the decision-making level, but also to fulfil a necessary general ideological function of producing 'interest-free' justifications for the continuance of social practices which actually serve particular *political* interests. (Original italics; Harris, 1980, p. 31)

Although radical critics typically characterize their target as 'liberal' philosophy of education, since the perpetuation of existing social practices is a feature of conservatism rather than liberalism, it would perhaps be more accurate, as Penny Enslin (1985) has suggested, to identify these tendencies as *conservative* rather than liberal.

For our purposes, of pivotal importance in these value-laden analyses is the opposition created between intrinsic and extrinsic value; this is a distinction closely identified in the orthodoxy with that between education and training (see, for example, Peters, 1964, 1966), where, in contrast to VET, a liberal education 'can have no ends beyond itself. Its value derives from principles and standards implicit in it' (Peters, 1964, p. 47). Edel (1985) has noted that the intrinsic–extrinsic distinction is just one of a number of polarities employed to elucidate the notion of a liberal education. It is possible, as he says, to discern various such polarities in the literature; for example, the liberal might be contrasted with the narrow and the technical, or alternatively it might be regarded as broadly synonymous with the humanities and thus contrasted with the sciences, or yet again, the liberal arts and sciences might together be contrasted with the applied sciences such as engineering or studies related to business, etc. While for Edel the intrinsic–extrinsic distinction is just one more such polarity, it might be more appropriate to see the intrinsic–extrinsic distinction as fundamental to all such polarities in the sense that the 'technical', 'scientific' or 'applied' are variously differentiated from the liberal by virtue of their being directed at extrinsic ends.

Yet the distinction between intrinsic and extrinsic ends might itself be interpreted in terms of a further, perhaps more fundamental notion, that of utility; for, while extrinsic ends are characterized by their usefulness, intrinsic ends seem to be most readily distinguishable by their 'lack of utility' (*ibid.*, p. 313). Among all the various intersecting polarities employed to elucidate the concept of a liberal education it would seem that the most fundamental distinction of all is between knowledge that is deemed to be useful and that which is not.

The division of knowledge into that which is deemed to be of intrinsic value and that which is directed at extrinsic ends and characterized by its utility, has long been associated with distinctions of social class. Some would trace the association back at least as far as Socrates' observation that skilled craftsmen did not have philosophical capabilities, with the association maintained through the universities of the Middle Ages and 'continually vindicated' (Maskell, 1999, p. 157) through generations of teachers and writers from the Renaissance onwards. The distinction is found in both Plato and Aristotle where the ancient Greek ideal of liberal education for leisured freemen is contrasted with training, which was associated with slaves (Brown, 1985; see also Schofield, 1972). In *The Politics* Aristotle specifically contrasts learning that is 'liberal and something good in itself' (1952, p. 337) with occupational subjects which 'should be regarded merely as means and matters of necessity' (p. 336), adding that 'To aim at utility everywhere is utterly unbecoming to high-minded and liberal spirits' (p. 337).

Dewey (1966) characterized the modern inclination to distance liberal education from the useful or vocationally relevant as a tendency which 'accompanied the conservation of the aristocratic ideals of the past' (p. 319), ideals which, as Silver and Brennan (1988) also suggest, seem to be the source of many of education's dualisms. These ideals can be seen to have a particularly significant role in British cultural history where the gentrified, classical ideals of an early landowning aristocracy were embodied in the education system (Wilkinson, 1970) and fostered a cultural bias of anti-industrial values (Wiener, 1981). This cultural schism, centred on the distinction between intrinsic and extrinsic ends, has long been associated with the 'historic failure of the English education system to integrate the academic and the practical, the general and the vocational' (Maclure, 1991, p. 28). It has been said that there is, in Britain, a 'disdain for the practical intelligence – indeed, for the technological and the useful' (Pring, 1995, p. 186), a disdain long since exemplified by Keats when he famously lambasted Newton, accusing him of 'unweaving the rainbow' – claiming that he had destroyed all the poetry of the rainbow by showing that it could be reduced into the prismatic colours (see Dawkins, 1999).

Indeed, it might be said that there is a specifically British genealogy for the humanities–science variant of the 'intrinsically valuable–extrinsically useful' distinction in the form of a certain cultural and institutional hostility to science. It is not insignificant, for example, that the sciences were only gradually introduced into Oxbridge as late as the mid- to late nineteenth century and, even then, the applied sciences continued to be regarded as inferior (Ashby, 1958). In 1867 a sub-committee of the British Association for the Advancement of Science bemoaned the fact that scientific education in universities was not 'on a par' with, nor attracted the same 'rewards' as, a mathematical or classical education (Roderick and Stephens, 1972, p. 11).

Of course, this cultural bias was not without its critics. The dispute between T. H. Huxley (1880) and Matthew Arnold (1882) about the role of the sciences in education prefigured the later exchange, on precisely the same lines, between C. P. Snow and F. R. Leavis. Huxley suggested that the traditional classical education should give way to a more scientific education, arguing that science was equally a part of culture and that it not only provided a rigorous mental training, but also contributed to national economic well-being. In response, Matthew Arnold (1882) conceded that 'literature' might include the great works of science but nevertheless maintained that it was an education based on great literature – particularly the classics – which was necessary for cultivating the 'educated man'. As Collini notes, the dispute between Huxley and Arnold:

symbolised the ways in which social and institutional snobberies clustered around this topic ... Not for the last time in British cultural history, questions about the proper place of the sciences and the humanities in the nation's educational system appeared to be inextricably entangled with elusive but highly charged matters of institutional status and social class. (Collini, 1964, pp. xv–xvi)

C. P. Snow's famous Rede Lecture of 1959, 'The two cultures', highlighted still further the division between the 'literary intellectuals' and the natural scientists, each of whom regarded each other with mutual suspicion and incomprehension.[13] In a paper which was a precursor of his 1959 lecture, Snow had rounded on what he saw as the snobbish and nostalgic social attitudes of the literary elite:

The traditional culture, which is, of course, mainly literary, is behaving like a state whose power is rapidly declining – standing on its precarious dignity, spending far too much energy on Alexandrian intricacies, occasionally letting fly in fits of aggressive pique quite beyond its means, too much on the defensive to show any generous imagination to the forces which must inevitably reshape it. (Snow, 1956, p. 413)

In *The Two Cultures* Snow (1964) argued that the continued dominance of this elite over the social and political order was profoundly damaging not only to individual cultivation but also to social well-being; the many potential benefits of science were being lost through political mismanagement and the cultural and educational disparagement of science. To this day there are heads of industry who, similarly, would 'blame the teachers' for their 'anti-industry bias' in placing the 'life of the mind over the practical life' (Weinstock, 1976, p. 2; cited in Hyland, 1994, p. 4).

Snow was to suggest that this kind of division was an inherent feature of any advanced industrial society (see Snow, 1960). Though in which direction the snobberies run seems to be a somewhat more contingent matter: as Fuller (1989) has noted, it is common in American universities for humanities students to be disparagingly referred to as 'non-science majors' (p. 6), and in Britain there are undoubtedly scientists, industrialists, engineers, and the like, who would snobbishly exalt the scientific and the practical and regard the humanities and the academic with disdain.

At one level these divisions appear trivial: nothing more than a kind of scholarly group inclusiveness fired, perhaps, by a mixture of loyalty and anxiety. Nevertheless, their consequences for the philosophy and theory of education should not be underestimated. It would not be unreasonable to suggest that the orthodox conceptions of skill and training – purposefully depicted as epistemologically and cognitively impoverished and set in contrast to a 'rich' conception of a liberal education – can be seen to reflect many of these very same cultural and social divisions. The putative epistemic differentiation of the vocational and the liberal, one which the linguistic analysts contrived to substantiate using little more than spurious linguistic reasoning, can often be seen to be motivated by the selfsame cultural divisions.

But there is another equally divisive feature within the orthodoxy, for wrapped up with the more overt epistemological claims we can recognize a certain kind of metaphysical presumption. In its naïve form it has the simplistic appeal of a truism: that instrumentalist means are well suited to instrumental ends. We see, for example, that the precepts of instrumental reason were deemed to be entirely apposite in relation to the concepts of skill and training. Here, it was claimed, was learning which was inert, value-free and rightly conceived of in terms of clear-cut specifications, identifiable rules and behaviourist descriptions of performance; a kind of knowledge appropriately framed by empirical science or just sheer common sense. This was in stark contrast to an account of the liberal enterprise which, with the arts and humanities at its head, was held to have a 'monopoly of value and the imagination' (Edel, 1985, p. 259). Technical rationality – that 'heritage of Positivism' (Schön, 1996, p. 31) – was implicitly invoked by the linguistic analysts, not universally as the logical positivists would have had it, but *selectively* – effectively a metaphysics of partiality designed to accommodate the social, political and cultural prejudices of the age. But, again, this purported metaphysical divide, like its epistemological counterpart, appears to be supported by nothing more than linguistic sleight of hand, by the use of a priori and legislative linguistics, ultimately derived from a misconceived view of philosophy as the arbiter of meaning.

Of course, it would be tempting to conclude from all this that

> this differential basis for vocational and academic studies has nothing more than historical association to support it. Beyond the contingent fact that the classical gentry ideal came to be associated with the most powerful political and economic groups in Britain, there are no intrinsic or logical reasons for the liberal/vocational dichotomy in education. (Hyland, 1994, p. 117)

However, caution is needed. Even acknowledging that the methods of the linguistic analysts fail to substantiate the claim that there are epistemic grounds for the distinction between the vocational and the academic, we cannot take this as equivalent to there being no grounds. In other words, it remains possible that there may be grounds for the distinction. This is a possibility we shall return to later.

The difficulties associated with Oxford philosophy were to dog philosophy of education long after they had been exorcized from mainstream philosophy, and even to this day they continue to exert a discernible influence, as we shall see when we turn to the recent debate about competence-based education and training. Whatever misgivings we might have as regards the way in which the linguistic analysts characterized the liberal–vocational divide, the fact is that one of its most salient features remains stubbornly intact. The idea that the vocational is somehow epistemologically distinctive, that it is marked off by a certain kind of knowledge, a 'knowing how' as opposed to a 'knowing that', is one which has persisted in the literature. Our next task will be to challenge the claim, one which is fundamental to the orthodoxy, that it is possible to make an epistemological distinction between 'knowing how' and 'knowing that'.

Notes

9   On this point see Scruton, 1997.
10   See, particularly, Austin, 1962, 1970.
11   The contingent if not capricious nature of these analyses and the meanings they attribute to particular 'concepts' is borne out by instances where conspicuously conflicting accounts might be arrived at using the same methodology. For example, Atkinson (1972), in contrast to Peters and nearer to Ryle, contrasts 'trained' with 'drilled' and ascribes to the 'drilled' man the characteristics which Peters attributes to 'trained'. Sometimes the analyses have the appearance of being completely arbitrary; for example, while one (e.g. Maskell, 1999) might specifically identify instruction *with* training, another might deem training to be 'wider than instructing but narrower than educating' (Akinpelu, 1981, p. 196).
12   Typically, these analyses are littered with phrases such as 'X always suggests ...', 'we might describe someone as X but not as Y', 'to say of someone that they are X is to ...', 'we often say that ...', 'we speak of ...', etc.
13   There is little reason to think that much has changed on this score. Richard Dawkins (1999) relates the following exchange further to Bernard Levin's article in *The Times* on 29 July 1994:

> Bernard Levin had made light of the idea of quarks ('The quarks are coming! The quarks are coming! Run for your lives ...'). After further cracks about 'noble science' having given us mobile telephones, collapsible umbrellas and multi-striped toothpaste, he broke into mock seriousness: *Can you eat quarks? Can you spread them on your bed when the cold weather comes?* This sort of thing doesn't really deserve a reply but the Cambridge metallurgist Sir Alan Cotterell gave it two sentences, in a letter to the editor a few days later. *Sir, Mr Bernard Levin asks 'Can you eat quarks?' I estimate that he eats 500,000,000,000,000,000,000,000,001 quarks a day ... Yours faithfully ...* (pp. 31–2)

3

Knowing How and Knowing That

Of all the works of linguistic analysis one of the most consummate and almost certainly one of the most influential was Gilbert Ryle's *The Concept of Mind* (1949), a work dedicated to exposing the alleged misuse of a single concept. Ryle sets out to demonstrate that 'when we describe people as exercising qualities of mind, we are not referring to occult episodes of which their overt acts and utterances are effects; we are referring to those overt acts and utterances themselves' (p. 25). Ryle's prime concern, then, in the Oxford manner, is with our *descriptions* of the mental, with what we *mean* when we use words such as 'intelligent', 'clever' or 'logical'. *The Concept of Mind* is expressly a work of linguistic analysis, and with its frequent allusion to the ordinary usage of words, and close regard to the distinctions implied by our choosing to employ one term in particular circumstances rather than another, it is a model of its kind. As is typical of work of linguistic analysis, it tends to assimilate questions about things in the world to questions about the meanings of words, often conflating the two and treating answers to the latter as though they were answers to the former. Even Ryle's title is ambiguous as to its intended focus, for to claim that a 'concept' is the object of attention is to evade the crucial matter of whether the chief concern is some epistemological/ ontological feature of the world or whether the primary interest is one of semantics.

Chief among the linguistic distinctions which Ryle draws attention to, and the one which has been so influential in philosophy of education, arises from his observation that in talking about 'knowing' we tend to distinguish between knowing *how* and knowing *that*. Famously, Ryle's purpose in drawing attention to this distinction was to debunk the 'intellectualist legend', the official doctrine that we can assimilate knowing how to knowing that and that the former is essentially and logically subordinate to the latter in the sense that intelligent performance is necessarily guided by, or involves, the prior consideration of rules, maxims, regulative propositions, etc. For Ryle, this customary way of thinking about the mental is patent nonsense. The idea that a chef should have to recite his recipes before being able to cook, or that someone must first rehearse the appropriate moral imperatives before being able to save a drowning man, is manifestly not the case. The presumption that acting involves doing two things, that we are required first to 'do a bit of theory and then to do a bit of practice' (*ibid.*, p. 29), is, on Ryle's view, mistaken for a number of reasons. First, he reminds us that we are often unable to cite the regulating principles which guide our actions.[14] Second, he points to the fact that there are many cases where our abilities precede the articulation of explanatory theory, where theory can be seen to follow practice: 'Rules of correct reasoning were first extracted by Aristotle, yet men knew how to avoid and detect fallacies before they learned his lessons' (*ibid.*, p. 30). Third, and for Ryle the most crucial objection to the prevailing view, is that if choosing and applying regulative propositions is itself an operation required to be carried out intelligently, then this too, according to the official dogma, must be guided by further propositions. Accordingly, if the intellectualist legend were true, any and every performance would be preceded by an infinite regress of principles guiding principles.

So, Ryle argues, contrary to the official doctrine that intellectual operations are primarily instances of knowing *that*, intelligence consists primarily in knowing *how* to do things. The long-standing assumption that the mind's 'defining property' is its 'capacity to attain knowledge of truths' or that mental-conduct concepts are properly defined 'in terms of concepts of cognition' (*ibid.*, p. 26) is, according to Ryle, simply mistaken. Intelligence cannot consist in the accumulation of facts for the simple reason that 'there is no incompatibility between being well-informed and being silly'; neither can it consist in some 'capacity for rigorous theory' (*ibid.*, pp. 25–6) for theorizing is just one practice among many that may be done more or less intelligently. All this is not to deny the existence of the mental but rather to challenge the assumption that the 'core of mental conduct' consists of 'intellectual operations' (*ibid.*, p. 26). We should therefore, on Ryle's view, recognize that when we use mental–conduct concepts such as 'intelligence' or 'stupidity', or related adjectives such as 'clever', 'sensible', 'careful', 'stupid', 'dull' or 'careless' – terms we habitually use to predicate the mental – we are actually indicating complexes of behaviour: 'Overt intelligent performances are not clues to the workings of minds; they are those workings' (*ibid.*, p. 58).

Ryle was, of course, all too aware that this left him open to being stigmatized as behaviourist (*ibid.*, see p. 327), and, since he clearly takes statements about the mental to *mean* the same as statements about behaviour, it would certainly be appropriate to see him as subscribing to logical behaviourism (see Rorty, 1980). In this respect his position is closely related to the neo-positivist idea that the meaning of propositions consists in the way in which they can be publicly verified. Notwithstanding any reservations Ryle might have had about the behaviourist implications of his argument, ultimately he believed his to be the only tenable account if the only alternative was, as he believed it to be, a choice between either a Hobbesian mechanistic conception of mind or the Cartesian dualism which characterizes the official doctrine.

Even if behaviourism were substantially true, one difficulty for Ryle is that it would be impossible to give an account of the requisite dispositions to behave unless we were able to provide 'infinitely long lists' of possible behaviour (Rorty, 1980, p. 98). And it is worth noting here the congenitally reductionistic tendencies of competence-based education and training in attempting just such accounts. However, there are even more serious difficulties which beset Ryle's account. For while behaviourism, at a stroke, solves the problem of other minds – the question of how it is possible for us to have knowledge of the mental states of others – it nevertheless, as Quinton (1973) has objected, does it rather *too* well; for, if our observations of behaviour really are sufficient on this count, it leaves us in need of an explanation as to why we often have the level of doubt we do about the mental states of others. Why, for example, we doubt whether descriptions of the observable aspects of a performance really are sufficient to provide a complete account of a particular ability (see, for example, Moss, 1981). The crucial problem for Ryle, and for behaviourism generally, is that behaviour is neither a sufficient nor a necessary condition for the mental (Marres, 1989). Behaviour is not a *necessary* condition, for there are many instances where mental states occur without being accompanied by behaviour. Feelings, for example, do not have to give rise to behaviour. Neither is behaviour a *sufficient* condition, for it can be simulated, faked, etc. Moreover, it is not possible for specific behaviour to be non-problematically associated with particular mental states. Alisdair MacIntyre (1971) makes the point that feelings of resentment might be accompanied by virtually any type of behaviour. In such cases it is not possible to determine specific characteristics which would enable us to identify certain types of behaviour with resentment. Since the relationship between many mental states and behaviour is in this sense contingent, it might also be said that the identification of mental states with future behaviour is problematic since such behaviour need not necessarily follow: as Marres (1989) notes, 'When connected behaviour does occur, it is evidence of, and not identical with, the mental states' (p. 38).

But these are not the only difficulties which beset the argument of *The Concept of Mind*. As has already been indicated, it is a work which has all the features we might expect of a work of linguistic analysis. First, there are claims relating to facts of language usage, not least of which is the fact that in ordinary language we distinguish between knowing how and knowing that. While we can readily acknowledge such facts per se, it is quite another matter to claim to derive from them anything of major epistemological significance. If, as has been argued, contingent facts of ordinary language usage cannot provide us with non-contingent truths about the world, then the fact that we make a distinction in ordinary language between knowing how and knowing that, cannot of itself constitute a basis for any epistemological distinction. Second, there are claims about what is *meant* by certain words and in many of Ryle's pronouncements we find the legislative overtones characteristic of Oxford philosophy, i.e. claims to the effect that when we use particular words we must or can only mean certain things. Enough has already been said to cast doubt on the legitimacy of such claims. Third, and perhaps most serious, throughout *The Concept of Mind* there is a systematic conflation of questions of an ontological nature with questions about the meanings of words – treating answers to the latter as though they were answers to the former. Even Ryle's account of dispositions, which is central to his overall argument, is conspicuously ambiguous on this score and, as William Lyons has pointed out, this ambiguity is a major flaw in Ryle's argument:

> If Ryle were merely giving us a semantic account of dispositions, that is, telling us what the term 'disposition' means or how it is used linguistically, then his account is adequate ... But if, as Ryle seems to believe, his account is also or chiefly meant to be what I shall call a genetic account of dispositions, that is, an explanation of what they are ontologically and how they arise, then his account is inadequate. I suspect Ryle believed that his account was not merely an account of how we use the term 'disposition' or of what we mean to say when we attribute a disposition to someone or something, because he argued from his account of dispositions to ontological conclusions, not to mere semantic conclusions. He did not claim to be merely pointing out what we mean by the term 'dispositions', he claimed to be telling us what they were and how they worked. (Lyons, 1980, pp. 49–50)

There seems little doubt, then, that Ryle's linguistic methodology presents him with serious difficulties. Yet, wrapped up in his analysis of ordinary language are several claims which remain cogent after we have untangled them from the linguistic elements of his argument. First, and of major importance, there is the claim that any knowledge we have about the mental states of others is essentially constituted of and necessarily delimited by the sort of evidence it is possible for us to have access to. We cannot, for example, simply look inside someone's head. On this view the only evidence we can possibly have with respect to the mental states of others is their outward behaviour or dispositions to so behave. Seen thus, we might say that the entire problem of mind–body dualism against which Ryle militates is more properly regarded, as Rorty (1980) has rightly argued, as a conflict about the sort of access we can have to the mental, i.e. between privileged and public access; the crucial gap is, therefore, epistemological rather than ontological as Ryle has it, with his famous analogy of the 'ghost in the machine'. Ryle's argument about the sort of evidence we have access to when we make claims about the mental attributes of others is certainly compelling; our sense of unease about it stems from its apparently inescapable behaviourist consequences. One challenge which *The Concept of Mind* poses is how we might acknowledge this important point about access without also having to subscribe to behaviourism. Without anticipating too much, suffice it to say for the moment that if we adopt Ryle's view of the agent as a disengaged, passive, neutral spectator – a view which, for Ryle, is a corollary of his logical positivism (see Rorty, 1980) – such behaviourist consequences do indeed follow. However, these consequences might be avoided if we are able to reject this view in favour of a conception of human agency characterized more by what Charles Taylor (1997) has described as being 'engaged with or at grips with the world' (p. 23), a view of the agent as essentially embodied, an agent whose world is shaped partly by such embodiment and partly by being engaged in shared social practices and forms of life.

A further challenge posed by *The Concept of Mind* concerns the way in which Ryle depicts what he perceives to be the mentalistic alternative to his behavioural–dispositional account: how he identifies the mental with the notion of 'theory' and how he conceives of this in relation to practice. For Ryle, any attempt to reinstate the mental back into the picture of intelligent performance necessarily involves us in a view of the mental as something which is divorced, and at some remove, from practice. The predominant feature of the mental on this view is 'theory', i.e. the conscious and explicit application of maxims, rules, avowals, stores of propositions, etc., a sphere of activity which is ontologically distinct and temporally prior to action. The challenge here will be to develop an account of human capability which not only avoids Ryle's behaviourism, but at the same time avoids resort to an account of the mental as something divorced from practice, as an ontologically and temporally distinct sphere of activity concerned with the explicit and conscious manipulation of theory or propositions.

But the most immediate issue here is Ryle's centrally important distinction between knowing how and knowing that. It is a distinction which continues to be highly influential in much theorizing about education. Not only is it a prominent feature of the orthodox conception of skill/training but it also corresponds closely with some of the basic assumptions underpinning current policy in relation to competence-based education and training. Yet the prevailing assumption that such terms denote an epistemological distinction turns out to be fundamentally mistaken.

Applying the 'knowing how–knowing that' distinction

It is useful to recognize that there are two senses in which we make a distinction between knowing how and knowing that: one trivial and one not so trivial. The trivial sense of the distinction arises merely from the rules of grammar: it is simply grammatically correct to say that someone knows *how* when we happen to be talking about their doing something, and that someone knows *that* if we happen to be talking about their being in possession of some fact or piece of information. Our aversion to saying 'he knows *that* to drive a car' derives less from a point of epistemology or even semantics than it does from grammatical correctness. At the risk of appearing frivolous we might say that such formalities no more demonstrate the existence of two forms of knowledge than the gender of French nouns indicate the sex of everyday objects. Any inclination to derive epistemology from syntax evaporates when we consider that the rules of grammar also allow us to say that someone knows *how* to state a fact.

The rules of grammar aside, however, there are prima facie instances where we do seem to apply the distinction to differentiate between two types of knowing, where we purposefully designate someone's knowledge as an instance of knowing *how* as opposed to knowing *that*, or vice versa. Perhaps the first thing we should note is that while the distinction appears credible with the sort of examples chosen by Ryle and Peters, it is not necessarily as convincing in all cases. Edel (1973; see also Hager, 1999), for example, has argued that many occupational activities elude classification as instances of knowing how, for example those where complex skills are applied in teamwork situations using complex technologies. Nevertheless, the distinction is one which persists in the literature with even those who treat it with ambivalence conceding that the distinction is one which 'remains' (Eraut, 1994, p. 107). Although there is, as we shall see, a wide divergence of opinion about precisely what kind of knowledge is indicated by each of these terms, nevertheless, the basic assumption that in using them we are referring to two different kinds of knowledge has, ever since Ryle brought the distinction to philosophical prominence, gone largely unquestioned.

Yet I want to suggest that it is a mistake to assume the distinction to have an epistemological basis, not least because by Ryle's own account our use of the distinction is clearly not about distinguishing two distinct modes of knowledge but about distinguishing the kinds of *evidence* we have when we make judgements about the knowledge of others. The point here is that our judgements – as Ryle himself was keen to point out – are necessarily based on inferences from available evidence: usually either from people's actions or from their making some kind of declaration (written or verbal) about what they know. What Ryle seems to have missed – as have many others who have assumed an epistemological basis for the distinction – is that we employ the phrases knowing how and knowing that respectively, according to *how* the fact of someone's knowing was made evident to us. It might be said that Heidegger (1962) conveys something of this in his insight that 'Assertion communicates entities in the "how" of their uncoveredness' (p. 266).

Of course, the distinction is not restricted to being expressed in terms of knowing how and knowing that – for example, Bartram's (1990) distinction between 'procedural knowledge' and 'declarative knowledge' and Eraut's (1994) distinction between 'process knowledge' and 'propositional knowledge' amount to much the same thing. What is odd here is the way in which an epistemological basis for these distinctions is assumed even while employing terms which reveal that the distinction is really about the way in which we *determine* whether someone is knowledgeable, i.e. whether we discern it from some declaration of knowledge or whether, as Bartram himself says, it is 'inferred from one's actions' (p. 55).[15]

Michael Oakeshott makes what appears at first sight to be a similar distinction in *Rationalism in Politics* when he distinguishes 'practical' and 'technical' knowledge, the first being the kind which 'exists in use' and the second the sort of knowledge to be found in textbooks or manuals (see Oakeshott, 1991, p. 12). Eraut (1985) has taken Oakeshott to task for attempting to classify knowledge according to its source, for example from books or from personal experience. Yet Oakeshott would be justified to make this kind of distinction if by so doing, his intention was to draw attention to the kinds of evidence we have for judging someone to be knowledgeable. Certainly it would be a mistake for Oakeshott to assume an epistemological as well as an evidential basis for the distinction although, *pace* Eraut, it is not entirely clear that Oakeshott actually does assume this.[16] But the main point here is that when various commentators refer to different kinds of knowledge, the distinction can often be seen to be more about how we come to know about someone's knowing rather than about the kind of knowledge someone has.

What is of interest is why we should choose to make this kind of distinction if it refers not, as is commonly assumed, to two different kinds of knowledge but to the kinds of evidence upon which our inferences are based. It would seem that one reason for applying the distinction arises when there is a conflict between the sources of evidence. For example, we use the distinction to characterize those cases where a person, though being able to recite the facts, propositions or rules which relate to a performance, is nevertheless unable to carry out that performance. Thus we might say that a person 'knows that' but does not 'know how'. Conversely, we might also use the distinction as a way of articulating the apparent incongruity in those cases where, despite a performance being executed correctly, there is evidence to suggest that a person lacks the knowledge or understanding expected – as, for example, when a person is unable to explain the rationale behind his or her actions. It would seem, therefore, that we distinguish between knowing how and knowing that where we wish to apply some kind of caveat or proviso to our judgements about the knowledge of others by drawing attention to the *kind* of evidence we have – for example, where we want to say that contrary to what might be inferred from *one* source of evidence we are disinclined to judge someone as being knowledgeable, in some particular sense, because of countervailing evidence from the other. As we shall see, our drawing attention to the kind of evidence we have is one way of indicating more precisely what it is that is known.

It is perhaps worth emphasizing again Ryle's commitment to the view that our judgements about the mental states of others are profoundly dependent upon and necessarily limited by the kind of evidence it is possible for us to have access to; indeed, it might be said that this constitutes the most cogent part of his argument. Moreover, on this point Ryle was surely correct. The question, then, is whether this evidence is the *only* determining factor in our arriving at such judgements or, more precisely, whether our explanatory accounts of what it is to know must necessarily correspond to, and be exhausted by, our descriptions of the performative and declarative evidence to which we have access. Ryle assumed it was and his behaviourism was a direct corollary of this assumption.

Of course, our acknowledging that when we refer to knowing how and knowing that we are really indicating the kinds of evidence we have access to does not rule out the possibility that there are two fundamentally different forms of knowing, forms which in some sense happen to coincide with these evident, outward manifestations. The important thing for the moment is that the fact of such usage in itself does not constitute proof of any corresponding epistemic distinction. Nonetheless, the prevailing assumption that there *is* a meaningful epistemological distinction turns out to be of profound consequence for education.

Thick and thin conceptions of knowing how and knowing that

Despite the frequency with which references to knowing how and knowing that appear in the literature, there are widely differing ideas about what it is to know how as opposed to that. Out of the many diverse opinions it is possible to discern two tendencies, each arising from an inclination to emphasize or give priority to either one or other form of 'knowing'. While some commentators can be seen to stress the conceptual thickness of knowing how, others, conversely, draw attention to the thickness of knowing that.

As we have seen, Ryle was at pains to emphasize the conceptual thickness of knowing how; according to him it is in knowing how that intelligence primarily resides, whereas knowing that plays a lesser part in the scheme of things. It is not difficult to see how this thick–thin configuration of knowing how and knowing that might be understood in the context of education. Many would share Max Black's (1973) view that 'All education aims, in the first instance, at "know how"' (p. 92). They would recognize the limitations of an education confined to propositional knowledge – the kind of knowledge delineated by Ryle's knowing that or William James' 'knowledge about' – and point to the richness of knowing and learning how (Aiken, 1966).

But perhaps more important here are the similarities between Ryle's position and the sort of assumptions implicit in the competence approach – similarities which have certainly not gone unnoticed in the literature. The parallels are perhaps at their most striking in Ryle's declaration that: 'In ordinary life ... as well as in the special business of teaching, we are much more concerned with people's competences than with their cognitive repertoires, with the operations than with the truths that they learn' (Ryle, 1949, p. 28). As Terry Hyland (1994) has noted, it is a statement which could serve as a philosophical justification for NVQ apologists were they, as Hyland aptly says, actually ever to seek theoretical justification for their methods. The important point here is that the thick–thin configuration of knowing how and knowing that formulated by Ryle corresponds with the sort of aims adopted by CBET. Just as Ryle gives pride of place to behaviour and behavioural dispositions, seeing intelligence, competence, etc. as residing primarily in knowing how, similarly, CBET affords overriding priority to competence, performance – to knowing how.

Although Ryle and CBET might be said to share the same thick–thin conceptions of knowing how and knowing that, it is important to recognize that they are motivated by quite different concerns. For Ryle the thick–thin configuration arises from what he saw as the necessary limits imposed on what it is possible for us to mean by our statements about the mental. CBET's conception, on the other hand, might more properly be regarded as a purposeful reaction to what some would see as the 'previous domination of knowledge' in education (Mansfield, 1990, p. 21), a domination perceived to be at the expense of the more practical, 'doing' aspects of human affairs. Where Ryle and CBET converge is at the point where Ryle's invocation of ordinary language usage – with what we mean, for example, when we say that someone 'knows how' to do something intelligently – coincides with CBET's naïve attempts to ground educational practice in the selfsame aphoristic commonplaces. It may appear somewhat anomalous to identify CBET with a thick conception of knowing how, for a frequent complaint directed at CBET is that it is characterized by a conception of 'know-how' which is conspicuously narrow and mechanistic and thus perhaps more appropriately described as thin. But CBET's defects are more convoluted than they first appear and, as will be argued later, it is necessary to distinguish between CBET's aims and its methodology. While we might correctly characterize CBET's aims as incorporating a Rylean thick–thin conception of knowing how–knowing that (and hence open to the charge of having an insufficient regard for knowing that), it will turn out that the methodological strategy employed by CBET necessarily engenders a thin formulation of knowing how. Consequently, if pressed to describe CBET in terms of the knowing how–knowing that distinction we might say that what CBET substantively delivers is a thin–thin configuration.

Of course, the danger, for both Ryle and CBET, in affording knowing how such a broad conceptual remit is that knowing that, by implication, becomes conceptually diminished. To the extent that 'know-how' is regarded as epistemologically sufficient for (or indeed equivalent to) consummate performance, then knowing that – indeed knowledge and theory generally insofar as they are seen as equivalent to knowing that – comes to be regarded as superfluous to intelligent action. Those who begin to think of knowing that in such impoverished terms, perhaps merely as the ability to state facts, are likely to succumb to the idea that such knowledge is extraneous to vocational capability and largely irrelevant to VET's purposes. They might come to think that 'Knowledge – simply stated as knowledge – means little' (Mansfield, 1990, p. 21) and that there is little value in learning 'bucketfuls of facts', (Wolf, 1989, p. 41; a phrase Wolf borrows from the Higginson Report). Certainly, Ryle was correct when he observed that people do not normally preface their actions with a recital of relevant propositions, so if this is what knowing that consists of, then it appears to be of little vocational significance. It would be difficult to think of many vocational activities for which it is necessary to employ propositional knowledge in this way. Thus it is that those who conceive of knowledge in such terms ultimately come to believe that 'even in the most professional occupations the proportion of "knowledge-heavy" competences is quite few' (Moran, 1991, p. 8), even going so far as to cast doubt on the idea that knowledge is 'an essential prerequisite for competent performance' (*ibid*).

It would seem, then, that to take this thick–thin configuration of knowing how and knowing that to its logical conclusion is to accede to the extraordinary idea that knowledge is of little importance to vocational capability. And it is precisely this thick–thin configuration of knowing how and knowing that which has effectively become enshrined in the aims of the NVQ system, where the unabashed aggrandizement of performance or knowing how stands in stark contrast to the grudging admittance of 'underpinning knowledge' and where we witness a 'persistent downgrading' (Hyland, 1994, p. 74) of knowing that in favour of knowing how.

Whatever reservations we may already have about this thick–thin configuration of knowing how–knowing that, its soundness is further put in doubt by indications that we might equally conceive of knowing that as the thicker or richer of the two, and knowing how as the thinner concept. This is precisely the line taken by R. S. Peters in his explication of knowing how and knowing that, and if anything, it is this account rather than Ryle's which has had the most enduring influence in philosophy of education. What has not been widely acknowledged is the important fact, one which Peters omits to mention, that although clearly influenced by Ryle's use of the dichotomy (see Peters, 1980, p. 95, note 9), his account expressly reverses Ryle's original emphasis. Knowing how in Peters' version of the dichotomy – far from being the wellspring of intelligence and intelligent operations – is exemplified by such things as riding bicycles, swimming and playing golf. Indeed, to know how is to not really know very much at all; it is to have 'knack rather than understanding' (1966, p. 159; see also Peters, 1973, p. 6). Know-how, as Peters understands it, is to be identified with merely physical abilities, the kind of capabilities which have a 'close connexion with bodily movements' (*ibid.*), rather than with any extensive conceptual grasp of things.

In marked contrast to this starkly impoverished notion of knowing how, knowing that is understood as denoting the considerably richer, deeper and broader kind of understanding which characterizes the wider educational enterprise: we are told that a necessary aspect of education (as opposed to training) is that it 'involves "knowing that" as well as "knowing how"' (Peters, 1980, p. 96). In similar vein Pring (1995) identifies 'knowledge that' with 'school learning' (p. 146) and elsewhere (Pring, 1976) with the 'belief-type' knowledge which characterizes the school curriculum. Knowing that, on this view, is no mere capacity to recite propositions but rather a 'body of knowledge and some kind of conceptual scheme to raise this above the level of a collection of disjointed facts' (Peters, 1966, p. 30).[17]

On this account the contrast between knowing how and knowing that is further emphasized by drawing attention to perceived differences in the modes of learning implied by the two forms of knowledge. As we have already seen, for Peters, knowing how is predominantly the stuff of training, and even training may on occasion require 'much more than the mere mastery of a "know how" or "knack"' (Peters, 1973, p. 16). In contrast to the substantial educative processes involved in providing for the kind of conceptual understanding associated with knowing that, 'know-how' might merely be 'caught' or 'learnt by practice and imitation alone' (*ibid.*, p. 15). Similarly there are those who would see 'know-how' as distinctive by virtue of being the kind of knowledge which can be instilled by means of conditioning, in contrast to knowing that which could never be conveyed by such means (Vesey, 1973).

Suffice it to say, then, that there is little common ground between Ryle's account of knowing how and knowing that and that given by Peters. Although both would claim to derive justification for their particular conception of the distinction from the facts of ordinary language usage, there the similarities stop. If ever proof were needed that the vagaries of language usage might be recruited to any and every cause – even those that are diametrically opposed – the knowing how–knowing that distinction is a case in point. While Ryle is determined to counter any attempt to reduce knowing how to knowing that, his argument is acutely dependent upon his being able to show that intelligent capacities are rightly assimilated to his thick conception of knowing how. Conversely, while Peters is keen to avoid reducing intelligent capacities to mere 'know-how' or 'knack', he is more than amenable to the idea that such capacities be assimilated to his thick conception of knowing that.

These attempts to assimilate one form of knowing to the other are a logical corollary of the 'conceptual gerrymandering' (to borrow a phrase from Richard Rorty) by which means these two camps vie to give overriding epistemic priority to either dispositional- or propositional-based conceptions of intelligent capability. But the main point here is not simply that the facts of ordinary usage are unable to provide sufficient grounds for making a legitimate epistemological distinction. It is rather that such contrary accounts cast doubt on there being any clear, non-controversial criteria by which we might either define the concepts or draw a distinction between them.

The absence of any such criteria is further evidenced by the fact that it seems entirely feasible, by extending the logic of either argument, to conceive of either knowing how or knowing that in such thick terms as to largely divest the other of any substantive epistemological content. In other words, if either conception is taken to its logical conclusion the distinction between them disappears altogether. Indeed, even as it stands, Peters' account of knowing how, diminished to the status of mere 'knack' or 'bodily movements', is so epistemologically impoverished that to know how is not really to know at all. Conversely, by emphasizing the performative aspect of propositional knowledge, Ryle's argument might be extended so as to acknowledge that when we judge that a person knows *that* we do so on the basis of whether he or she knows *how* to make a statement or answer questions.[18] Thus it might be argued that, by Ryle's own account, there should not really be a distinction between knowing how and knowing that because all instances of knowing are really cases of knowing how (Hartland-Swann, 1955–6). In this vein, Jane Roland (1958; see also Roland Martin, 1961) has argued that all instances of knowing that can be reduced to knowing how to make statements or answer questions, and that a more germane distinction is to be made between different kinds of knowing how.

Of course, none of these attempts to reduce one kind of knowing to the other are at all tenable. As Godfrey Vesey (1973) puts it, knowing how to skip is not reducible to knowing that if one jumps when the rope is horizontal it will pass under one's feet. And it is equally wrong-headed to assume that knowing that can be assimilated to knowing how to state facts or answer questions. We can immediately recognize that the assimilation of either one to the other necessarily entails a radical depreciation of knowledge. To suggest that the ability to skip is equivalent to knowing certain facts about skipping, or that knowing about the French Revolution is equivalent to knowing how to make appropriate propositional utterances, is to profoundly misunderstand what is involved either in skipping or in knowing about the French Revolution. The important thing here is to recognize that the reason why these attempts at assimilation are mooted at all is that they follow from a certain ontological confusion – a failure to distinguish between knowledge and its outward manifestations. When one kind of 'knowing' is implicitly understood to be an epistemic state of the person but the other is taken to be an outward manifestation of knowing, then it appears feasible to claim that the latter is the consequence of the former and therefore reducible to it.

The crucial mistake here would be to assume that our aversion to assimilating one form of knowing to the other testifies to the existence of two distinct modes of knowledge. Our intuition that there is something fundamentally wrong with such assimilation derives less from our being able to discern two epistemologically distinct categories of knowing, than from the fact that it leaves us incapable of accounting for those cases where there is a conflict between one source of evidence and the other. In other words, we are reluctant to reduce 'knowing how to skip' to knowing certain facts about skipping because we wish to admit of those cases where a person can recite the facts pertaining to skipping but cannot skip. The need here is to differentiate not between two forms of knowledge, but between knowing one thing and knowing another. *This* distinction is one missed by descriptions which might equivocally conjoin the words 'know' and 'skipping'. What is highly significant here is that, ultimately, our need to refer to the kind of evidence we have – to knowing how or knowing that – is symptomatic of the profound difficulties we have in using language to describe intelligent capabilities. This, as we shall see, will prove to be a crucially important issue when we come to consider competence-based approaches to education and training in more detail.

In the same way that we resist the reduction of knowing how to knowing facts, similarly, we are not prepared to reduce knowing that to knowing how to make statements or answer questions, because, for example, it would leave us incapable of accounting for those cases where we are disinclined to judge someone as knowledgeable even though that person can make appropriate utterances, or, conversely, those instances where we might have good reasons to judge someone as knowledgeable despite the fact that he or she cannot express that knowledge. Importantly, then, we distinguish between knowing how and knowing that in such cases not because we are able to differentiate two fundamentally different kinds of knowledge, but because it allows us to draw attention to the kind of evidence we have for judging someone to be knowledgeable and in so doing indicate more clearly *what* it is that is known.

Consequences of the knowing how–knowing that distinction

Before considering some of the consequences of maintaining the knowing how–knowing that distinction, let us sum up the argument so far. First, it has been argued, contra both Ryle and Peters, that the fact that we refer to knowing how and knowing that in ordinary language does not of itself demonstrate the existence of two corresponding and distinct forms of knowledge. Moreover, I have suggested that our use of the distinction might more properly be seen to refer to the kinds of evidence upon which we base our judgements about the knowledge of others, rather than to two epistemologically distinct kinds of knowing. Indeed, I have suggested that this is in part corroborated by Ryle's own assertion that what we mean when we make statements about the mental states of others is essentially delimited by the kinds of evidence it is possible for us to have access to. Second, we have seen that there is little consensus in the literature as to how knowing how and knowing that are to be distinguished or where the line between them is to be drawn. Where individual commentators draw the line is entirely dependent upon their wider purposes. While Ryle's thick–thin configuration of knowing how–knowing that is intended to support his thesis about what it is possible for us to mean when we make statements about the mental, Peters' thin–thick configuration is designed to alert us to the shortcomings of an education which emphasizes doing at the expense of understanding.

Each account has its own failings. To be disposed, with either Ryle or CBET, towards a thick–thin conception of knowing how and knowing that is to compound two kinds of mistake. First, it is to lean towards a behaviourist account of human agency: towards the idea that descriptions of behaviour provide a sufficient account of intelligent capability. Ultimately, to adopt this thick–thin conception is to suffer what Dearden (1984) has called 'the absurd consequence of ignoring the understanding which accompanies and indeed importantly constitutes human behaviour' (p. 140). When this preoccupation with the operational is at its most extreme even propositional knowledge comes to be regarded as the mere capacity to make utterances. The difficulty with this, as Terry Hyland (1994) rightly says, is that it 'not only seriously underestimates what is involved in knowing facts, but also provides ammunition for those who wish to portray knowledge and understanding as inert and passive' (p. 70). Indeed, the second mistake entailed by the thick–thin conception of knowing how and knowing that consists in its tendency towards an impoverished conception of propositional knowledge and of theory, towards the idea that knowledge and theory are in some sense extraneous or even irrelevant to intelligent capability.

On the other hand, to adopt Peters' thin–thick conception of knowing how and knowing that is to veer towards a conception of knowing how as consisting in physical action or 'bodily movement'. This is not only to profoundly underestimate the epistemological richness of human action but it is also to revert to the very mind–body dualism which Ryle was at pains to avoid. When knowing how is made this thin, the distinction is no longer between two different kinds of knowledge but, rather, between having knowledge and not having knowledge. Aside from any philosophical incoherence, when conceived of in these terms the distinction between knowing how and knowing that will not even serve its intended purpose of epistemologically distinguishing the liberal enterprise from those undertakings directed at vocational or instrumental ends. The idea that vocational and the liberal are distinguishable by physical action and knowledge respectively is so manifestly untenable as to hardly need rebuttal:

> In reality of course each encompasses the other. No competence at anything above a purely instinctual level can be gained without some knowledge and some understanding about the application of that knowledge. Electricians without knowledge and understanding quickly become ex-electricians. (Smith, 1996)

Yet, many remain strangely reluctant to relinquish this dichotomy of physical action and formal knowledge, and when its use to characterize the vocational–liberal distinction becomes untenable the dichotomy is turned to other purposes and invoked as a way of discriminating – on putatively epistemic grounds – between different occupations. Hence Ronald Barnett tries to persuade us that

> actions can be distinguished in terms of the balance between formal knowledge and physical activity. At the polar ends of this axis we have, for instance, the pure mathematician and the grand prix racing motorist. In between, but towards the respective ends just indicated, would lie the medical surgeon and the opera singer. (Barnett, 1994, p. 56)

Despite the prima facie plausibility of this kind of claim there is much here of which we should be deeply suspicious. First, there is the highly dubious assumption that knowledge and action can be polarized in this way. Ryle himself did enough to cast doubt on the validity of this divide; in this he is echoed by Bantock (1963) when he writes: 'There is not knowledge *and* activity; there is only activity guided by knowledgeable insight' (original emphasis; p. 142). Yet Barnett's positioning of occupations along an 'axis' of this kind clearly suggests an *opposition* between physical activity and knowledge; it even seems to imply that physical activity and knowledge are mutually exclusive in the sense that a role which is substantially composed of one must of necessity involve less of the other.[19]

Second, and equally questionable, are the assumptions involved in the positioning of particular occupations on the axis. Barnett does not reveal the extent of his own expertise in motor racing or opera singing but we might suspect that there may well be substantially more to know about Grand Prix racing than might be immediately apparent to the uninitiated. Certainly, many would be unconvinced by the suggestion that, say, a recital of Schubert *lieder* could properly be approached with anything less than a wealth of knowledge and the profoundest understanding. But equally, there is also something bizarre about the suggestion that the role of the mathematician or surgeon should be distinguished in part by virtue of being disposed towards inactivity. Of course, such pronouncements probably say more about their author's personal affinities or antipathies towards certain occupational or social groups than they do about the kinds of knowledge involved in any particular occupation. While not wishing to suggest that all occupations are epistemologically equivalent, we should perhaps be prepared to treat with suspicion claims to the effect that the more 'physical' occupations involve little or no knowledge.[20] The main point here, again, is that when knowing how is made this thin, the distinction is no longer between two different kinds of knowledge, but rather between having knowledge and not having knowledge at all.

This kind of discrimination between occupational groups – on ostensibly epistemic grounds – is not the only divisive consequence to derive from the knowing how–knowing that distinction. Closely related to the assumption that there are two forms of knowledge is the widely held view that knowledge which is characterized by its extrinsic utility or economic relevance somehow places fewer demands upon the learner; that knowing how is more easily attained than knowing that. This is not merely to the express the commonplace that learning one thing may be more or less difficult than learning another, or that learning may be at higher or lower levels, for this is equally a feature of any kind of learning, vocational or liberal. Rather, it is to suggest that a distinguishing feature of the vocational curriculum is that it is somehow less demanding than the liberal curriculum, that knowing how lacks, as Peters would put it, the 'cognitive implications' of knowing that. At first sight this might appear to be corroborated by instances where students with a history of underachievement in mainstream education subsequently prove able to apply themselves successfully to learning in a vocational context. It is presumed that the difference in attainment is due to a difference in *what* is learned, that the vocational involves a kind of knowing which is qualitatively different from the academic: a knowing how as opposed to a knowing that. Accordingly, many would see it as entirely appropriate that the 'vocational way of thinking and speaking may, on occasion, be intended only for the less able, even though they might be the majority' (Pring, 1995, p. 188) and that work-related learning be 'confined to the less able for whom training rather than continued education is deemed more appropriate' (*ibid.*). In similar vein, the Chief Inspector of Schools, Chris Woodhead, was reported as suggesting that 'failing pupils', post-14, should 'learn a trade' (O'Leary, 1999) and that 'many young people would be better off training as plumbers than taking GCSE courses' (Poole, 1999, p. 1).

Such views are so widespread as to be almost prosaic. And yet, even prior to any serious philosophical examination, there are several things here which should strike us as rather odd. To begin with, we might question whether the nation's economic interests are best served by this alignment of the vocational with the 'less able' and how this sits with calls for ever more complex vocational skills, capabilities and knowledge. We might wonder whether such views are founded on a sufficient understanding of what is required in 'learning a trade' – would employers, for example, similarly be of the view that the 'less able' or the 'failing' are suitable candidates for such training? But perhaps most telling of all, it might strike us as odd that pupils who have difficulty with, say, mathematics and physics in the school curriculum, suddenly, when faced with remarkably similar subject matter in a vocational context, are able to demonstrate a capacity for learning which previously seemed lacking. To draw attention to this kind of anomaly is not only to cast doubt on the idea that the vocational and the liberal really are as epistemologically distinct as is often assumed; it is also to be obliged to look elsewhere for explanations as to why 'failing pupils' are apparently able to succeed in work-related learning. We might begin to suspect that differences in attainment are due more to differences in the *modes* of learning rather than in *what* is learned – for example, the fact that vocational learning tends to be situated and relevant; we might also acknowledge differences in certain motivational factors. Against this background, the fact that the 'less able' are capable of succeeding in work-related learning might appear more an indictment of mainstream education than it is evidence that education and training are characterized by two distinct kinds of knowledge.

Aside from such epistemic matters there are also undesirable political implications to these kinds of arguments, as Dewey recognized all too well:

> at the present juncture, there is a movement in behalf of something called vocational training which, if carried into effect, would harden these ideas into a form adapted to the existing industrial regime. This movement would continue the traditional liberal or cultural education for the few economically able to enjoy it, and would give to the masses a narrow technical trade education for specialized callings, carried on under the control of others. The scheme denotes, of course, simply a perpetuation of the older social division, with its counterpart intellectual and moral dualisms. (Dewey, 1966, p. 319)

There are many others too who, sharing Dewey's concerns, would strenuously oppose the idea that 'failing pupils' should be directed towards vocational learning, but, significantly, these objections would tend to be made on egalitarian rather than epistemic grounds. For example, John Dunsford, General Secretary of the Secondary Heads Association, responded to the Chief Inspector's suggestion by declaring that: 'We do not simply have two sorts of children, one for whom academic education is appropriate and one better suited to vocational courses' (quoted in O'Leary, 1999). Crucially, to make this kind of objection is not to deny that training and education are characterized by two distinct forms of knowledge – rather, it is to deny, on ethical or political grounds, that it is right to discriminate between pupils with a view to providing one kind of learning rather than the other. The orthodox assumption that education and training entail two fundamentally distinct kinds of 'knowing' goes unchallenged, even by those who recognize the potentially divisive and damaging consequences of maintaining such a distinction.

The widely held assumption that there are two fundamentally distinct forms of knowledge certainly has far-reaching consequences for our understanding of how the vocational enterprise stands in its relation to mainstream education. But the more immediate difficulty here is that any attempt to provide a coherent epistemological account of vocational capability is severely thwarted by the pervasive tendency to frame knowledge in these terms. Michael Eraut's (1985) account of the difficulties associated with 'mapping' the knowledge requirements of a profession is pertinent here. Eraut notes that invariably we are inclined to base such a map either on the sort of knowledge we find listed in the syllabus of a programme of training or, alternatively, on some kind of specification of professional practice. Yet, as he points out, neither kind of account would seem to be sufficient. Attempts to create such a map by reference to the appropriate programme of training will invariably be structured in accordance with traditional assumptions about the likely modes of provision and couched in the language of the syllabus. The problem with this is that areas of knowledge not normally included in the syllabus will tend to be omitted. On the other hand, attempts to avoid such associations and map directly from the study of professional practice are also, as Eraut says, fraught with difficulty, not least because of the implicit nature of much professional knowledge. Accordingly, there will tend to be a wide discrepancy and 'limited overlap between practice-derived maps and syllabi' (p. 119), and even those areas where there *is* overlap will often be structured and described in different ways, with mapping outside these common areas too imprecise to be useful.

What Eraut describes as 'the mapping problem' is essentially a problem caused by thinking of knowledge in terms of the 'knowing how–knowing that' dichotomy. We have noted the fact that, in attempting to describe the knowledgeable states of others, we invariably resort to describing the kind of evidence we have access to: in this case, descriptions of professional practice (knowing how) or descriptions of syllabi (knowing that). Eraut rightly recognizes that neither is sufficient to describe what it is to be vocationally capable. If anything, he understates the problem, for it is clear that what the 'mapping problem' demonstrates is that our conceiving of knowledge in such dichotomous terms stands in the way of providing any coherent account of occupational knowledge.

By way of illustration imagine the following scene. A factory production line is in full swing when suddenly the machines grind to a halt. Alarm bells ring and warning lights flash; a maintenance technician arrives and makes his way to one of a hundred electrical control panels each interconnected perhaps with several miles of cabling. He opens the control panel, takes a screwdriver from his pocket and makes a small adjustment to just one of several hundred components. Closing the control panel he presses some buttons and the production line bursts into life. The question is, how is it possible to account for what the technician knows? His performance did not require the conscious manipulation of propositions or facts – and neither did it require any particular physical dexterity. Here is a kind of expertise much sought after by employers, one that would require no small amount of training, and yet we are unable to account for it in terms of the knowing how–knowing that dichotomy. And this is by no means a special or unusual case; indeed, it would seem that most if not all occupations are exactly the same in this respect.

One of the challenges here will be to develop an account of occupational capability such as it *is* possible to account for just this kind of expertise. But if we are to abandon the knowing how–knowing that dichotomy as epistemic points of reference, we face the question of what conception of knowledge we might put in its place. A preliminary indication of how it might be possible to escape the divisive and obstructive consequences of dividing knowledge in this way is to be found in the work of Michael Oakeshott.

Avoiding the knowing how–knowing that dichotomy

In an important though rarely cited paper, 'Learning and teaching', Michael Oakeshott (1973) provides an account of knowledge which gives an indication of how we might avoid resort to the knowing how–knowing that dichotomy. Oakeshott argues that knowledge should be regarded, not as mental items we carry around with us to be used as necessary, but rather as powers of certain kinds. He suggests that the entirety of what we know should more properly be thought of as a 'manifold' of abilities, with more complex abilities comprising simpler abilities. Similarly, the abilities associated with a particular occupation might be regarded as a manifold of simpler abilities which are 'grouped and given a specific focus' (p. 164). Crucially, in contrast to Ryle, Oakeshott does *not* intend this to be an indication of how we gain access to, or make claims about, other people's knowledge. Indeed, he purposefully avoids just this pragmatic reading, and hence the behaviourism which besets Ryle's account, by emphasizing that abilities of different kinds cannot be assimilated or reduced to one another. For example, 'the ability to understand or to explain cannot be assimilated to the ability to do or make' (*ibid.*).

Oakeshott goes on to suggest that knowledge can be thought of as a conjunction of 'information' and what he calls 'judgement'. Information is the explicit ingredient of knowledge, consisting of facts about the world of the sort typically found in textbooks and encyclopaedias. It is neither inherently useful nor useless – it can only be relevant or irrelevant to the matter in hand. However, as Oakeshott points out, the facts, propositions or rules which constitute information cannot on their own provide us with the ability to do, make, understand or explain anything. For us to have abilities, information has to be selected and interpreted, and we also have to be able to discern when and where to use it.

> What is required in addition to information is knowledge which enables us to interpret it, to decide upon its relevance, to recognise what rule to apply and to discover what action permitted by the rule should, in the circumstances, be performed; knowledge (in short) capable of carrying us across those wide open spaces, to be found in every ability, where no rule runs. (*Ibid.*, p. 168)

So information is never entirely sufficient for knowledge: as Oakeshott puts it, 'it never constitutes the whole of what we know' (*ibid.*, p. 167), for any ability also requires 'judgement':

> that which, when united with information, generates knowledge or 'ability' to do, to make, or to understand and explain. It is being able to think – not to think in no manner in particular, but to think with an appreciation of the considerations which belong to different modes of thought. (*Ibid.*, p. 173)

Clearly, Oakeshott is not using the term 'judgement' here in the ordinary performative sense of the word as, for example, when someone explicitly makes a decision or expresses a preference. Rather, he uses 'judgement' to signify the tacit component of knowledge – that component of knowledge which is unspecifiable in propositions, and it is for this reason that it cannot be regarded as just another form of information. Neither can it be resolved into information, or be expressed or itemized as such. Where *abilities* are unspecifiable, as Polanyi and Schön famously identified, then this for Oakeshott would indicate a lack of informatory content in what is known, rather than the existence of a special category of knowing.

On Oakeshott's view it is a mistake to hypothesize a knowing how which can be separated from, and dichotomously set in opposition to, a knowing that. For knowing how, in this sense, should more properly be regarded as a component part of *all* knowledge and it is for this reason, specifically to avoid this all-too-common misconception, that Oakeshott uses the term 'judgement' to denote this ubiquitous, non-informatory component of knowledge.[21] The two 'components' of knowledge, i.e. information and judgement, should be seen not as two fundamental forms or categories of knowing but rather as a 'synthesis'. The distinction between them, such that it is, is 'a distinction between different manners of communication rather than a dichotomy in what is known', for each cannot be communicated separately, but neither can they be communicated in the same manner. For Oakeshott the distinction is of educational rather than epistemological import; for what it means is that the processes of learning consist of a 'two-fold activity of acquiring "information" and coming to possess "judgement"' (*ibid.*, p. 170).

Importantly, Oakeshott's thesis runs counter to those who would see judgement as characteristic of a liberal rather than a vocational education (e.g. Maskell, 1999), or as a characteristic feature of the professional as opposed to the technical or vocational (see Eraut, 1994, pp. 48–9). On the contrary, according to Oakeshott, with the most practical or technical skills it is precisely judgement, rather than information, which is the *greater* part of what is known. That said, it would be a mistake to identify this component of knowledge primarily with the manual or sensual skills since 'its place in art and literature, in historical, philosophical or scientific understanding is almost immeasurably greater' (Oakeshott, 1973, p. 168). In textual criticism, for example, judgement is what 'comes into play where the information to be got from the collation of MSS and recension stops'. It is what 'escapes even the most meticulous list of the qualities required for practising the craft of the textual critic' (*ibid.*).

Later we shall take up certain other aspects of Oakeshott's paper, but we can already see that it has several important implications. First, it indicates how we might begin to think of knowledge without having to resort to the knowing how–knowing that dichotomy, a dichotomy which would seem to be inimical to any coherent account of vocational capability. Second, it raises the possibility of being able to emphasize the 'doing' aspects of human affairs, i.e. abilities, without sliding into behaviourism. Third, in stressing the centrality of certain mental processes, what Oakeshott here refers to as judgement, it points to the essentially mentalistic nature of such abilities.

We might say, with Bantock (1963), that to conceive of knowledge in terms of knowing how and knowing that is to perpetrate a 'false distinction' (p. 143). Contrary to the orthodoxy, we have seen that the distinction more properly refers to the evidential conditions of our claims about the knowledgeable states of others. The fact that the literature contains such widely conflicting interpretations of knowing how and knowing that serves to demonstrate the incoherence of the distinction and the implausibility of the idea that it corresponds to two forms of knowledge.[22] Moreover, it is a distinction which is inherently divisive – providing a fulcrum around which so many other distinctions can be seen to revolve, for example training–education, physical–mental, theory–practice, and one which seems to be fundamentally inimical to providing a coherent account of occupational capability. Oakeshott's account of knowledge as a 'manifold of abilities' indicates that it is possible to shake free of this dichotomy, a dichotomy which, buttressed by the logic of ordinary language philosophy, stands at the very centre of the orthodoxy. Before considering how we might build on Oakeshott's notion of knowledge in order to construct a more coherent account of what it is to be vocationally capable, we must turn to consider one further legacy of ordinary language philosophy: its impact on the recent debate about competence-based education and training.

Notes

[14] Here Ryle might be regarded as prefiguring the likes of Michael Polanyi or Donald Schön in acknowledging that certain aspects of knowledge are essentially tacit.

[15] One of the earliest examples of this tendency is Aristotle's (1975) distinction in *Ethica Nicomachea* between practical and theoretical reason.

[16] Oakeshott is obviously reluctant to admit of two separate epistemological

categories, speaking as he does of the 'distinguishable but inseparable ... twin components of knowledge' (1991, p. 12). As we shall see, in another paper Oakeshott modifies and greatly clarifies his argument regarding the 'twin components' of knowledge.

[17] Given Peters' references to such things as 'understanding' and 'conceptual schemes' as distinct from knowing how, the Rylean critic would presumably accuse Peters of attempting to reinstate the 'intellectualist legend' – we might say that, by Peters' account, the 'ghost in the machine' is alive and well.

[18] Some might see Searle's (1969) 'speech acts' or Austin's (1970) 'performative utterances' (p. 233) as providing a precedent for a performative account of propositional knowledge.

[19] It is not exactly clear whether Barnett intends this axis to operate on a proportional or a qualitative assessment of knowledge against physical activity: in other words, whether his positioning of the role of medical surgeon towards the knowledge end of the axis is based on the *relative* amount of knowledge compared with physical action; a low-skilled job requiring little knowledge and even less physical action might, in this view, feasibly occupy the same point on the axis as the surgeon. Or, alternatively, whether built into this classification of occupations is an overriding value placed on knowledge as against action; an occupation's position on the axis is substantively determined by the extent of formal knowledge presumed to be involved, regardless of the extent of physical action.

[20] Barnett introduces a second and equally questionable way of classifying occupations, that of communication: 'At the polar ends of this axis would lie the psychoanalyst and the clay-pigeon shooter. In between, and towards those respective ends, would lie the physiotherapist and the currency dealer in the dealing room' (1994, p. 56). Again, we might suspect partiality: it is perhaps not entirely coincidental that the role of an academic would rate highly on both counts, i.e. 'formal knowledge' and 'communication'; it might reasonably be objected that there are other, equally pertinent grounds for classifying occupations, for example imagination, creativity, judgement, productivity, responsibility, leadership, to name but a few.

[21] Gribble (1969) can be seen to make a similar point when he says that 'knowing something involves judging that something is so, and judging is a complex mental operation' (p. 58).

[22] Elsewhere (Lum, 2007) I have demonstrated the *logical* incoherence of assuming that it is possible to derive a meaningful epistemic distinction from the fact of there being a division in the 'consequent conditions' of knowing (such as that between knowing how and knowing that).

4

The Competence Problem

If ever proof were needed of the continuing influence of Oxford philosophy in the philosophy of education, we need look no further than the literature surrounding the recent debate on competence-based education and training. Here, in their eagerness to apply analytical techniques to a 'concept', many commentators took at face value CBET's naïve identification of its methodology with the notion of 'competence'. Beguiled by CBET's use of the word, critics have thus far concentrated their efforts on explicating 'the concept of competence', not realizing that in so doing they were not only misperceiving their target but also inadvertently vindicating CBET's arrogation of the term. So widespread has been the inclination to identify CBET with the notion of 'competence' that it will be useful to examine the debate in some detail before proposing a more appropriate characterization.

Advocates of the competence approach would regard it as a truism to say that it is an approach characterized by the primacy afforded to competent performance, combined with a concern to make explicit and public the criteria by which we gain the measure of competence. This identification of CBET with the notion of competence has gone largely unquestioned; certainly the bulk of critical attention has been firmly fixed on 'the concept of competence', with critics variously highlighting the inconsistency, ambiguity or incoherence of what is generally perceived to be CBET's central, distinguishing feature. Much has been made of the fact that there is 'no agreed definition of the term' (McAleavey and McAlleer, 1991, p. 20). It has been famously identified as an 'El Dorado of a word with a wealth of meanings' (Norris, 1991, p. 331), a term which 'attracts many different shades of interpretation' (Debling, 1989, p. 80). Out of such indeterminacy there has arisen a plethora of disparate interpretations with commentators differentiating variously between competence as 'enhanced performance' and competence as a 'deep structure responsible for the surface performance' (Wood and Power, 1987, p. 409), between 'behaviourist', 'generic' and 'cognitive' constructs (Norris, 1991), between competence as 'capacity' and competence as 'disposition' (Carr, 1993), between 'operational' and 'academic' competence (Barnett, 1994), and even between 'competence' and 'competency' (Hyland, 1994). Given the nebulous nature of the concept it is hardly surprising that one commentator has asked 'how can a system which claims to be based on precise standards and explicit outcomes be allowed to get away with such confusion about the basic terms which are at the heart and foundation of the whole process?' (Hyland, 1994, p. 21).

Suffice it to say, then, that 'the concept of competence' has become the focus of critical attention with critics generally denouncing CBET on the grounds that this, its supposed central concept, is fundamentally flawed. In so doing, however, critics would seem to have misperceived their target. Indeed, I want to suggest that in spite of its deceptive appellation CBET is more properly characterized, not by the notion of competence, but by its highly idiosyncratic and philosophically naïve methodological strategy. Certainly the tactic of attempting to demonstrate the implausibility of CBET by highlighting the inadequacies of 'the concept of competence' has had little practical impact and this, I want to suggest, is due in no small part to certain difficulties with the critical position.

A problem with the critical position

One of the predominant critical themes in the competence debate is the idea that the very notion of competence somehow compromises knowledge and understanding. But attempts by critics to pin down a particular conception of competence in order to demonstrate the concept's shortcomings in this regard are invariably met by insistent counter-claims from the competence strategist that what *he* means by 'competence' is specifically such as to encompass all that is required by way of knowledge, understanding, or indeed 'whatever else it takes' (cf. Bridges, 1996). On this view it is a paradox to ask 'is competence enough?' (Williams, 1994, p. 6), or suggest that we go 'beyond competence' (Barnett, 1994, p. 172) or query whether it is 'good enough' (Ashworth, 1990) because competence, for the competence strategist, is by definition all-inclusive and necessarily sufficient – anything less would *not be* 'competence'.

This impasse – centred upon rival interpretations of a single word – has become one of the abiding features of the 'competence debate', where, in the tradition of linguistic analysis, attempts have been made to resolve the dissension by appealing to the facts of ordinary language usage. But, as we might expect given our previous discussion of the linguistic approach, such facts do not help us here. There is little to be gained by our noting – true though it is – that 'competent' is used in ordinary language as a 'lower order kind of concept' (Hyland, 1994, p. 20), one which denotes mere sufficiency or some form of basic minimum, when by the same token we must also acknowledge that the word is equally used as a term of approbation. We witness an almost palpable frustration on the part of CBET's critics, who must ultimately concede that since 'we talk naturally of individuals being competent, and with some sense of praiseworthiness ... There can be no objection *in principle* to the application of the terms (competence and

outcomes) to educational processes' (original emphasis; Barnett, 1994, p. 71).
If anyone has the last word in the ordinary language argument it must be the
competence strategist simply because, as Norris (1991) rightly acknowledges,
'competence and standards are good words, modern words; everybody is for
standards and everyone is against incompetence' (p. 331). Much of the
cogency of the competence strategist's position derives from this simple fact of
language usage, hence for the critic to allow the debate to be framed in these
terms is to effectively relinquish the argument.

Ultimately, the strategy of selecting, from the range of possible
interpretations of 'competence', those which fortuitously support our wider
educational purposes is unlikely to enable us to arbitrate between such
competing claims. Again, we might recall Ruth Jonathan's insight that:

> Scrutiny of what we 'know', as revealed in how we think and speak, will . . .
> not reveal significant non-contingent truths about reality. It will not reveal
> whether or not our beliefs are right and our purposes justified: it will simply
> help us appreciate the interconnections between our beliefs and their
> relation to our purposes. (Jonathan, 1985, p. 17)

Indeed, it is precisely because ordinary language usage will not enable us
to arbitrate between conflicting interpretations of 'competence' that the
critical case against CBET is severely weakened by allowing the disputation to
be reduced to one of semantic sparring. Not least because even those who
acknowledge the shortcomings of existing models of CBET may be seduced
into thinking that a 'more generic and cognitively laden' (Bridges 1996, p.
361) concept of competence remains at least a theoretical possibility and that
CBET can be exonerated by the simple expedient of adopting a definition of
competence which sufficiently includes knowledge, understanding, values or
'whatever else'. The fact that 'knowledge and understanding is . . . treated in a
paltry way by the advocates of the competence model' (Ashworth, 1992, p.
10) thus comes to be regarded as a description of contingent circumstance –
and hence open to piecemeal modification and improvement – rather than an
indication of some more serious, underlying, non-contingent difficulty.

But the real problem here is not simply that we lack the means to arbitrate
between conflicting definitions of competence, but rather that in making 'the
concept of competence' the object of attention, we allow an obstructive
conflation of two logically distinct constructs: on the one hand competence as
an educational *aim*, and on the other, competence as a construct *inferred* from
methodology. When Gilbert Jessup (1991) tells us, for example, that someone
'who is described as competent in an occupation or profession is considered to
have a repertoire of skills, knowledge and understanding' (p. 26), we can take
it that he is attempting to delineate competence as an educational aim – an
end towards which the educational enterprise, or at least the business of
assessment, should be directed. In contrast, when critics make reference to,

say, the behaviourist foundations of the competence approach (Ashworth and Saxton, 1990; Marshall, 1991; Hodkinson, 1992; Hyland, 1993a, 1993b, 1994, 1997) and draw attention to CBET's insufficient regard for knowledge and understanding, the 'concept of competence' being presented is essentially that of a construct inferred from the de facto consequences of CBET's methodological strategy, what we might call the 'critical construct' of competence. There is thus a sense in which advocate and critic have simply been talking at cross-purposes.

The crucial thing here is the fundamental non-commensurability of these two configurations of competence, the point being that no matter how conclusive the evidence stacked up against the 'critical construct' this does not carry over to, or detract from, 'competence' as an educational end. Certainly, such evidence may render questionable the likelihood of attaining such ends given the particular strategies employed, but this cannot detract from the validity or coherence of the end itself, nor rule out the possibility that an alternative strategy may more effectively attain that end. This is precisely why the critic, in characterizing CBET in terms of 'the concept of competence', is unable to be rid of the spectre of 'alternative models' (Hyland, 1997, p. 492) of CBET, models or strategies which are claimed to avoid by some means or other the inadequacies of existing strategies. We need to be clear, therefore, about what it is that constitutes both necessary and sufficient condition for an educational approach to be identified as 'competence based'. For only when CBET is correctly characterized can we determine the extent to which critical attention should be directed at the conceptual integrity of 'competence' as an educational aim, or towards CBET's methodological strategy.

The identifying features of CBET

Insofar as we are clear that we are considering competence as an aim there appears to be little reason not to allow the competence strategist an extended, all-embracing notion of competence, one which by definition is epistemologically and cognitively all-inclusive. Recognizing that this will be an anathema to many of CBET's critics, I should quickly emphasize that to allow this is not to allow very much at all. For, when competence is defined in such comprehensive terms, the demand by proponents of CBET that competence should form the focus of our educational endeavour becomes nothing more than an empty platitude, a slogan devoid of any significant content.

There are two important points to be extricated from this. First, when defined thus CBET certainly cannot claim to have a monopoly over such ends: *any* educational strategy might be equally justified in claiming to have equivalent concerns – though without CBET's jargon it might be less obvious. In the very broadest sense of the word every educational activity and every form of assessment might ultimately be regarded as aimed at the provision or measurement of competence of some kind. Thus when we allow the competence strategist an all-embracing notion of competence, it becomes difficult to see how the concept of competence is any more a unique identifying characteristic of CBET than it is of any other approach, or how having such an aim constitutes sufficient condition for us to be able to identify an educational approach as 'competence based'.

The second point is that notwithstanding the abundance of competence-orientated jargon within CBET literature – the incessant references to 'competence' and 'competences' – the capacity of CBET to substantively achieve its ends, given that competence is conceived of in such comprehensive terms, is an entirely contingent matter and one which remains to be demonstrated. This point should be obvious, but the competence slogans continue to be extremely persuasive for those who fail to correctly distinguish between educational ends and strategies merely *labelled as those ends*. It is clear that the competence strategist fails to see any difficulty here and assumes a correspondence between competence as an aim, and the so-called 'competences' which constitute CBET's modus operandi. This identification of method with aim allows the competence strategist to arrogate for his method terms such as 'competence' with total impunity. Furthermore the critic, who in denouncing 'the concept of competence' similarly fails to distinguish between method and aim, merely sustains the deception. For CBET's claim that it has a special association with competence to be substantiated we would require evidence, first of a correspondence, and second of a causal relationship between methodological strategy and aim. In the absence of such evidence 'competence' could not be regarded as an analytic feature of CBET.

But competence is not the only analytic feature claimed for CBET. There are those who, while never having been endeared by the concept of competence, nevertheless find it difficult to shake off the conviction that there must be something of value in an approach which is ostensibly directed towards a capacity or disposition to act in the world, and which is concerned to make explicit and public the criteria by which we gain the measure of such capacities or dispositions. Of course, nowhere is this conviction likely to be more assured and such priorities appear more appropriate than in relation to vocational education and training. But when 'doing' is thought of in the widest social, cultural and even moral sense then there is also a prima facie case for the application of CBET to the wider educational enterprise. Just such a case is put by David Bridges when he notes that:

> One of the features that is common to all forms of competence-based education, training and assessment is the highlighting of what people can *do* ... such concerns are not merely compatible with, but required by, a commitment to an education that is liberal or liberating. (Original emphasis; Bridges, 1996, p. 364; see also UDACE, 1989)

Now surely Bridges is right to assert that a concern for the 'doing' dimension of a human being is an indispensable constituent of a truly liberal education, and that the emancipatory aims of such an education would be severely compromised were it to leave individuals 'incapable of acting in and upon a social world' (*ibid.*, p. 364). Against this background the competence strategist's assertion that priority should be attached to 'what people can *do*' is incontrovertible, particularly when applied to educational endeavours within a vocational context. The question here, however, is what exactly the competence approach has to offer in this respect. Indeed, what all of this hangs on is our being prepared to accept at face value this identification of CBET with some kind of special aggrandizement of human action: its having some intrinsic, unique or at least enhanced capacity to attend to the 'doing' aspects of human affairs that is found lacking in alternative approaches. I want to suggest, *pace* Bridges, that this is not the case and that 'doing' is not an analytic feature of CBET.

The competence lobby would find this difficult. They would regard CBET's association with 'doing' as self-evident – given their lists of 'can do's' and their free use of terms such as 'performance'. To be frivolous we might say that if this is all that is meant when it is said that CBET 'highlights what people can do' then we would have to agree. But the serious point here is that, again, in accepting – as the competence strategist would have it – that CBET's aims consist of the most comprehensive conception of 'doing', then it remains to be demonstrated that its methods correspond to and are causally related to such ends. The putative association with 'doing' is not, in any but the most trivial sense, an analytic feature of CBET.

At the risk of being tedious, the same point has to be made concerning the notion of 'outcomes'. Perhaps it was the hope of distancing CBET from criticism directed at 'the concept of competence' which led some of its main protagonists to lessen their emphasis on 'competences' in favour of 'outcomes';[23] perhaps it was partly because the notion of 'outcomes' was thought to lend itself more readily to wider, non-vocational applications. But the point here is exactly the same: it is not that we might object to the idea of education having 'outcomes' but rather, assuming that the competence strategist would have us understand 'outcomes' in the fullest sense, it needs to be demonstrated that CBET's methods correspond to such ends.

It would seem, then, that where competence and non-competence approaches differ is not in their declared ends but in the strategies employed to delineate and attain such ends. What distinguishes the competence strategist's position is not any *purposefully* distinctive notion of human capability, competence or skill, but simply the claim that the educational enterprise can be meaningfully and sufficiently specified by means of 'statements of outcome', 'performance criteria', 'range statements', and the like. Such statements are so patently essential to the competence approach that without them there would be little else to distinguish CBET. Indeed, it might be altogether more appropriate for CBET to be identified as a 'statement-based' approach. Importantly, if the use of such statements constitutes a sufficient condition for us to be able to identify an approach as being 'competence based', then it follows that the putative associations with 'competence' or with 'doing' are not necessary conditions. We can thus acknowledge the logical possibility that the use of such statements is insufficient for, or even antithetical to, the task of specifying competent performance. For the moment, however, I simply want to suggest that if there is one feature which characterizes CBET – the attendance of which constitutes both necessary and sufficient conditions for an approach to be identified (in spite of the misnomer) as 'competence based' – it is the singular assumption that the educational enterprise can be unequivocally, accurately and sufficiently delineated by means of such statements. If there is a case to be made against CBET it must be made here.

Competence statements and the problem of 'ontological shift'

For the competence strategist, the capacity to create statements of outcome is a prerequisite of any educational endeavour: 'If you cannot say what you require, how can you develop it and how do you know when you have achieved it?' (Jessup, 1991, p. 134). The entire competence project is buttressed by the apparently unassailable logic of this question. But by Gilbert Jessup's own account if for any reason we are unable to *accurately* state what we require, in *precise* terms, the competence approach is effectively bankrupt:

> statements must accurately communicate their intent. For accurate communication of the outcomes of competence and attainment, a precision in the use of language in such statements will need to be established, approaching that of a science. The overall model stands or falls on how effectively we can state competence and attainment. (*Ibid.*)

This proclamation effectively sets the arena for the debate proper. First, it clearly demonstrates the role expected of language; second, in its overt reference to science, it hints at the empiricist assumptions which, as we shall see, underpin CBET; and third, it acknowledges the measure against which the competence approach must ultimately be judged.

In considering the extent to which it is possible for such statements to 'communicate their intent' the first thing we should note is that they have two different uses and hence two different meanings. First, they are used to *prescribe* the commitments and priorities required or expected of educational practitioners. To issue a statement of competence is to make a particular form of demand upon the educator; it is to require the educative process to be directed towards a particular goal. Second, statements of outcome are intended to be used in a *descriptive* capacity – this is most obvious when they are used as criteria for assessment. Whatever their perceived merits when used prescriptively, it is their capacity to *describe* the educational enterprise which is of paramount importance within the CBET scheme of things. The political and managerial appeal of such descriptions consists in the fact that they provide the means to hold educators to account. The distinction, one evaded by Jessup in his elliptical references to 'communicating' or 'stating' competence, is not at all clear-cut.[24] But it is important because while such statements may be tenable in their prescriptive capacity, as descriptions their feasibility seems to be a very different matter.

Certainly there is much to recommend the use of such descriptions if they are possible. On the face of it they hold the promise of giving direction to the educational enterprise, of providing clarity of purpose and a curriculum unencumbered by the irrelevant or merely autochthonous. Having clear and precise descriptions of the skills or capabilities required might help counter the not uncommon tendency for the vocational curriculum to accumulate theory for theory's sake. Such descriptions might foster not only a more effective enterprise, but also one which is more open, more accountable and more democratic, one in which the student can benefit from knowing in advance what is to be learned and what is to be assessed. Indeed, the prospect of precise descriptions is of particular import in the context of assessment where it has one especially important consequence. For if such descriptions are possible then it would seem that we are duty bound to dispense with considerations relating to the kind of preparation a person has received as a measure of fitness to practise in an occupation. Fairness, not to say common sense, would require us to disregard such 'inputs' and afford priority to the overriding issue of whether a person has attained the capabilities described – whether he or she is competent.

Such sentiments go a long way towards explaining the appeal and increasing prevalence of 'competence', 'outcomes' and 'skills-based' approaches; indeed, it might be said that the entirety of present policy-making and practice in education, not only in the UK but increasingly elsewhere, is underpinned by the assumption that such descriptions are possible. It is extraordinary that these strategies have gained such widespread acceptance and been afforded such unqualified official approval while the very assumption upon which they are based seems hardly to have received any attention. What makes this all the more remarkable is that there would appear to be profound and irrevocable difficulties with the idea that competence can be specified in clear and precise terms.

Now it is not being suggested that we are incapable of indicating the ends of vocational education in some broad or general way. Indeed, some expression of ultimate aim might reasonably be regarded a prerequisite to any meaningful educational endeavour. There is nothing unduly problematic, for example, in our determining that a maintenance engineer should, among other things, be able to 'maintain engineering assets' and that training should be directed towards that end. However, for those anticipating a precise and unequivocal description of what the engineer should be capable of, a statement such as this is disappointingly devoid of content; as vacuous as it is innocuous, it raises more questions than it answers. 'What kind of "engineering assets" are to be maintained?' it will be asked. Under what circumstances or in what contexts might this task be performed? What exactly is meant by 'maintain'? While those familiar with the role in question would doubtless find such a statement replete with potential meanings and pregnant with educational possibilities, it could hardly be said to specify, in clear and unambiguous terms, what it is to be competent.

It is at this juncture that those intent on arriving at a more precise description will take a characteristic and, it will turn out, quite crucial step. For it will be presumed that this ambiguity is to be remedied by the creation of further, more specific statements intended to stand in relation to the first, we might say, as sub-statements. On this view the specification that the student be able to 'maintain engineering assets' might be given requisite substance by adding further statements specifying, for instance, the kind of assets to be maintained, the various circumstances or contexts in which the task might be carried out, perhaps detailing along the way any relevant standards, health and safety regulations, and so on. The perception is of an hierarchical, vertically structured framework in which generic statements derive meaning from more specific or more detailed sub-statements. This is the stock approach of 'functional analysis' and it is a strategy very much in evidence in the 'learning outcomes', 'range statements' and 'performance criteria' that characterize outcomes-based curricula and competence-based assessment procedures.

Yet this supposed breaking down of educational objectives is not at all what it seems. The idea that this second group of statements represents simply a more specific or more detailed rendering of the first is thrown into doubt when we consider *what* these statements describe. In the case of an occupation such as engineering, for example, they will inevitably be centred on the various equipment, machines, tools, in other words the *things* the engineer may encounter. Few would find anything surprising or untoward about this and, significantly, many would find it difficult to conceive of how else such an occupation might be specified. Certainly, such descriptions have the advantage of allowing an inordinate degree of precision. Nonetheless, it might be said that there is something distinctly odd about the idea that protracted lists of artefacts and equipment can somehow constitute an *educational* specification. It might reasonably be asked how an inventory of equipment, however detailed, can represent what it is to be skilled or competent.

The issue is brought into sharper relief when we contrast this with the function of the originating, generic statement. For to state, as an expression of educational intent, that the student should be able to 'maintain engineering assets' is above all to say something about the *person*, it is to say something about what we as educators aim to achieve with respect to that person and his or her capabilities. There is thus a quite radical ontological disparity, between what is intended by the generic statement and what is described by its ostensible sub-statements. In moving from one kind of statement to the other we shift not to a more precise description of the same thing, but, rather, to a description of something else; there is, we might say, an 'ontological shift' in focus. The implicit assumption that these two kinds of statement stand in some hierarchical relation to each other is mistaken, for what we take to be sub-statements will often be such as to facilitate a *sideways* shift in our attention towards an ontology which is at some remove from the object of our original intentions.

Clearly, not all occupations would or could be described in terms of artefacts and equipment; indeed, if we were to scrutinize a range of specifications for different roles we would find references to any number of things including processes, procedural rules, behavioural traits, items of factual knowledge, values, attitudes, kinds of physical dexterity, documents or texts, to name but a few. But the fact that different occupations might be specified in such ontologically disparate terms only underscores the profoundly contingent nature of such descriptions. The elliptical notion that such statements simply describe 'tasks' obscures the substantive issue of *what* is being described and *why*.

Any human involvement presents, potentially, an array of manifestations which, in teleological terms, might be thought of as forming a continuum stretching outwards from the person to his or her intended end, i.e. from person to object. It is not without significance that from the perspective of instrumental rationality the direction of this continuum is reversed, i.e. from object to person. Notwithstanding this contrariety, if we trace the path of this continuum we can see that it may involve any number of distinct ontologies each of which may or may not be included in a specification. In describing the work of a craftsman, for example, we may choose to specify the finished product, or we might describe the kinds of materials worked to achieve that end, or the various tools or machines employed; we might describe the procedures adopted, the rules followed; we might detail the kinds of dexterity needed to use the equipment; we might choose to itemize certain behavioural traits; at the far end of this continuum, we might try to articulate what it is the craftsman understands, and the kinds of judgements or other mental processes that might be brought to bear in carrying out the task. Now we might choose to describe all or just some of these manifestations. But the crucial point here is that we are involved unavoidably in making certain decisions, we have to *choose* what to describe and how to describe it.

Our aspiring to produce the most comprehensive specification does nothing to rid us of this choice. For as Friederich Waismann recognized, there is no logical solution to the question of what counts as a sufficient or complete description:

> If I had to describe (this) right hand of mine, which I am now holding up, I may say different things about it: I may state its size, its shape, its colour, its tissue, the chemical compound of its bones, its cells, and perhaps some more particulars; but however far I go I shall never reach a point where my description will be completed: logically speaking, it is always possible to extend the description by adding some detail or other. (Waismann, 1951, pp. 121–2)

So in specifying just one aspect of a task a line has to be drawn somewhere and hence a decision has to be made where it is drawn. It follows, then, that implicit in any specification are a whole range of judgements, not only about which aspects are to be regarded as relevant, but also about what counts as a sufficient description of any aspect and thus, by inference, the relative emphasis placed on each aspect. Once we become sensitive to their substantive ontological focus – rather than accepting at face value the idea that they simply describe 'tasks' – we can see that specifications are often far from comprehensive; indeed, we begin to appreciate just how narrow and highly selective their focus may be. To take our previous example, by listing in great detail the equipment to be worked on while simultaneously leaving unarticulated and indeterminate the issue of what is meant by 'maintain', the ontological focus of the statement 'maintain engineering assets' is shifted away from the person towards the object. Such a statement might typically be disparaged as a 'behavioural objective' yet it is not even focused on behaviour. In fact, a specification might often be focused on surprisingly few of the many different manifestations of capability that lie between the person and his or her intended end. But the important thing here is what it is that determines that focus, why priority is ascribed to one thing rather than another, and why different occupations might come to be described in very different terms.

It is true, of course, that different roles require us to do and know different things, but this commonplace serves to conceal the extent to which radically different modes of description come to be accepted as appropriate for different occupations. To take just one example, the entirely contingent matter of whether or not an occupation happens to have some clearly identifiable, concrete outcome such as a manufactured product will invariably have a significant bearing on how that occupation is specified. An occupation which has such an outcome will almost certainly be described, to a greater or lesser extent, in terms of that object. Yet a role which might be acknowledged to be not dissimilar in terms of the understandings and skills required, but having some far less tangible outcome, necessarily will be specified in very different terms – perhaps in terms of behaviour, rules, procedures, or some other feature. Not only is this sufficient to controvert the often implicit assumption that specifications are always directed at instrumental ends, but it serves to indicate what it is that determines the substantive focus of any specification, what it is that causes the focus to settle on one thing rather than another. For if such ontologically diffuse specifications can be said to have anything in common, any shared rationale, it is that they are inclined to describe the most readily discernible features of an occupation, those features most favourably disposed to precise description. In short, they gravitate towards what *can* be described rather than perhaps what *ought* to be described.

Of all the various manifestations of human capability the least tangible and the least disposed to precise explication are those centred in the person. Michael Polanyi famously provides the first indication that there is something wrong-headed about the assumption that such capabilities can be unequivocally described and accurately communicated by means of language:

> I shall reconsider human knowledge by starting from the fact that *we can know more than we can tell*. This fact seems obvious enough; but it is not easy to say exactly what it means. Take an example. We know a person's face, and can recognize it among a thousand, indeed among a million. Yet we usually cannot tell how we recognize a face we know. So most of this knowledge cannot be put into words. (Original emphasis; Polanyi, 1983, p. 4)

For Polanyi, even the simplest physical skills are not given to being described in precise terms: '... a skill combines elementary muscular acts which are not identifiable, according to relations that we cannot define' (*ibid.* p. 8). The point is reiterated by Donald Schön:

> When we go about the spontaneous, intuitive performance of the actions of everyday life, we show ourselves to be knowledgeable in a special way. Often we cannot say what it is that we know. When we try to describe it we find ourselves at a loss or we produce descriptions that are obviously inappropriate. (Schön, 1996, p. 49)

There is thus an important sense in which the demand for precise and unambiguous specifications is fundamentally incompatible with the need to take account of the understandings, the capacities for judgement, imagination, problem-solving and the host of other propensities and proficiencies which are so vital for competent action. The practical repercussions of this are far-reaching. Inevitably, the more ungainly and rudimentary specifications – of which there are many examples within the UK's system of National Vocational Qualifications (NVQs) – will focus upon the more readily discernible features of performance and neglect these all-important attributes. Such specifications will be described by their critics as behaviouristic – which in their effects, of course, they are. But these are shortcomings engendered more by philosophical naïvety than by any distinctive conception of mind or capability – motivated only by the bureaucratic imperative for clarity and precision.

Our first instinct might be to suppose that this neglect would be most deleterious for those occupations more obviously reliant upon these less tangible attributes - the professions, perhaps. But the skewing of specifications towards the more concrete manifestations of capability might be seen to be of greater detriment to those occupations involved with making and doing – i.e. the crafts and blue collar occupations – simply because those occupations present far greater opportunity for resort to descriptions of artefacts, equipment, etc. Competence in plumbing is likely to be regarded as sufficiently delineated by descriptions of boilers, wrenches and temperature settings, in contrast to competence in, say, law or management, where there is not the same recourse to an equivalent ontology. It is not difficult to recognize the potentially divisive consequences of this, how easy it is to become ensnared in the socially and educationally damaging dualisms that have long beleaguered vocational education. Yet again, circumstances can be seen to conspire to endorse a denigration of those occupations more readily associated with physical ontologies and concrete outcomes, with the understandings and attributes substantively required by those occupations systematically being understated. Indeed, in practice – barely credible though it may seem – the inclusion of person-centred attributes within a specification may derive less from any coherent conception of those attributes than from the contingent fact of there being little else to describe.

Yet whatever difficulties are faced in using language to describe human capabilities the use of competence-based approaches is invariably accompanied by the conviction, one which we would all to some extent share, that whether or not someone is competent, skilled or capable is something which can be treated as a matter of fact. By this I mean that we tend to regard our judgements about such matters as being objective in a sense which distinguishes them from certain other kinds of judgement. For example, we would tend to consider our claim that 'X is a competent builder' as in some sense immune from the subjectivity involved in claiming that 'that is a beautiful sunset' or 'act A is morally preferable to act B'. Of course, the distinction is really one of degree as indicated by statements such as 'X is a competent artist'. Nevertheless, it is compelling, particularly in a vocational context, to want to be able to say, as a matter of fact, that someone either can or cannot do a job, perform a task or demonstrate an ability. The statements which characterize CBET might be said to be an expression of just such facts.

CBET's critics have not been slow to seize upon the distinction intimated here between fact and value. Indeed, one of the more counter-productive features of the 'competence debate' has been the not infrequent attempts to defend against the encroachment of CBET by stressing the role of values in a particular educational sector or occupation.[25] On these grounds the universities might be contrasted with further education, the professions with the crafts, arts with sciences, white collar with blue collar, and so on. However, we should remain alert to the perspectival, interested and potentially divisive nature of such claims; the inclination of educationalists to thus argue a special case for the teaching profession, for example, while certainly understandable, should be sufficient to raise our philosophical hackles. In any case, such arguments do not dissuade those who would simply advocate a more 'integrated' (Hager and Beckett, 1995) or holistic conception of competence. Put more precisely, in view of what has been said above, this amounts to the claim that statements of outcome can just as readily state the fact of someone having certain values or attitudes as the fact of their having a particular skill. So, while some critics have perhaps been guilty of oversimplifying the fact–value distinction, the competence strategist simply ignores it, confident in the assumption that all features of human capability are equally disposed to being represented by statements of outcome.

Of course, the very notion of 'fact' is problematic, a notion aptly described by Alisdair MacIntyre (1981) as 'a folk-concept with an aristocratic ancestry', not least because it tends to carry with it the erroneous assumption 'that the observer can confront a fact face-to-face without any theoretical interpretation interposing itself' (p. 76). The oversimplistic opposition we tend to create between fact and value, a salient feature of modernity, can be regarded as a by-product of a certain paradigm of knowledge, one which is deeply ingrained in our culture and derived from an essentially empiricist metaphysical view of the world. John Halliday has rightly identified just such empiricist presuppositions in the competence approach, noting that:

> Competence is assessed as if it were a state that is objectively described by the competencies. In that way written descriptions of behaviour may be seen as substitutes for the elusive notion of objective reality. (Halliday, 1996, p. 54)

Elsewhere, Halliday has criticized empiricist epistemology:

> on the grounds that 'experience' cannot provide the foundations necessary to support the claim that scientific knowledge is 'objective' knowledge. (Halliday, 1990, p. 8)

Certainly we might question 'the whole mode of thinking whereby we take the "subjective" and the "objective" as signifying a basic epistemological or metaphysical distinction' (Bernstein, 1983, p. 12) and Halliday has comprehensively demonstrated the difficulties posed for CBET once we begin to challenge its inherent empiricist/objectivist assumptions. However, it may be unnecessary to prove empiricism false in order to demonstrate the incoherence of CBET for, as we shall see, it is in part the improper application of empiricist assumptions and methodologies which renders the competence approach untenable, and this is consistent with empiricism being true.

When we talk about the facts of someone being competent, capable or skilled, and we begin to query what kind of fact these facts are, our attention is drawn from the epistemological towards the ontological, away from issues relating to what is *known* towards questions about what it *is* to be competent skilled, capable or skilled. It was Martin Heidegger who, in effectively putting aside what had been the central project of modern philosophy, insisted on turning from epistemology to ontology, arguing that since knowing is a mode of human 'there-being' ('Dasein'), questions about Being are more fundamental than questions about knowledge; for Heidegger, ontology precedes epistemology:

> Knowing is a mode of Dasein founded upon Being-in-the-world . Thus Being-in-the-world, as a basic state, must be Interpreted *beforehand*. (Original emphasis; Heidegger, 1962, p. 90)

Following Heidegger's example we might now turn to the question of what it is, ontologically speaking, for someone to be capable, a performance to be competent or an object to skilfully made. When we have considered this question we will be able to respond more fully to the competence strategist's implicit assertion that outcome statements can be used to describe the facts of someone's capability, skill or competence.

Notes

[23] Compare, for example, Burke (ed.) 1989, with Burke (ed.) 1995 and Jessup, (1991).

[24] There is a basic sense in which statements employed in a descriptive capacity might generally be required to contain a greater level of detail than when used prescriptively. For example, a customer's *prescription* to a garage mechanic to 'repair the engine' of his car can make perfect sense even though it conveys the barest information about the work to be done and could not be said to *describe* what is to be done. A precondition of such statements being able to fulfil their prescriptive role is that the recipient of the prescription is able, so to speak, to fill in the detail. In other words, they must have an understanding sufficient to allow them to *infer* what is required. In contrast, to the extent that statements are required to fulfil the role of complete and unequivocal *descriptions*, it is generally assumed that there must be no such preconditions – an assumption we will later have cause to controvert.

[25] It is often the suggestion that some aspects of a vocation may be 'contestable' that holds out the promise of exemption from the competence agenda. But such considerations tend to get short shrift from those who are convinced that specific goals or purposes can be set in the form of competence statements (see, for example, Tomlinson, 1996; cited in Blake, Smeyers, Smith and Standish, 1998, p. 132).

5

Towards an Ontology of Occupational Capability

We have noted that underlying the competence strategist's use of outcome statements is the conviction that whether or not someone is competent, skilled or capable is something which can be treated as a matter of fact; he or she wants to be able to state, as a matter of *objective* fact, that someone either can or cannot do a job, perform a task or demonstrate an ability. Here we will take up the issue of what kind of fact these facts might be.

In *Speech Acts* John Searle (1969) makes a distinction between two sorts of fact: brute facts and institutional facts. He notes that we generally tend towards a particular metaphysical conception of the world in which there are certain paradigms of knowledge and that these paradigms, although widely varied, nevertheless have certain features in common – namely, that they derive from an empiricist model of knowledge. The natural sciences form the model for this system of knowledge, one which is embodied in our culture, and from which we derive facts as widely varied in kind as: 'This stone is next to this stone', 'Bodies attract with a force inversely proportional to the square of the distance between them, and directly proportional to the product of their mass', or 'I have a pain' (*ibid.*, p. 50). Such facts he dubs 'brute facts'. However, there are many kinds which are difficult to assimilate into this empiricist metaphysical view of the world. Clearly, statements relating to aesthetics or ethics do not fit easily or non-controversially into this picture; indeed, it would be an altogether contentious matter to talk of aesthetic or ethical 'facts'. But there is another kind, one which is generally regarded as objective, which appears to be not at all a matter of subjective opinion or individual preference, for which it is nevertheless difficult to provide an adequate account in terms of the empiricist model.

Searle notes that we constantly refer to objective facts about such things as money, property, marriage, government or games, and yet it seems that the classical empiricist model of brute facts is insufficient to describe such things. The fact that someone is married, or owns a particular property, or wins a game of chess, or the fact that Clinton was the president of the USA, are all clearly objective facts, and yet they cannot be accounted for in terms of the brute facts of the natural sciences. In contrast to the notion of brute facts

Searle calls these 'institutional facts'. The characteristic feature of institutional facts is that, unlike brute facts, they seem to be dependent upon some kind of human agreement or institution. Brute facts, such as the fact that this pen is made from materials which have a certain molecular structure, that it is 13.5 centimetres long, that it contains a certain amount of ink – these facts are independent of whether or not we happen to agree about them. On the other hand, the fact that a person has a five-pound note in his pocket is an institutional fact. The brute facts of physics and chemistry can provide an account of the composition of the piece of paper and the ink markings on it - but *not* the fact that it is a five-pound note. As Searle would say, take away the institution of money and all I have is a piece of paper with ink markings on it. It is, in other words, a five-pound note by human agreement.

Institutional facts not only permeate every area of human activity, but they are also indispensable for explaining many areas of human experience where brute facts appear to be entirely ineffectual. By way of illustration Searle asks us to imagine that a group of observers were attempting to describe a game of American football in statements only of brute facts:

> What could they say by way of description? Well, within certain areas a good deal could be said, and using statistical techniques certain 'laws' could even be formulated. For example, we can imagine that after a time our observer would discover the law of periodic clustering: at statistically regular intervals organisms like colored shirts cluster together in a roughly circular fashion (the huddle). Furthermore, at equally regular intervals, circular clustering is followed by linear clustering (the teams line up for play), and linear clustering is followed by the phenomenon of linear interpenetration. Such laws would be statistical in character, and none the worse for that. But no matter how much data of this sort we imagine our observers to collect and no matter how many inductive generalizations we imagine them to make from the data, they still have not described American football. (*Ibid.*, p. 52)

There are striking parallels here with the competence strategist's stated ambition of describing competence with a precision 'approaching that of a science'. The point here is that that no matter how detailed the empirical analysis of either objects or behaviour (i.e. brute facts), we nevertheless fail to sufficiently describe the phenomenon. For Searle, what would unavoidably be missing from such a description are those concepts (in the case of football, notions such as touchdown, offside, etc.) which cannot be explained in terms of the brute facts because they only exist by virtue of human agreement: they are *social constructs* rather than intrinsic features of reality. It seems to me that, similarly, the facts relating to competence, skill, capability, etc. are just this sort of fact.

More recently, in *The Construction of Social Reality*, Searle (1995) has examined the phenomenon of institutional facts more closely, asking how it is possible for there to be an 'objective' reality which exists in part by human agreement. To convey the extent of the problem he describes a fairly straightforward social situation: his going into a café in Paris and ordering a beer (in French), drinking it, and then leaving some money on the table before departing. An innocent scene he suggests, 'but its metaphysical complexity is truly staggering, and its complexity would have taken Kant's breath away ...' (*ibid.*, p. 3).[26] There is, Searle tells us, a huge invisible ontology which cannot be represented by the brute facts of physics or chemistry, despite the fact that 'restaurant', 'waiter', 'sentences of French', 'money', 'chair' and 'table' are all physical phenomena. The fact that the waiter doesn't himself 'own' the beer, and yet it was he who 'served' it; the fact that he is 'employed', that the restaurant is 'licensed' and 'regulated' by the 'government', that there are certain 'prices', 'taxes', etc. are all such as to constitute a social reality of almost limitless extension which cannot be accounted for in empiricist terms.[27] Furthermore, there is likely to be an extensive normative content to such an experience which, again, brute facts would be unable to explain. The beer may be flat, warm, tasty or delicious, and other factual claims might similarly be made about the restaurant, the chair or the table; the waiter may be rude or polite, competent or incompetent, etc. All of this complexity arises from just this one simple social situation; as Searle says, if he were to go on to attend a lecture or go to a party the extent of this immense 'metaphysical burden' is increased still further. It would seem that much of our ordinary, everyday experience is constituted of a social reality of astonishing metaphysical complexity.

Of interest here is the fact that the kind of ontology Searle is trying to get at is one which seems to be missed by the Cartesian distinction of *res cogitans* (thinking thing) and *res extensa* (the thing of extension or substance). Descartes' notion of *res extensa* allows no ready distinction between those features of the world which lend themselves to empirical explanation and are describable in terms of brute facts, and the kind of social reality Searle is trying to explain which, on his view, can only be described by institutional facts. For those who maintain some attachment to the basic Cartesian picture, this social reality might almost suggest a third ontological realm. Indeed, this is roughly the position adopted by Karl Popper in *The Self and Its Brain* (Popper and Eccles, 1986), where he postulates the existence of three 'worlds'. In addition to the 'World 1', of physical entities or objects, of atoms and molecules, and the 'World 2' of mental states, including conscious and unconscious psychological states and dispositions, Popper claims there is a 'World 3' which consists in such things as:

> the products of the human mind, such as stories, explanatory myths, tools, scientific theories (whether true of false), scientific problems, social institutions, and works of art. World 3 objects are of our own making,

although they are not always the result of planned production by individual men. (*Ibid.*, p. 38)

Popper emphasizes that the components of World 3 – a 'world' which seems to correspond closely with Searle's constructed social reality – are not to be regarded as mere figments; he argues to the contrary that they are very 'real', not just by virtue of the World 1 aspects in which they might be embodied (e.g. a work of art might be embodied in canvas and pigment), but they are real in the sense that they are able to interact with or induce effects in any one of the three 'Worlds'. For example, a work of art (World 3) may influence the World 2 experiences of another artist who then works on World 1 materials to produce a further World 3 object. Or again, a system of numbers might begin as an invention but then develops a life of its own, raising new problems which have an objective, independent existence, one which exerts real and concrete influences on the world.

In similar vein, Michael Oakeshott (1973) speaks of a 'world' of human achievement, a 'civilised inheritance' (p. 173) to which human beings can succeed only by learning; in so doing he hints at a perhaps more unified ontological conception than that suggested by Popper:

> The components of this world are not abstractions ('physical objects') but beliefs. It is a world of facts not 'things'; of 'expressions' which have meanings and require to be understood because they are the 'expressions' of human minds ... this is the only world known to human beings. The starry heavens above us and the moral law within, are alike human achievements. And it is a world, not because it has itself any meaning (it has none), but because it is a whole of interlocking meanings which establish and interpret one another. (*Ibid.*, p. 158)

This world is contingent and positive rather than necessary, a world of

> feelings, emotions, images, visions, thoughts, beliefs, ideas, understandings, intellectual and practical enterprises, languages, relationships, organizations, canons and maxims of conduct, procedures, rituals, skills, works of art, books, musical composition, tools, artefacts and utensils – in short, what Dilthey called a *geistige Welt*.' (*Ibid.*)

While, for Popper, it is the capacity to induce effects which makes World 3 objects 'real', Searle invests his notion of social reality with metaphysical substance by ascribing to it a particular kind of objectivity. He reminds us that the terms 'objective' and 'subjective' can be used in both ontological and epistemic senses. When used epistemically the terms are primarily predicates of judgements, while their use in an ontological sense entails their predicating entities of some kind. Moreover, we can recognize that it is possible for something to be simultaneously both objective and subjective in the sense that we can make epistemically subjective statements about ontologically objective entities, and conversely, epistemically objective statements about ontologically subjective entities. On Searle's view the social objects which constitute social reality are of this latter kind: epistemologically objective but ontologically subjective. The next stage in Searle's argument is to acknowledge that it is possible to make a distinction between intrinsic and observer-relative features of the world:

> It is, for example, an intrinsic feature of the object in front of me that it has a certain mass and a certain chemical composition. It is made partly out of wood, the cells of which are composed of cellulose fibers, and also partly of metal, which is itself composed of metal alloy molecules. All these features are intrinsic. But it is also true to say of the very same object that it is a screwdriver. When I describe it as a screwdriver, I am specifying a feature of the object that is observer or user relative. It is a screwdriver only because people use it as (or made it for the purpose of, or regard it as) a screwdriver. (Searle, 1995, pp. 9–10)

Searle acknowledges that the distinction between intrinsic and observer-relative features is not always straightforward. The test, he tells us, is to ask; 'Could the feature exist if there had never been any human beings or other sentient beings?' (*ibid.*, p. 11). The important thing here is that while we can recognize that the addition of these observer-relative features does not add any new material objects to the world, we can acknowledge that it does add features to reality which are at once epistemically objective (e.g. it isn't just my opinion that it is a screwdriver) and ontologically subjective (i.e. it is only a screwdriver insofar as people regard it as such).

For Searle, brute facts have a logical priority over institutional facts: it is not possible for there to be institutional facts without there existing brute facts of some kind. In the case of money, for example, there must be some physical form whether it be paper, metal, or magnetic trace on computer disc. Similarly, in the case of vocational capability there must be some form of physical realization – either physical objects, movements of the body, sounds coming out of people's mouths, or neurological activity in people's heads. Searle also emphasizes the primacy of social acts over social objects – of processes over products. On this view, five-pound notes, screwdrivers – and, I would suggest, competent performances and skilfully made artefacts – are all social objects constituted *by* social acts: the object is just the continuous possibility or recognition of the activity. In the absence of the requisite social acts these objects, qua social objects, cannot exist – although they would, of course, retain their brute ontologies as pieces of paper, wood or metal, etc.

According to Searle, then, we construct social reality by overlaying the ontologically objective, intrinsic features of the world with a subjective ontology of observer-relative features. Even the most familiar objects and experiences have an ontology which we create, using processes of which we are largely unconscious. The educational implications of Searle's thesis are immense for it would seem that social reality is something which we have to *learn* to see; for example, we *learn* to see moving cars, dollar bills and bath tubs – as opposed to 'masses of metal in moving trajectories, cellulose fibers with green and gray stains, or enamel-covered iron concavities . . .' (*ibid.*, p. 4). To so learn is a prerequisite to effective action; we can only deal with this vast, complex metaphysical structure when it becomes 'weightless and invisible' (*ibid.*) by virtue of our *not* recognizing its profoundly non-intrinsic, contingent nature. But it is precisely this invisibility which makes the analysis of social reality so problematic. As Searle explains, the simplistic and partly illusory objectivity we unconsciously ascribe to such things as football, cars and money (and, I would add, such things as skilfully made objects and competent performances) stands in the way of our getting to the essential underlying ontology.

I should stress that Searle is not directly concerned with educational matters, or indeed with such things as skill or competence, so my interpretation of him in this respect is not one he would necessarily share. Nonetheless, I want to suggest that when we refer to the facts of someone being vocationally capable or of something being skilfully made it is essentially to an ontology of the kind outlined by Searle that we are referring to, one which cannot be described adequately in empiricist terms and which in some very fundamental sense exists by virtue of human agreement. Moreover, also like Searle, I want to suggest that this is an ontology which we learn to regard as a simple phenomenon. The problem, as Searle says, is that it becomes 'tempting to think of social objects as independently existing entities on analogy with the objects studied by the natural sciences' (*ibid.*, p.36). We are then deceived into thinking that we can provide an account of human skill or vocational capability by reference to certain ontologically objective features of the world. In talking about the facts of such things we forget that we are dealing with facts which 'exceed the physical features of the underlying physical reality' (*ibid.*, p. 228). In other words, we come to regard them in the manner of the orthodoxy: as simple, discrete, inert, behavioural or physical phenomena; intrinsic features of the world disposed to being narrowly specified in terms of brute, empirical facts.

Searle identifies three parts to the apparatus required to construct social reality:

1 **The assignment of function:** the function of objects, behaviour – and, we might add, of competent performances, skills, etc. – is imposed by the observer; in other words, function is not an intrinsic feature of the world but one ascribed by us within a framework of prior assignments of value.
2 **Collective intentionality:** by which is meant the capacity we have to

share beliefs, desires, intentions, etc., a 'We Consciousness' in the sense that
I do something only as part of *our* doing something. This 'biologically
primitive phenomenon' (*ibid.*, p. 24) is fundamental to explaining variously
the collective activities of primitive hunters or musicians in an orchestra.

3 **Constitutive rules:** characteristically of the form 'X counts as Y in
context C', such rules don't merely regulate activity, they actually create
its possibility. Obvious examples are such things as money, for example
'This note counts as having a certain value when used in this country.'

Later we shall return to examine these 'building blocks' of social reality in
more detail, considering how they might add to our understanding of
vocational capability. For the moment, however, I want to consider some of
the more general features of Searle's argument and their wider implications.

We have seen that Searle's account rests on the distinction he creates
between facts which are entirely dependent upon human existence and those
which are independent of us. He intends his account of social reality to be
consistent, first, with a position which approximates to philosophical realism
('the idea that there is a real world independent of our thought and talk'
(*ibid.*, pp. xii–xiii)), and second, with a version of the correspondence theory
of truth ('the idea that our true statements are typically made true by how
things are in the real world that exists independently of the statements' (*ibid.*,
p. xiii). Searle believes that his account of social reality resolves the traditional
but 'misguided' opposition between biology and culture and that it is possible
to resolve the mind–body dichotomy by understanding the mental as
consisting in 'higher-level features' (*ibid.*, p. 227) of more basic physiological/
physicochemical phenomena – in much the same way that wetness and
liquidity might be said to be 'high-level features' of water but are not
discerned as characteristics of H_2O at the molecular level. Similarly, he argues
that rather than there being a fundamental opposition between culture and
biology, 'culture is the form biology takes' (*ibid.*); hence, on Searle's view it
ought to be possible to discern a 'continuum from the chemistry of
neurotransmitters such as seretonin and norepinephrine to the content of
such mental states as believing that Proust is a better novelist than Balzac'
(*ibid.*, p. 228); it ought to be possible, in other words, to outline a 'more or less
continuous story that goes from an ontology of biology to an ontology that
includes cultural and institutional forms; there should not be any radical
break' (*ibid.*, p. 227).

It is not my intention here to either strenuously defend or attack Searle's
position vis-à-vis his stance on philosophical realism or his correspondence
conception of truth. For our present purposes the important thing here is that
the position Searle adopts can be regarded as representative of the prevailing
consensus in modern Western societies, a consensus centred on the
foundational status of empirical science. Ultimately, I will want to suggest

that the account of social reality Searle proposes has profound implications for our understanding of vocational capability and that it allows us to repudiate the kind of assumptions which constitute the orthodox conception of vocational capability and which also underpin competence-based approaches to education and training. However, we can recognize that Searle's realist/correspondence stance does present him with certain difficulties, not least the way it ensnares him in the Cartesian dichotomies of objective–subjective, object–subject, fact–value, intrinsic–observer-relative, etc. Indeed, as we have seen, the distinctions between objective–subjective and intrinsic–observer-relative play a major part in his account. Even where he claims to be able to resolve certain polarities by claiming to discern a 'continuum' between the extremes, the unity which obtains might more properly be regarded as an explanatory unification rather than an ontological one. But what is remarkable about Searle's account is how close its ontological insights come to some of those found in certain strands of continental philosophy while still retaining an attachment to those empiricist foundations which remain so much the common currency in the Anglo-Saxon tradition. In particular, much of Searle's ontology of social reality can be seen to be prefigured by Martin Heidegger's account of Being-in-the-world, an account which not only avoids the dichotomies which beset Searle's narrative, but arguably also provides a more coherent and comprehensive ontological conception of human capability.[28]

What I want to suggest, then, is that Searle's account of social reality – because it is generally consistent with the prevailing realist, correspondence, empiricist orientated view of the world – provides us with a useful default position from which to critique the orthodoxy. But I also want to suggest that the case against the orthodoxy and CBET will be even further substantiated if, using Heidegger's conception of Being-in-the-world, we are able to ameliorate Searle's account. There is, of course, space here to give only the briefest outline of Heidegger's vast undertaking, but in what follows I hope to highlight some of the main features of Heidegger's conception of Being-in-the-world, sufficient at least to indicate its significance for our account of vocational capability.

Heidegger and Being-in-the-world

While Searle's interest lies in explaining how we can ascribe 'objectivity' to institutional facts, in how we construct social reality, Heidegger's (1962) project in *Being and Time* was no less than that of examining the very nature of Being. Being, he tells us, is 'that on the basis of which (*woraufhin*) entities are already understood' (pp. 25–6). It is the difference it makes that there is something rather than nothing. Being is what it is for entities to show up or disclose themselves; it is that which is prior to the ontical,[29] the background against which the ontical is perceived, and Heidegger takes Dasein, the 'there-being' of human existence, as the focus of his investigation of Being.

Heidegger rejects the Cartesian – and we might even say Searlian – notion of *res cogitans* as mind or ego ontologically distinct from the world; that is, the conception of mind as an internal phenomenon set apart from an external world which it strives to describe in terms of 'objective', quantifiable facts. For Heidegger, the 'worldless *res cogitans*' (*ibid.*, p. 254) postulated by Descartes has several unacceptable consequences. Not least, it encourages a technological approach to the world and to human being, the idea that the world can be non-problematically and accurately quantified and manipulated. Descartes' instrumentalist ambitions are clearly evident in the following passage from the *Discourse on Method* (1890), where his allusion to the skills of 'artizans' effectively amounts to an exposition of the orthodoxy:

> I perceived it to be possible to arrive at knowledge highly useful in life ... to discover a Practical (philosophy), by means of which, knowing the force and the action of fire, water, air, the stars, the heavens and all the other bodies that surround us, as distinctly as we know the various crafts of our artizans, we might also apply them in the same way to all the uses to which they are adapted, and thus render ourselves the lords and possessors of nature. (Descartes, 1890, pp. 60–1)

A further difficulty with the Cartesian distinction of *res cogitans* and *res extensa*, one which we have already noted, is that the latter is not sensitive to the substantial ontological difference between such things as, say, atoms and mountains on the one hand, or tools and chess pieces on the other. Accordingly, the notion of 'objectivity' becomes increasingly strained as we try to apply it to those features of the world which seem more dependent upon human purposes – what Searle would call observer-relative features – and we are led to characterize such features as somehow constituting an 'ontologically subjective' realm which is then projected onto some more fundamental, 'ontologically objective' reality. Heidegger rejects the Cartesian notion of *res cogitans* along with the dichotomies it generates, for example objective–subjective, external–internal, fact–value, and instead posits a conception of Dasein as essentially 'in-the-world':

> to Dasein, Being in a world is something that belongs essentially. Thus Dasein's understanding of Being pertains with equal primordiality both to an understanding of something like a 'world', and to the understanding of the Being of those entities which become accessible within the world. (Heidegger, 1962, p. 33)

Dasein's world is not just the geographical position it happens to occupy, a world of concrete things and objects; rather, it is first and foremost constituted by the sphere of meanings and purposes by which Dasein engages with other 'beings' – objects, tools, artefacts or other human beings. So while we can acknowledge that, ontically, existence is necessarily an internal phenomenon – the brain is manifestly located inside the skull – Dasein's existence is fundamentally about its interaction and involvement with the world. The world is thus a fundamental component of Dasein's Being; Dasein *is* the world it reveals to itself: '*Dasein is its disclosedness*' (original emphasis; *ibid.*, p. 171). If Dasein's very existence is constituted by its Being-in-the-world, then it is not possible, as Descartes and others have assumed, for it to exist as a disinterested mind or ego detached from the world, able to examine itself by introspection and 'cross over' into the world via perception. Writing of the 'transcendence of Dasein' in *The Metaphysical Foundations of Logic*, Heidegger explains:

> To be a subject means to transcend. This means that Dasein does not sort of exist and then occasionally achieve a crossing over outside itself, but existence originally means to cross over. Dasein is itself the passage across. And this implies that transcendence is not just one possible comportment (among others) of Dasein towards other beings, but is the basic constitution of its being, on the basis of which Dasein can relate to beings in the first place. (Heidegger, 1992a, p. 165)

Indeed, if we somehow lose our connections with the world, we do not simply end up with a separated mind; we end up with no mind at all: as Richard Polt (1999) points out, experiments with sensory deprivation demonstrate all too clearly what happens to the brain when it is deprived of the opportunity to be 'in the world'. On Heidegger's view it is profoundly mistaken to regard ourselves as detached, disinterested viewers; we are engaged actors who relate to our Being by acting, interacting and generally having dealings with the beings in the world around us.

Heidegger's 'analytic of Dasein' centres on Dasein's 'average *everydayness*' (original emphasis; 1962, p. 38): 'the kind of being which is *closest* to Dasein' (original emphasis; *ibid.*, p. 94). It is fortuitous for our purposes that he takes the case of a craftsman in his workshop with his everyday use of tools and equipment and his relation to his materials, customers, etc. as an archetype through which to explore the essential ahistorical structures of Dasein's Being. Just as Searle is struck by the way in which we seem oblivious to the ontological complexity of everyday experience, the way in which it seems to be 'weightless and invisible', so too Heidegger (1962) draws our attention to the fact that 'That which is ontically closest and well known, is ontologically the farthest and not known at all; and its ontological signification is constantly overlooked' (p. 69). Indeed, again like Searle, Heidegger claims that the ontological character of 'average everydayness' has been ignored by previous philosophers. He argues that the long-standing philosophical tendency, persisting from antiquity down to Hegel, has been to homogenize the being of entities into a 'common or average concept of being' (Heidegger, 1982, p 22) equivalent to 'present' and it is this metaphysics of presence which deceives us into thinking that a complete and final understanding of beings is possible: we become obsessed with the idea of *re*-presenting beings in an 'objective', definitive way, assuming that we can always measure, manipulate and control beings by technological means.

Against this view Heidegger claims that it is possible to discern different ways or modes of being. Dasein, as Being-in-the-world, is itself one such mode but there is also an important distinction to be made between the 'present-at-hand' (*Vorhandenheit*) and the 'ready-to-hand' (*Zuhandenheit*). All entities can be regarded in a disinterested way as present-at-hand: this is the kind of being implicitly assumed in referring to 'intrinsic' features of the world; it is a kind of being which is understood as neutral, disengaged from human purposes, where 'the perception of the object is imagined to be somehow isolated from any context of human practice' (Standish, 1997, p. 445). In contrast, ready-to-hand is a kind of being inextricably related to human activities and purposes; it is the primary Being of things of use, of tools, equipment, etc. The craftsman's tools are revealed to him as ready-to-hand as he goes about his work; for example, in the activity of hammering the hammer is revealed as ready-to-hand. This is not the detached, 'theoretical' kind of being that is revealed when it is regarded as a present-at-hand shaft of wood with a steel head, as a thing of a certain molecular structure or mass, or verifiable dimensions. Rather, in use the hammer has a being which is unobtrusive, even inconspicuous:

> No matter how sharply we just look at the 'outward appearance' of Things in whatever form this takes, we cannot discover anything ready-to-hand. If we look at things just 'theoretically', we can get along without understanding readiness-to-hand. But when we deal with them by using them and manipulating them, this activity is not a blind one; it has its own kind of sight, by which our manipulation is guided and from which it acquires its specific Thingly character. (Heidegger, 1962, p. 98)

As we operate within the world we are surrounded by equipment which is revealed to us in this way. The furniture, the walls of the building we are in, or if we go outside, the street signs, the road bridge, pavements, etc., all constitute an equipmental totality which is significant for us, which is ready-to-hand. There is an important sense in which things are 'there' for us even though we may not be explicitly or consciously directing our attention towards them, a point emphasized by Heidegger in *The Basic Problems of Phenomenology*:

> Sitting here in the auditorium, we do not in fact apprehend the walls – not unless we are getting bored. Nevertheless, the walls are already present

even before we think them as objects. Much else is also given to us before any determining of it by thought. (Heidegger, 1982, p. 163)

In contrast, beings are more likely to be revealed to us as present-at-hand if they break, if they become unusable, if they are not where we expect to find them, or if we just try to reflect on them 'objectively'. To see things as present-at-hand thus requires a '*deficiency* in our having-to-do with the world concernfully' (original emphasis; Heidegger, 1962, p. 88); it requires us to refrain from 'any kind of producing, manipulating, and the like' (*ibid.*). In one sense we might say that it is easier to regard things as present-at-hand, imagining that we can focus on entities in isolation from their context, relations or uses, and describe them precisely and sufficiently in terms of what Searle would call brute facts.

There are interesting parallels between Heidegger's distinction between the ready-to-hand and the present-at-hand and Michael Polanyi's distinction between what he calls 'subsidiary' and 'focal' awareness. Polanyi notes that one of the striking features of any skill is that it seems to involve our having two kinds of awareness:

> I know the feelings in the palm of my hand by *relying on them for attending to the hammer hitting the nail*. I may say that I have a subsidiary awareness of the feelings in my hand which is merged into my focal awareness of my driving the nail. (Original emphasis; Polanyi and Prosch, 1975, p. 33)

It may be that the phenomenon Polanyi describes indicates that we have the ability to shift the focus of the ready-to-hand, and that it is not necessarily, as Heidegger might say, that which is 'ontically closest'.

The kind of distinction Heidegger makes when distinguishing the present-at-hand and the ready-to-hand appears also to be borne out by certain clinical evidence which suggests that similarly distinct ways of experiencing the world might be identified with different parts of the brain. For example, there are rare cases in which patients who have suffered localized damage to the brain may lose their capacity to see the world in terms of the ready-to-hand while retaining their ability to perceive present-at-hand abstractions. The neurologist Oliver Sacks relates an account of a patient who, though able to describe the world around him in very precise abstract terms, had nevertheless lost the ability to see things in their relations to human involvements. On being presented with a glove and asked to say what the object was, the patient could only describe what he saw as 'A continuous surface ... infolded on itself ... It appears to have five outpouchings' (1986, p. 13). The patient was still unable to recognize it as a glove even when prompted that it might fit a certain part of the body; only later, after accidentally putting it on his hand, did he exclaim: 'My God, it's a glove!' (*ibid.*). Sacks cites other cases of patients 'who could only recognise objects by trying to use them in action' (*ibid.*), and who otherwise appear to 'construe the world as a computer construes it, by means of key features and schematic relationships' (*ibid.*, p. 14).[30]

It is possible to see loose parallels between Heidegger's comparison of the present-at-hand with the ready-to-hand and Searle's distinction between intrinsic and observer-relative features. However, there are a number of crucial differences. On Searle's view the intrinsic, ontologically objective features are more fundamental – the ontologically subjective social reality is seen as overlaying this more fundamental realm. In contrast, Heidegger ascribes no such ontological priority to the present-at-hand: unlike Searle he insists that we do not see an object such a hammer as first present-at-hand and then interpret this as ready-to-hand equipment; rather, we implicitly and immediately see it as *zuhanden*:

> we do not, so to speak, throw a 'signification' over some naked thing which is present-at-hand, we do not stick a value on it; but when something within-the-world is encountered as such, the thing in question already has an involvement which is disclosed in our understanding of the world, and this involvement is one which gets laid out by the interpretation. (Heidegger, 1962, pp. 190–1)

Heidegger's insight is that the distinction between what Searle would call the ontologically objective and the ontologically subjective, between what is so in itself and what is so only for us, is itself a distinction which comes from our own understanding of being. It is not a distinction which can be drawn from the Dasein-independent nature of the world. Without Dasein there is no background or foreground to the nature of things, no state or kind of being which inherently has priority over some other. In other words, if there were no Dasein there would be beings but no being. Not only could beings not be *zuhanden* but they could not even be *vorhanden*, the world of atoms and molecules – the 'projections' revealed by science.

Indeed, for Heidegger, science is just another mode of Dasein's Being, one which is secondary to and derivative of more everyday ways of being. So to give priority to descriptions of molecules and atoms, to make this ontology, this kind of being, in some sense more fundamental is, on Heidegger's view, simply to give unwarranted precedence to the scientific viewpoint. For one thing, we can recognize that scientific method rests upon certain ontological assumptions; it requires some prior understanding of Being.[31] Moreover, the data science provides cannot clarify this prior understanding no matter how much information we gather; the ontological is inescapably prior to and more fundamental than the ontical. We might also note that Searle's notion of the ontologically objective is further undermined by Heidegger's point that present-at-hand features are revealed only as part of a wider signification that cannot itself be accounted for in terms of the 'ontologically objective' or the present-at-hand. The brute facts of natural science by which a screwdriver might be described only have meaning within a wider sphere of signification; so rather than the lifeworld being created by overlaying an apparently objective world of brute facts with a subjective realm of human values, to the contrary it is the lifeworld, on Heidegger's view, which gives such facts their meanings (see Heidegger, 1962, pp. 96, 131–2). So, in contrast to the kind of view held by Searle, Heidegger would insist that readiness-to-hand is how things are 'in themselves' (*ibid.*, p. 101) and that intuiting the present-at-hand is a secondary and derivative form of understanding. He would agree with Searle that without human involvement this thing would not be a screwdriver; however, as far as Dasein is concerned it *really is* a screwdriver. The fact that it is Dasein-related does not mean that it is the creation of my will, a product of Dasein's 'subjectivity'; rather, it is the 'relational totality' (*ibid.*, p. 120) of 'significance' which is so fundamental to our being and which structures our world, which opens up the possibility of our encountering the ready-to-hand.

Of course, Heidegger is also at variance with Searle with regard to the latter's attachment to philosophical realism and the correspondence theory of truth. For Heidegger, our access to entities is absolutely fundamental to our way of being: 'Along with Dasein as Being-in-the-world, entities within-the-world have in each case already been disclosed' (*ibid.*, p. 251). He acknowledges that in some respects this might seem to be in accord with the philosophical realist's claim that ultimately 'the external world is Really present-at-hand' (*ibid.*). On Heidegger's view, however, the philosophical realist makes the mistake of assuming that reality is first, something which needs to proved, and second, something which is capable of being proved; accordingly the realist attempts to 'explain Reality ontically by Real connections of interaction between things that are real' (*ibid.*). Popper's claim that World 3 objects are 'real' by virtue of being seen to have causal (present-at-hand) effects on other (present-at-hand) features of the world is a case in point. For Heidegger, then, realism is characterized by a 'lack of ontological understanding' (*ibid.*), an inability to recognize that while it is possible to acknowledge the existence of a Dasein-independent reality, what it *means* to be real is necessarily Dasein-dependent:

> Entities *are*, quite independently of the experience by which they are disclosed, the acquaintance in which they are discovered, and the grasping in which their nature is ascertained. But Being 'is' only in the understanding of those entities to whose Being something like an understanding of Being belongs. (Original emphasis; *ibid.*, p. 228)

Present-at-hand entities do have properties which are independent of us but in order to understand this independent way of being, the way in which things are in themselves, we have to first interpret our own way of being – as

Heidegger puts it: '*Reality is referred back to the phenomenon of care*' (original emphasis; *ibid.*, p. 255). This is not, however, to subscribe to any radical idealism for 'the fact that Reality is grounded in the Being of Dasein, does not signify that only when Dasein exists and as long as Dasein exists, can the Real be as that which in itself it is.' (*ibid.*).

Another point on which Heidegger may be seen to be at odds with Searle is on the issue of the latter's assumption of a correspondence conception of truth, i.e. the idea that statements are true if they correspond to facts about the world. Heidegger rejects this kind of position and posits instead a conception of truth as unconcealment or uncovering. It is Dasein rather than correspondence which is the primary 'locus' of truth: '"*There is*" *truth only in so far as Dasein is and as long as Dasein is*' (original emphasis; *ibid.*, p. 269). Hence, Heidegger tells us, 'Before Newton's laws were discovered, they were not 'true'; it does not follow that they were false, or even that they would become false if ontically no discoveredness were any longer possible' (*ibid.*). So while according to correspondence theory assertions must correspond to facts, for Heidegger, an assertion or a statement should be recognized as an artificial construct: 'What is expressed becomes, as it were, something ready-to-hand within-the-world which can be taken up and spoken again' (*ibid.*, p. 266). The danger – as we shall see when we turn to consider the assumptions implicit in the use of competence statements – is that such statements come to be regarded as present-at-hand. We are then deceived into thinking of truth as a present-at-hand relationship between a present-at-hand statement and a present-at-hand entity; indeed, according to Heidegger, this is how we mistakenly come to think of truth as a correspondence between statements and the world:

> if this conformity is seen only as a relation between things which are present-at-hand ... then the relation shows itself as an agreement of two things which are present-at-hand, an agreement which is present-at-hand itself. (*Ibid.*, p. 267)

On this view, then, falsehoods are not assertions which fail to correspond to reality but rather a matter of concealment or distortion; truth, on the other hand, consists in uncovering.

There are, then, a number of quite important and fundamental differences between Searle and Heidegger. Yet there are also important and substantial areas of correspondence. Both point to the extraordinary ontological complexity of our everyday experience and testify to an ontology which defies empirical description. Searle's thesis demonstrates that, even for those who are reluctant to relinquish empirical science's foundational status, these are features of the world which demand a different kind of explanation and a different conception of 'objectivity'. For Heidegger, on the other hand, these clues to worldhood ultimately highlight the profound inadequacy of the entire objectivist, empirical standpoint. Seen thus, there appears to be a remarkable unanimity from these two contrasting perspectives, viewpoints which might even be seen as representative of the two grand and antithetical readings of our time. In what follows we will explore how Searle's notion of social reality and Heidegger's conception of Being-in-the-world might allow us to construct a more coherent account of what it is to be vocationally capable.

Notes

26 Searle points out that Kant's preoccupation with epistemological questions meant that he did not attend to these ontological complexities. Indeed, Searle expressly doubts whether there has ever been any satisfactory consideration of these features of reality, apparently unaware of relevant contributions in later continental philosophy, particularly from Heidegger.

27 Berger and Luckmann (1991) have indicated the important role of language in this objectification of social reality:

> The reality of everyday life appears already objectified, that is, constituted by an order of objects that have been designated as objects before my appearance on the scene. The language used in everyday life continuously provides me with the necessary objectifications and posits the order with which these make sense and within which everyday life has meaning for me. I live in a place which is geographically designated; I employ tools, from can-openers to sports cars, which are designated in the technical vocabulary of my society ... (pp. 35–6)

28 Searle himself does not acknowledge this connection and likewise, Finn Collin (1997), in his recent review of constructivist arguments, omits to acknowledge parallels between Searle's account and continental philosophy but, rather, places Searle in the tradition of contract theorists.

29 In other words, entities and facts relating to them; see Macquarrie and Robinson's footnote in Heidegger (1962), p. 31.

30 Richard Polt, similarly, has recognized the relevance of such cases for Heidegger's distinction (see Polt, 1999, p. 50).

31 It might even be said, perhaps, that a lack of some elemental sense of this makes for bad science. The biologist Richard Dawkins (1999) has attacked the prevailing conception of science as cold, detached from human purposes and lacking in poetry; there is, he complains, 'an anaesthetic of familiarity, a sedative of ordinariness, which dulls the senses and hides the wonder of existence' (p. 6).

6

An Alternative Conception of Vocational and Professional Capability

In Chapter 3 we considered Michael Oakeshott's conception of knowledge as 'manifolds of abilities' and his claim that abilities, in turn, might be thought of as a synthesis of 'information' and 'judgement'. Here I want to explore how we might expand upon Oakeshott's account of knowledge by locating our conception of vocational capability within the kind of ontological framework considered in the last chapter.

We noted that part of Searle's account of how we construct social reality centres on our apparent capacity to assign functions to things: on his view the assigning of function is one of the 'building blocks' of social reality. According to Searle, human beings are able to assign or impose functions equally on man-made artefacts and on naturally occurring objects but in either case functions are always observer-relative, they are *never* intrinsic features of the world. Importantly, Searle emphasizes that to state the function of something is not simply to describe a causal relationship; for example, this is a screwdriver because it turns screws. Rather, by imposing the function of 'screwdriver' on this object I am in effect assuming that it *should* be suitable for certain uses even though in the event it may turn out not to be suitable; for example, the screwdriver blade may not have been tempered correctly and therefore be useless for its intended purpose, in other words it may *malfunction*. There is thus an important normative aspect to the imposition of function; it would seem that the imposition of function, even the 'discovery' of function in nature, can take place only within a context of previously determined interests, values or purposes. As Searle (1995) says, 'Whenever the function of X is to Y, X and Y are parts of a *system* where the system is in part defined by *purposes, goals, and values generally*' (original emphasis; p. 19).

While few would have difficulty with the idea that the function of a five-pound note is somehow imposed by the people who use it, the idea that the function of the heart (i.e. to pump blood) is similarly assigned appears counter-intuitive. Nevertheless, Searle insists that even biological functions of this kind are not intrinsic features of the world; rather, the apparent 'discovery' of a function in nature substantively consists in the discovery of some causal connection to which *we* assign a teleology of our own invention. Our conviction that the function of the heart is to pump blood and thereby keep us alive is a reflection of the values and priorities which we bring to the phenomenon.

It is worth noting that it need not always be the person directly using an object who assigns function to create the 'social object'. As Searle says, the driver of a car may be totally unaware of the existence of a drive-shaft, let alone its function; but the person who designed the car *has* assigned function to it. We can expand on this idea and say that a car mechanic who has cause to work on the car may also assign function to the drive shaft and *this* function may not necessarily be identical to the function imposed by the car's designer. The designer's understanding of the drive shaft may, for instance, include the fact that it has undergone certain special hardening treatments and that it should be able to cope with certain conditions of torque – treatments and characteristics which the mechanic may not or need not necessarily be aware of. It would seem that, potentially at least, one physical phenomenon could give rise to several different assigned functions, thereby effectively creating several different social objects, each aligned with the values, goals and purposes of different agents.

It is not difficult to begin to appreciate the acute relevance of the notion of function for our understanding of vocational capability. We might, for example, think of the craftsman's facility to assign function to his workshop, his tools and materials. The producer of an artefact must have some conception of function in relation to the object he is making and be capable of directing his activities to that end. Importantly, it would seem that this is something that has to be learned; for example, in mastering his craft the apprentice must learn to assign functions which are 'appropriate' or in some sense aligned with those designated by the wider community of practitioners. We might also think of the way in which we assign functions to people, or more precisely, to people in particular roles. It is significant, as Searle points out, that while we ascribe functions to teachers, engineers and architects, we do not assign functions to humans as such. This is because whenever we assign function we do so in the context of an evaluative system, and humans have no function per se 'unless we think of humans as part of some larger system where their function is, e.g., to serve God' (*ibid.*).

For us to begin to understand how it is possible for us to assign function it is necessary to consider Searle's conception of intentionality,[32] i.e. the capacity of the mind to represent objects or states of affairs in the world. We might say that to assign a function to something is to have an intentional state, but on Searle's account it is important to recognize that such states are far more complex than they first appear.

An intentional state only determines its conditions of satisfaction – and thus only is the state that it is – given its position in a *Network* of other Intentional states and against a *Background* of practices and preintentional assumptions that are neither themselves Intentional states nor are they parts of the conditions of satisfaction of Intentional states. (Original emphasis; Searle, 1983, p. 19)

Thus, on Searle's view, in order for me to have the belief that the object in my hand is a hammer, that belief has to be embedded in a Network of other intentional states. We can understand the belief only within that context. A similar point is made by Peter Winch, in *The Idea of a Social Science* (1965), when he emphasizes that an idea derives its sense 'from the role it plays in the system' and that ideas cannot be understood once they have been 'torn out of their context' (p. 107).

Heidegger's 'analytic of everydayness' provides an indication of just how pervasive and extensive this 'network' or 'context' might be. The craftsman's immediate, environing world is constituted by his workshop and the ready-to-hand tools and equipment he uses; for the carpenter, for example, this would include such things as the hammer, nails and wood that he uses. According to Heidegger (1962), the hammer implicitly refers to a whole range of other entities such as, for instance, the nails which might be 'hammered', the bench on which the hammering is done, the wood which is fastened. There is thus a profound sense in which a single tool, 'an' equipment, 'is ontologically impossible' (p. 404), for each ready-to-hand entity is substantively one part of an inter-referential totality of equipment. My understanding of the hammer is interdependent on my understanding of the other items in the workshop and, indeed, the workshop itself; it is only by means of such references that equipment can make sense to us. Moreover, we can recognize that this referential context is not restricted to Dasein's immediate surroundings. The immediate world which Dasein inhabits (*Umwelt*) inevitably testifies to a larger world (*Welt*), for example, to the other Dasein who supply the materials, the customers for whom the carpenter makes things, even to the trees from which the wood came and the forests in which they are grown, and so on. In the activity of hammering, this larger world is retained for Dasein, if only as a muted awareness.

For Heidegger, the function of any ready-to-hand entity such as a hammer is circumscribed by the totality of its 'involvements':

With the 'towards which' of serviceability there can again be an involvement: *with* this thing, for instance, which is ready-to-hand, and which we accordingly call a 'hammer', there is an involvement in hammering; with hammering there is an involvement in making something fast; with making something fast, there is an involvement in protection against bad weather; and this protection is for the sake of providing shelter for Dasein – that is to say, for the sake of a possibility of Dasein's Being. (Original emphasis; *ibid.*, p. 116)

This chain of involvements necessarily culminates in an ultimate 'for-the-sake-of-which': something which 'always pertains to the Being of *Dasein*, for which, in its Being, that very Being is essentially an *issue* ...' (original emphasis; *ibid.*, pp. 116–17). Thus, for Heidegger, as for Searle, our understanding of the hammer *as* a hammer is irredeemably grounded in our wider purposes, goals and values. Since the ready-to-hand is 'always understood in terms of a totality of involvements' (*ibid.*, p. 191), we might say that Dasein understands not so much individual or discrete entities or activities but, rather, its environment as a whole. Worldhood, for Dasein, is effectively a realm of significance: the 'relational totality of this signifying ... This is what makes up the structure of the world' (*ibid.*, p. 120). Dasein's world is a totality of references and possibilities, a network of significance which, although an *existentiale* of Dasein, cannot be created by any one Dasein as an act of will. It is constituted by the sphere of purposes and meanings which structures what we do and who we are, and within which beings can be revealed and make sense to us.

Reverting to Searle's way of speaking for the moment, we might say that my intentional state that this is a hammer, only is the state that it is, given its position in a network of other inter-related states about the totality of equipment, the sphere of related involvements, my overall purposes and intentions and the kind of possibilities which are revealed to me. Moreover, the realm towards which these intentional states might be directed would appear to have an almost limitless extension, radiating far beyond my immediate environment into the world at large. Yet, according to Searle, even this extensive network of intentional states is insufficient to explain how it is possible for such states to work; for on his view any intentional state only is the state that it is, given a certain Background of preintentional or non-intentional states. On this view, any explanation of how it possible to have intentional states about hammers, workshops, tools and customers must include an account of the Background.

The operation of the Background

In *The Metaphysical Foundations of Logic*, Heidegger (1992a) emphasizes that 'Transcendence, being-in-the-world, is never to be equated and identified with intentionality' (p. 168).[33] One reason why it should not be so identified, as Michael Inwood (1999) has explained, is that 'Intentionality makes everything too sharp and explicit, ignoring the background of which I am tacitly aware' (p. 160).[34] Indeed, we might already recognize that there is much in Heidegger's analytic of everydayness, his account of Being-in-the-world, which seems to imply the involvement of capacities which do not have the kind of directedness which normally characterizes the intentional. Rather, they constitute what Charles Taylor (1993) has described as the 'unexplicited horizon' (p. 325), which confers intelligibility upon the intentional; a kind of 'pre-understanding of what it is to act, to get around in the world, the way we do' (*ibid.*, p. 327). For Searle, as we have already said, the intentional is necessarily dependent for its operation upon a 'Background' of non-intentional, non-representational abilities, dispositions, tendencies or forms of 'know-how':

> beliefs, desires, and rules only determine conditions for satisfaction – truth conditions for beliefs, fulfilment conditions for desires, etc. – given a set of capacities that do not themselves consist in intentional phenomena. (Searle 1995, p. 123)

According to Searle, there are several ways in which we can see these kinds of 'capacities' at work. One important manifestation of the Background can be seen in the way it enables linguistic interpretation to take place. For, as Searle puts it, 'the literal meaning of any sentence can only determine its truth conditions or other conditions of satisfaction against a Background of capacities, dispositions, know-how, etc., which are not themselves part of the semantic content of the sentence' (*ibid.*, p. 130). If we take, for example, the sentence 'she gave him her key and he opened the door', Searle would hold that there is a '*radical* under-determination' (original emphasis; p. 131) of what is said by the sentence's literal meaning. There is nothing in the sentence which rules out interpretations such as: 'he swallowed the key and then forced the door open with a hammer' or 'she gave him the key and he returned three weeks later and opened the door'. As Searle says, there appears to be no limit to the range of possible interpretations of even the most simple sentence. It would seem that linguistic utterances and sentences only make sense or convey their intended meaning because we have a certain form of knowledge about how the world works and certain abilities for coping with the world, and this is something which is not and cannot be conveyed in the sentence itself.

Another way in which the Background can be seen to work is in the way it structures consciousness. Intentionality is essentially aspectual and we tend to recognize the things we see in the world around us in terms of what is familiar to us. Our perceptions and the majority of our experiences are essentially configured in terms of predetermined categories or patterns of familiarity and this, on Searle's view, is a function of the Background. If we are in a foreign country, we still recognize things as houses or clothing even though they might look very different from those we have seen before. Searle notes how difficult it is to break completely with this aspect of Background:

> Surrealist painters tried to do this, but even in a surrealist painting, the three-headed woman is still a woman, and the drooping watch is still a watch, and those crazy objects are still objects against a horizon, with a sky and a foreground. (*Ibid.*, p. 134)

The Background can also be seen to provide what Searle calls 'scenarios of expectation' (*ibid.*, p. 135); that is, an understanding of how things generally proceed: an understanding, for example, of what kind of things happen when we go shopping in a supermarket, take up employment or take part in an auction.

Another important function of the Background is the way it enables our interests, motives and general dispositions to have a determinative influence on our experiences. If we imagined, say, an engineer and a sociologist on a tour of a factory together, we might expect each to experience the occasion very differently; their Background capacities would structure their perceptions and experiences according to their divergent interests and concerns. They would most likely come away having perceived and experienced very different things.

Yet another feature of the Background relates to the way it apparently 'facilitates certain kinds of readiness' (*ibid.*, p. 136). For instance, there is a sense in which a craftsman repairing a gas appliance would be 'ready' for a leak of gas – even if he is not at all expecting it – in a way in which he would not be 'ready' for an electric shock, not because an electric shock would be a logical or pragmatic impossibility but because it would be counter to the sort of readiness he has. As Searle puts it, he would be 'ready' to see skiers on a mountainside and 'ready' to see rows of students in a lecture room – but not the other way round.

On Searle's view we can also recognize that Background disposes us to certain kinds of behaviour. For example, we are disposed to stand at a certain 'comfortable' distance from other people, have conversations at certain levels of loudness, etc. Similarly, M. L. J. Abercrombie (1989) notes the way in which we adopt behaviour patterns which are appropriate to our own culture, such things, for example, as gender-specific posture and ways of walking. We seem to take on such behaviour patterns 'as it were by the pores of the skin' (p. 57), absorbed in common with others from the wider culture in which we are immersed.

As Searle says, there are undoubtedly many other manifestations of the Background, many other ways in which our perceptions, understandings and our ability to operate competently in the world can be seen to be determined by our Background capacities rather than by any specific and explicit beliefs, rules, desires, intentions or other intentional states. However, one particularly important manifestation of Background is the way it apparently enables perceptual interpretation to take place. It enables us to see things *as* certain things, for example I see this object *as* a hammer. It should be emphasized that when Searle speaks of 'interpretation' in this way he does not mean that there is a separate act of interpretation being performed; on the contrary, as he says, 'we normally just see an object or understand a sentence, without any act of interpreting' (1995, p. 134). In his *Philosophical Investigations* Wittgenstein makes the point that it would not make sense for someone, on seeing some cutlery, to exclaim 'I am seeing this *as* a fork':

One doesn't '*take*' what one knows as the cutlery at a meal *for* cutlery; any more than one ordinarily tries to move one's mouth as one eats, or aims at moving it. (Original emphasis; Wittgenstein, 1968, part II, § xi, p. 195)

Similarly, Heidegger suggests that our interpretation of something *as* something is 'grounded existentially in understanding' (1962, p. 188), an understanding which is prior to and more primordial than the interpretation:

the 'world' which has already been understood comes to be interpreted. The ready-to-hand comes *explicitly* into the sight which understands ... we are not simply designating something; but that which is designated is understood *as* that *as* which we are to take the thing in question ... In dealing with what is environmentally ready-to-hand by interpreting it circumspectively, we 'see' it *as* a table, a door, a carriage, or a bridge ... (Original emphasis; *ibid.*, p. 189)

Although my interpretation might be focused on a particular object, it nevertheless presupposes an understanding of the wider environment. I *interpret* something as a hammer primarily in terms of its function, in terms of what I can use it for – and in order to do this I have to *understand* what tools or equipment are – and something about nails, wood, work-benches, etc. So instances of interpretation presuppose a wider and more fundamental understanding of the world. We might say that there is a sense in which we already 'have' the thing in question; we have already seen and conceived of it 'in advance' (*ibid.*, p. 191).

Whenever something is interpreted as something, the interpretation will be founded essentially upon fore-having, fore-sight, and fore-conception. An interpretation is never a presuppositionless apprehending of something presented to us. (*Ibid.*, pp. 191–2)

What seems clear is that as we move around in the world we do not *first* experience things as basic material or physical objects; we see screwdrivers, cars, bathtubs and five-pound notes rather than mere physical entities of wood, metal or paper. Still less do we experience the world as a series of sensations or stimuli; the world is first and foremost, as Heidegger would say, a world of ready-to-hand entities. Despite the ontological priority Searle ascribes to a realm of intrinsic, ontologically objective features, his conception of Background similarly allows him to acknowledge that the fact of our having assigned function, of having created a social object, is something which is basically 'invisible'. We do not have to consciously think 'we are now imposing a function on this' each time we use money, see a screwdriver, use a tool or regard a performance as being skilful; we do not encounter beings in some raw state which we then have to explicitly interpret. Indeed, as

Heidegger understood, it is surprisingly difficult for us to experience 'raw' sensations:

> What we first hear is never noises or complexes of sounds, but the creaking wagon, the motor cycle. We hear the column on the march, the north wind, the woodpecker tapping, the fire crackling. It requires a very artificial and complicated frame of mind to hear a pure noise ... Likewise, when we are explicitly hearing the discourse of another, we proximally understand what is said, or – to put it more exactly – we are already with him, in advance, alongside the entity which the discourse is about ... Even in cases where the speech is indistinct or in a foreign language, what we proximally hear is unintelligible words, and not a multiplicity of tone data. (*Ibid.*, p. 207)

Heidegger (1993a) reiterates the point in 'The Origin of the Work of Art': 'we never really first perceive the throng of sensations ... We hear the door shut in the house and never hear acoustical sensations or even mere sounds' (pp. 151–2). What seems to be at issue here is something so fundamental that it involves not simply our being able to ascribe functions to things but more our capacity to see, hear or feel things at all; the very possibility of our having experience seems to be dependent on the Background. As with visual and aural sensations so too with tactile ones as Michael Polanyi illustrates:

> as we learn to use a probe, or to use a stick for feeling our way, our awareness of its impact on our hand is transformed into a sense of its point touching the objects we are exploring. This is how an interpretative effort transposes meaningless feelings into meaningful ones, and places these at some distance from the original feeling. We become aware of the feelings in our hand in terms of their meaning located at the tip of the probe or stick to which we are attending. This is also so when we use a tool. We are attending to the meaning of its impact on our hands in terms of its effect on the things to which we are applying it. (Polanyi, 1983, pp. 12–13)

So even with a stick physically interposed between ourselves and the world we have the ability to transcend this sensory breach – to leap across into the world. Moreover, as Polanyi intimates, it would seem that this is something we have to learn and that in so learning we become, as Karl Popper puts it, the product of our own achievement; we become, at least in part, World 3 products:

> One learns not only to perceive, and to interpret one's perceptions, but also to be a person, and to be a self. I regard the view that our perceptions are 'given' to us as a mistake: they are 'made' by us, they are the result of active work. (Popper and Eccles, 1986, p. 49)

The idea that perception is an active process, that we have to learn to interpret our perceptions, is profoundly significant for our conception of vocational capability and it is an idea for which there is substantial evidence in the fields of cognitive psychology and the psychology of perception. One of the classic texts on the subject, and one which has a particular relevance for how these processes have a bearing on vocational capability is M. L. J. Abercrombie's *The Anatomy of Judgement* (1989). Given its acute practical relevance for the present discussion and the considerable support it lends to the kind of constructivist account we have been developing here it will be useful to consider Abercrombie's work in some detail.

Learning to see: the role of schemata

The work which led ultimately to the writing of *The Anatomy of Judgement* initially came about as a response to certain difficulties with the training of medical students. In 1944 the Report of a Committee of the Royal College of Physicians had expressed concern that the average medical graduate

> tends to lack curiosity and initiative; his powers of observation are relatively underdeveloped; his ability to arrange and interpret facts is poor; he lacks precision in the use of words. (Cited in Abercrombie, 1989, pp. 15–16)

Abercrombie's interest lay in researching the causes of and possible solutions to such problems and she came to believe that if students were more fully aware of the factors which influenced their observations, diagnoses and judgements, they may be able to improve their performance. It was with this in mind that she set about examining how we form judgements,[35] in particular drawing attention to the selective and interpretative nature of perception.

Contrary to the view that we passively receive perceptual information, Abercrombie argues that what we perceive depends not just on the state of the object being perceived, but also on the state of the perceiver – on what *we* bring to the act of perception. Drawing on evidence from a range of sources in cognitive psychology, she demonstrates that the way in which we perceive the world – the very having of experience – is profoundly affected by unconscious processes and that we come to the act of perception not with a blank mind but rather in a state of preparedness. Primed by experience, we are thus predisposed to perceive the world in particular ways. Abercrombie suggests that it is useful to think of this mental preparedness as being arranged in the form of 'schemata'. Indeed, more recently, Rumelhart (1980) has similarly suggested that schemata are the 'building blocks' of cognition and that learning is essentially about the development and application of schemata.

Abercrombie argues that while in our daily lives our senses are bombarded by raw data, the information we ultimately receive is that which is selected and conditioned by certain mental processes. The way we perceive the world is therefore dependent upon our making certain types of judgement, but this is done so quickly and automatically that we are rarely aware of the extent of our own involvement in the process; hence we assume that the information we receive is as 'given'. It is a view endorsed by Karl Popper when he suggests that:

> We learn to decode the coded signals which reach us: we decode them almost completely unconsciously, automatically, in terms of real things. We *learn* to behave, and to experience as if we were 'direct realists'; that is to say, we learn to experience things directly, as if there was no need for any decoding. (Original emphasis; Popper and Eccles, 1986, p. 45)

Abercrombie maintains that our seeing even the most ordinary things involves extraordinarily complex processes of which we generally remain unaware. The very act of perception involves us in unconscious processes in which we interpret and make judgements about the information we receive. By way of illustration she recounts experiments which demonstrate that visual stimulus patterns are interpreted differently according to the schema the observer brings to the act of perceiving. Our being able to see the image of a 'face', 'hidden' in a stimulus pattern of seemingly random blotches on the page, depends on our being able to select from the totality of blotches those which carry the information we want and reject those which are irrelevant to our purposes. On Abercrombie's view (1989) we can only discriminate in this way by choosing the appropriate schema, and in order to do this we may need some prompt or 'clue' (p. 31); of course, once we have had the 'face' pointed out to us we immediately adopt the appropriate schema and may then find it difficult *not* to see the image, and are probably surprised that we did not see it earlier.

It seems that the most ordinary, everyday activities involve our adopting those schemata which are appropriate to our purposes. The difficulty is that once attained, these abilities become so immediate and automatic that they are, to invoke Searle's terminology again, effectively 'invisible'. Of course, these are precisely the kind of abilities which are often associated with the idea of 'tacit knowledge' and we might recall here Polanyi's point about how we are unable to put into words how it is that we are able to recognize someone's face:

> There are many other instances of the recognition of a characteristic physiognomy – some commonplace, others more technical – which have the same structure as the identification of a person. We recognise the moods of a human face, without being able to tell, except quite vaguely, by what signs we know it. At the universities great efforts are spent in practical

classes to teach students to identify cases of diseases and specimens of rocks, of plants and animals. All descriptive sciences study physiognomies that cannot be fully described in words, nor even by pictures. (Polanyi, 1983, p. 5)

The important point here is not so much the difficulty we have putting these things into words (important though that is) so much as the idea that we are surrounded by features of the world, be they physiognomies, facial expressions, functional objects, meaningful behaviours, all of which we must *learn* to see. In coming to recognize features of the world around us, many of the capacities we develop we will have in common with others. Importantly, however, a considerable part of what it is to be vocationally capable consists in being able to apply schemata which enable us to 'see' those features of the world which are relevant and perhaps even unique to a particular vocational role.

Phil Hodkinson (1992) similarly suggests that 'schemas' (*sic*) can be seen to play an important role in what he sees as a dialectical interaction 'between the learner and the learned' (p. 33), arguing that 'schema theory' suggests a model of vocational competence very different from the behaviourist NVQ model. While the behaviourist model gives primacy to performance, Hodkinson's 'interactive' alternative recognizes three components: perfor-mance, intellectual processes and schemas, each intimately connected and mutually influential through continual dialectical interaction. The important point acknowledged by Hodkinson is that a change in performance may often require modifications to our schemata or the development of new, more appropriate ones.

As demonstrated in Abercromie's example of the 'hidden face', the act of perception often requires us to be able to discriminate between what counts and what doesn't, between, for example, background and foreground. We will ignore or reject the information which does not fit in with what our schemata lead us to expect. Quite often, skilled performance is very much about this capacity to selectively reject information. But this same capacity can mislead us if the schemata we choose are inappropriate for the task in hand: they may detrimentally limit our perception and we may be led to ignore useful or even vital information simply because it does not conform to the chosen schema. Abercrombie cites the example of a radiologist who, on X-raying a child who had presented with a persistent cough, at first failed to see anything of significance in the radiograph. Only subsequently was the shadow of a button in the throat area recognized as the cause of problem – it had been swallowed. The radiologist had previously overlooked it, assuming that the child had been X-rayed while wearing a vest. As Abercrombie says, the radiologist's schemata were based on his experience that people tend to wear buttons outside rather than inside their throats! Here we might bring to mind Heidegger's admonition that our first, last, and constant task is never to allow our fore-having, fore-sight, and fore-conception to be presented to us by fancies and popular conceptions, but rather to make the scientific theme secure by working out these fore-structures in terms of the things themselves. (Heidegger, 1962, p. 195)

In perceiving the world, our interpretation of sensory information involves us in selecting from our own store of information – from our own past experience.[36] We adopt a certain perspective based on past experience and this seems to be a central part of proficient performance:

> Because of the performer's perspective, certain features of the situation will stand out as salient and others will recede into the background and be ignored. As events modify the salient features, plans, expectations, and even the relative salience of features will gradually change. No detached choice or deliberation occurs. It just happens, apparently because the proficient performer has experienced similar situations in the past and memories of them trigger plans similar to those that worked in the past ... (Dreyfus and Dreyfus, 1986, p. 28)

In saying that we are predisposed by previous experience we should be clear that this is far from being equivalent to the behaviourist's notion of conditioned involuntary reflexes. Indeed, when we consider the way in which perception is profoundly value-laden we begin to understand just how inadequate the behaviourist account is. One experiment described by Abercrombie utilized a specially constructed, distorted room which, when viewed through a viewing hole, appeared to have a normal perspective. The viewer is deceived into seeing persons standing in the 'room' as oddly sized people in a room of 'normal' proportions – the schemata the viewer applies being based on his or her experience that rooms tend to be 'normal'. It might, of course, be objected that people, too, tend to be 'normal'. For Abercrombie, the likely reason why we intuitively opt for the 'normal room–oddly sized people' schema, rather than the (true) 'distorted room–normal people' schema, is related to our 'need to keep our environment stable' (1989, p. 47). She suggests that our capacity to move successfully around the world, estimate distances, get what we need, etc., relies on there being some general stability in those elements of our environment which we tend to regard as relatively static. In this sense, as Abercrombie says, we interpret raw information 'in terms of our past experience and present and future needs' (*ibid.*, p. 47); we thus get an important affirmation of how perception is intensely value-laden, of how our very perception of the world is fundamentally attuned to our wider purposes and priorities.

The selective nature of the processes of perception is underlined by experiments (D. R. Davis and D. Sinha, 1950; see Abercrombie, 1989, p. 32) which seem to indicate that it is possible for us to purposefully yet unconsciously misconstrue what we have seen in order to make it fit our chosen schema. In one, subjects were told a story before being asked to select, from a number of paintings, a picture which seemed most relevant to the story. Later, on being asked to describe the picture from memory, their descriptions (compared with those of a control group who had not heard the story) were clearly influenced by the story they had heard. Not only did they tend to recall those features of the painting which most closely fitted the story, but many aspects were wrongly perceived in an apparent attempt to make the picture 'match' the story. As Abercrombie says, the story provided a schema which the subjects then used in their perception of the painting, even to the extent that it appeared to distort their perception of what was there. Broudy (1988) has similarly suggested that a person's previous experience is one of the prime 'contaminants of sense perception' (p. 53). But the point here is not simply that we are fallible but rather that our perception of the world, as Hubert Dreyfus puts it, is never 'neutral':

> in the perception of objects there are no neutral traits. The same hazy layer which I would see as dust if I thought I was confronting a wax apple might appear as moisture if I thought I was seeing one that was fresh. The significance of the details and indeed their very look is determined by my perception of the whole. (Dreyfus, 1992, p. 238)

When it comes to 'seeing people' our use of schemata appears to be even more complex than it is when we perceive objects, images, etc. First, because our perception of other people seems to be more completely affected by our own personal past experience:

> According to their past experience and future intentions one person sees a policeman as a kindly figure who safeguards his passage across the road, another sees him as an enemy who may send him to the law-courts. (Abercrombie, 1989, p. 50)

Second, because the schemata we bring to bear tend to be self-confirming, our resulting behaviour will tend to bring about responses in others which tend to reinforce our original schema. The way in which a teacher's expectations may affect a pupil's performance is one example of how schemata might be thus reinforced, the teacher's implicit predictions acting as self-fulfilling prophesies.

Other visual experiments cited by Abercrombie demonstrate that our interpretation of one part of what we see may often be greatly affected by the other parts: i.e. by its visual context. As Merleau-Ponty (1992) recognized, 'The perceptual "something" is always in the middle of something else, it always forms part of a "field"' (p. 4). Abercrombie shows how this context will often provide 'clues' which influence our choice of schema and thus affect how things are perceived. So strong can this influence be that we remain deceived as to, say, the relative size of figures, when placed against a particular background in a drawing, even though we know their true size by having measured them. If we remove the background (and hence the clues) we are able to apply a more appropriate schema and avoid the deception. It would seem, then, that rather than perceiving features of the world in isolation, we unconsciously refer to the context in which those features are situated; we use the context to provide the necessary clues in order that we can select and apply appropriate schemata. But we are rarely aware that we are thus mentally predisposed, that our choice of schema is being determined by the context in which we perceive an object. Nevertheless, as Abercrombie suggests, this kind of unconscious perception 'may play an important role in many highly developed skills such as those involved in medical diagnosis' (Abercrombie, 1989, p. 53).

One important feature of schemata is the way in which they seem to enable us to go beyond the raw information we receive, information which may often be transient and otherwise unreliable. When, in a series of experiments by Ames (cited by Abercrombie, 1989, pp. 41–2), subjects were shown playing cards of different sizes in a darkened room – and thus deprived of information about visual background – they interpreted what they saw as similarly sized cards at different distances. As Abercrombie says, in normal life when we play a game of cards the images the cards make on the retina are continuously varying in size but we are able to interpret such changing images as representing cards of a uniform size. Our most basic physical skills, even our ability to move about in the world, depend on our making such assumptions by interpreting and 'going beyond' the sensory information we receive, and being prepared to modify our assumptions when they cease to be useful.

Another way in which it would appear we are able to 'go beyond' the information we receive is by applying complex compounds of schemata involving various senses. The schemata we have relating to apples, for example, is likely to comprise a complex of information not only about the way apples look in terms of their colour, size and texture, but also about how they feel to our hands, teeth or tongue; and how they smell and taste, and how they sound when bitten into or shaken. This 'compounding' of schemata allows us to 'go beyond' the information immediately given and make predictions on the basis of limited data.

When these complex schemata are used appropriately, we can take for granted a lot of other properties about which we have no direct evidence at the moment. When, for instance, we choose by sight what we think is the best apple from a dishful, we receive visually certain information about its size, shape and colour, and we choose that particular apple because we think it will taste nicer than the others. This means that we are going beyond the information immediately given (extrapolating or predicting)

by using our complex of schemata of apples, not only our visual one ...
(Abercrombie, 1989, pp. 47–8)

In practice, of course, we may not always be correct in our predictions,
hence in acting in and upon the world we engage in a continuing process of
reappraisal and modification of the schemata we use – in this way we
continue to learn to perceive the world by interacting with it. On Karl
Popper's view, our ongoing interpretation of, and interaction with, the
sensory information we receive is 'in many ways like problem solving by way
of hypotheses' (Popper and Eccles, 1986, p. 45). Similarly, Donald Schön
(1987; 1996) has acknowledged the way in which successful performance is
often related to the capacity to reflect on or in action. He notes the way that
professional baseball players apparently rely on 'finding the groove'; that is,
they learn to adjust their performance by reflecting on those aspects of their
performance which happen to work. Similarly, improvising jazz musicians
get 'a feel' for the piece they are playing; reflecting in action on their
collective music making:

> They can do this, first of all, because their collective effort at musical
> invention makes use of a schema – a metric, melodic, and harmonic
> schema familiar to all the participants – which gives a predictable order to
> the piece. In addition, each of the musicians has at the ready a repertoire of
> musical figures which he can deliver at appropriate moments. Improvisa-
> tion consists in varying, combining, and recombining a set of figures within
> the schema which bounds and gives coherence to the performance. (Schön,
> 1996, p. 55)

Schemata also seem to have an important effect on how we classify the
information we receive and, again, this appears to play an important role in
allowing us to extrapolate from available evidence and make predictions
about the future. In examining a patient, the doctor receives information from
signs and symptoms and uses this information as an indication of a particular
class of disease – one which can be identified and named. If the classification is
correct, the doctor knows vastly more than has been ascertained from the
examination, not only about things that he has not actually seen, for example
the presence of a particular virus, but also about the future; for example, he
can predict that certain symptoms will develop after a period of time. In using
the process of classification to extrapolate or predict the doctor is 'exploiting
his own and other people's schemata of similar cases' (Abercrombie, 1989, p.
115). However, the act of naming or classifying can affect our perception of
the available information because it affects our choice of schemata: being
committed to a particular classification effectively predetermines the
schemata available to us.

Judgement of the suitability of a system of classification is presumably based on the perception, not necessarily conscious, of a pattern of correlated features, and seems to involve the same kind of processes as aesthetic judgement. (Abercrombie, 1989, p. 118)

But our capacity to go beyond the information presented can lead us to make mistakes. In one experiment medical students were shown two X-ray images and asked to compare them. Rather than make statements relating to the directly observable features – for example, the relative size, shape, number and arrangement of shadows in the prints – students showed a marked tendency to make statements such as 'A is a young hand and B an old hand', 'The bones in B have fused' and 'A is a live hand, B is a skeleton'.

In making this kind of statement (an inference or conclusion) they are going beyond the information given, combining parts of their own store of common and biological knowledge with the information presented by the picture. The truth of such statements cannot be investigated by reference to the prints alone because they are made about the student's schemata, as well as the image on the retina. (*Ibid.*, p. 85)

Abercrombie cites research by E. Renbourn and J. Ellison (see Abercrombie, 1989, p. 91) which indicates that observer error in the reading of instruments (e.g. a burette) can be caused by individuals having a preference for certain digits or having prior expectations about what the result should be. There is also the suggestion that error might also be caused by parallax; that is, the observer might unconsciously shift the viewing position relative to the scale in order to obtain the expected result – or, as Abercrombie says, to make the information fit the schema.

Observation in science, whether during training, or in the practice of the most exquisitely developed skill, involves guessing, just as seeing in ordinary life does (and I use the word 'guessing' here to emphasise the precarious nature of the act, which the expression 'making a judgement' elides). (*Ibid.*, p. 92)

Indeed, we might note that those who are required to work with extreme accuracy and to very small tolerances, for example precision engineering fitters, often report that in learning to use instruments such as micrometers, vernier callipers, etc., the essential thing is for trainees to learn the correct 'feel' in applying instruments to the object being measured – a far from precise prescription. As Abercrombie says, what we are concerned with in such cases 'is learning to make the guess as good as possible' (*ibid.*).

It would seem, then, that there is substantial empirical evidence to support the idea that how we perceive the world around us is dependent not just on what is being perceived, but also on what we bring to the act of perception and that the very having of experience is thus profoundly dependent upon how we are disposed to deal with the sensory information we receive. In perceiving, we are unavoidably involved in complex processes of selection and interpretation, in making *judgements*, the outcomes of which are substantively determined by our past experience, by the context in which we receive the information, and by our own dispositions, purposes, interests and values. Even the most 'unequivocal' scientific 'facts' are not immune from such processes, but are equally subject to the interposition of human judgement and value; similarly, our dealings with other people are profoundly affected by the way in which we are predisposed to see them. It would seem that an understanding of such processes is crucial to any account of vocational and professional capability not least because, as Abercrombie clearly demonstrates, only then might we more fully comprehend the causes of fallibility.

But there is another equally important point to be derived from the evidence cited by Abercrombie, although it is not one she makes explicit herself. The evidence seems to indicate that in learning to see – in coming to adopt appropriate schemata – a person does not approach the world as a *tabula rasa*, merely taking on additional schemata here or there where none existed before. Rather, our learning to see would seem to involve us in a process of modifying, amending, perhaps in some cases being compelled to abandon the schemata we already have. The point here is that we are never 'schemata-less'; in order that we may see the world *at all* we have to make judgements and this entails our judging *from* some position. To borrow Thomas Nagel's (1986) evocative phrase, we might say that it is never possible for us to adopt a 'view from nowhere'. In Heideggerian terms there is an important sense in which we are always *already* in-the-world, already predisposed to experience the world in certain ways.

Seen thus, the learning process appears to be less about our being able to develop capacities sufficient to assimilate some external, 'objective' reality than it is about our being able to modify our interpretations so that *what* we see is appropriate to the priorities and purposes an occupation requires us to adopt. This has quite profound educational implications. At the very least it indicates that the complex physiognomies of materials and forms to which the craftsman directs his attention is something which he 'learns to see' not by reference to some precise, objective, empiricist mandate, but rather by coming to share the priorities and values of a community of practitioners. It would seem that in order for work to be good or bad, tools to be useful or useless, materials to be suitable or unsuitable – for him to *see* them as such – these things must come to *matter* to him; his perception of his work and the wider world in which it is situated would appear to be irredeemably grounded in the values he brings to it.

Knowledge, understanding and vocational capability

The three accounts we have considered in this chapter are clearly motivated by very different concerns. Searle's account of how we construct social reality is intended to explain how it is possible for formal institutions such as money, marriage or games of chess to constitute part of an 'objective' reality; Heidegger's 'analytic of everydayness' is, among other things, intended to establish the idea of existence as essentially Being-in-the-world and to 'reveal the primacy of the equipmental-instrumental understanding of the being of entities as opposed to the objective-scientific understanding' (Zimmerman, 1990, p. 137);[37] Abercrombie's work, on the other hand, is intended to demonstrate how perception is fundamentally affected by unconscious mental processes.

Yet, from these quite different perspectives it is possible to discern degrees of convergence and important areas of common ground. The respective accounts of 'function/background', 'understanding/Being-in-the-world' and 'schemata' all point to a primordial level of understanding which is of vital relevance for our conception of vocational capability. Together they indicate the means by which we come to understand how the world works, how we are able to perceive that world and structure our experience of it. Importantly, they also highlight the profound inadequacy of accounts of vocational capability couched in terms of descriptions of behaviour or physical operations. Rather, they seem to suggest, as Dearden (1984) has argued, that 'what someone is doing and why he is doing it are unintelligible without reference to his beliefs, desires, intentions, experiences, imaginings, attitudes, sentiments, or in general his understanding' (p. 142). And in this sense Michael Eraut (1989) is surely right when he says that 'people use theory all the time ... it is their personal theories which determine how they interpret the world and their encounters with people and situations within it' (p. 184).

But terms such as 'theory' and 'knowledge' are not really suitable here, for they suggest something far too explicit. The notions of Background and schemata expounded by Searle and Abercrombie are far from equivalent to explanatory theory or propositional knowledge.[38] Heidegger, too, is at pains to emphasize that his conception of 'understanding', partly constitutive of Being-in-the-world, is far more fundamental than 'knowledge': it is a *prerequisite* of such things as 'knowing', 'theorizing' or 'explaining'.[39] Being-in-the-world is essentially non-cognitive; it is not primarily about what beliefs or knowledge we have. Knowing is just one specialized kind of Being-in-the-world which is derivative of a more basic, non-cognitive kind of 'dwelling'. Our coming to 'objectively' know something can only arise from a purposeful 'thematizing' (Heidegger, 1962, p. 414) and objectifying of experience and this requires a pulling back from the world: 'a deficiency in our having-to-do with the world concernfully' (*ibid.*, p. 88). Richard Polt vividly illustrates

Heidegger's point with the following description of a taxi driver taking a passenger through heavy traffic:

> He is absorbed in the task of making his way through the stream of cars, buses and pedestrians. He is in his world, he dwells in it; his task and the things he encounters make sense to him in terms of a meaningful whole. This is not a matter of what he *believes* or *knows*; he is simply 'fascinated' (Heidegger, 1962 p. 88) by the process of being a cabbie. Suddenly he runs into a massive traffic jam. It becomes clear that he can make no progress at all. His passenger gets out, exasperated. Now there is nothing for our cabbie to do but wait, and he 'holds back from any kind of producing, manipulating and the like' (*ibid.*). He gives up on driving, and idly speculates on the causes of this traffic jam. He forms a *belief* that there is an accident ahead. He reviews the *grounds* for his belief in order to decide whether he really *knows* that there is an accident. (Original emphasis; Polt, 1999, p. 48)

Clearly, to conceive of vocational capability in these terms runs counter to the intellectualist conception of action – the conception against which Ryle militated – as something which is explicitly theory-guided. With Dreyfus and Dreyfus (1986), we might be inclined to concur with the existentialists who held that:

> Human understanding was a skill akin to knowing how to find one's way about in the world, rather than knowing a lot of facts and rules for relating them. Our basic understanding was thus a *knowing how* rather than a *knowing that*. (Original emphasis; Dreyfus and Dreyfus, 1986, p. 4)

Yet there are two urgent caveats to be added here. First, it will turn out that the notion of 'rules' is far more complex than the use of the term here suggests; this is something we shall explore in more detail in the next chapter. Second, it is crucially important to differentiate the kind of 'knowing how' invoked here from the 'knowing how' delineated by Ryle. Ryle's conception of 'knowing how', it will be remembered, was circumscribed by the evidential conditions of our coming to know about the knowledgeable states of others. In contrast to the line taken by Ryle, who effectively responded to the intellectualist legend by setting two types of knowledge (or more precisely two kinds of evidence) in opposition, here it might be said that we are simply acknowledging, with Dewey (1929), that 'things are objects to be treated, used, acted upon and with, enjoyed and endured even more than things to be known. They are things *had* before they are things cognized' (original emphasis; p. 21). As Heidegger (1962) points out: ' "Practical" behaviour is not "atheoretical" in the sense of "sightlessness" ' (p. 99).[40] Indeed, it would be more appropriate to see this kind of understanding as one which defies categorization in terms of a 'knowing how' or a 'knowing that', as Heidegger himself indicates with his description of an apprentice training to be a cabinetmaker:

> His learning is not mere practice, to gain facility in the use of tools. Nor does he merely gather knowledge about the customary forms of the things he is to build. If he is to become a true cabinetmaker, he makes himself answer and respond above all to the different kinds of wood and to the shapes slumbering in the wood – to wood as it enters into man's dwelling with all the hidden riches of its essence. In fact, this relatedness to wood is what maintains the whole craft. Without that relatedness, the craft will never be anything but empty busywork, any occupation with it will be determined exclusively by business concerns. Every handicraft, all human dealings, are constantly in that danger. (Heidegger, 1993b, p. 379)

Perhaps the predominant manifestation of this kind of relatedness, this kind of understanding, is judgement. As we have seen, at its most primordial it consists of the judgements we unconsciously make when we interpret sensory information. But judgement is manifest in all of our activities: it is integral to our competent dealings with the world. We might think of judgement as the means by which Heidegger's apprentice is able to 'answer and respond' to his materials. Indeed, an account of vocational capability in these terms is broadly consistent with Oakeshott's claim that the entirety of what we know can be thought of as a manifold of abilities which, in turn, consist of a synthesis of judgement and information. And just as 'judgement' might be interpreted in the very widest sense, so too the notion of 'information', for we can think of it as consisting in the most fundamental sensory information and the most abstract propositional knowledge alike.

As Oakeshott recognized, judgement is the tacit component of what we can be said to 'know'; it defies precise explication. Paul Standish indicates the important sense in which the very essence of skilled activity remains steadfastly opaque when exposed to the analytical techniques of technical rationality:

> The wood the carpenter works with is likely to present resistances – the occurrence of knots, the nature of the grain – against which his own activity will be progressively adjusted in a manner that cannot be altogether pre-planned. Not just resistances, however, for these same features become absorbed creatively into his making: he works with the grain. The craft activity does not seem so susceptible to the imposition of a calculative rationality or to formalism in terms of algorithmic processes. (Standish, 1997, p. 446)

Indeed, the different accounts we have considered here all testify to this opaqueness. It is corroborated in the 'weightless and invisible' ontology described by Searle and in the non-representational, non-intentional character of our most fundamental capabilities; similarly, in Heidegger's insight that 'that which is ontically closest and well known is ontologically the farthest and not known at all', and again in the profoundly 'unconscious' nature of the processes described by Abercrombie.

It is precisely this opaqueness which makes the task of determining the capabilities required for a particular vocation so problematic. Traditionally, those who have attempted the task have tended to set about describing the kinds of evidence that can be had about the knowledgeable states of others, thus gravitating towards an account in which the entirety of what someone can be said to know is couched in terms of the 'knowing how–knowing that' dichotomy or one of its variants: for example 'practice–theory', 'performance evidence–underpinning knowledge', and so on. On this view, it might be determined that the apprentice cabinetmaker would be required, for example, to know *how* to use a tenon saw, or know *that* certain kinds of wood have certain physical properties.

Yet, as Heidegger demonstrates, accounts of 'mere practice' and theoretical or propositional 'knowledge' fail to capture the essence of the cabinetmaker's understanding. It is not that there is a third mode of knowledge which needs to be added to the accounts of 'knowing how' and 'knowing that';[41] it is rather that these more evident manifestations of what is known should more properly be recognized *as* that – as manifestations of a more fundamental kind of understanding of which they are essentially *derivative*. It would seem that if the act of sawing, or the stating of facts about the properties of wood, is to be anything other than unthinking mechanical action or meaningless regurgitation of propositions, it must be grounded in this kind of understanding, this kind of dwelling. The apprentice must be able to develop an appropriate 'relatedness' to the materials and to the work if he or she is to be able to use a saw skilfully or really understand the properties of different woods. Accordingly, any amount of vacillation between descriptions of behaviour and accounts of propositional knowledge will inevitably fall short of describing what it is the cabinetmaker understands.

The difficulty for those inflicted with the 'knowing how–knowing that' myopia is not that they fail to spot the shortfall – the discrepancy caused by the ontological shift in attention away from knowledge to its outward effects – but rather that they mistakenly interpret it as a quantitative rather than a qualitative discrepancy. In recognizing the inadequacy of their description they assume that the remedy lies in elaborating still further what it is the cabinetmaker *does* or the *theory* required. In either case the problem is merely exacerbated: the one tendency leading towards reductionism and the other towards irrelevance. And the 'knowing how–knowing that' form of analysis gives rise to another kind of difficulty when, as is sometimes the case, the occupation being considered demands conspicuously little by way of practical deftness or propositional knowledge. For then there is the danger of a radical underestimation of the capabilities involved and the extent of the preparation required for that role.[42]

The conception of vocational and professional capability which has emerged from our discussion here stands in marked contrast to such evidential accounts of knowledge. On the view developed here, to become vocationally capable is first and foremost about learning to perceive, experience, cope with, in short, to *be* in a particular 'world'. As O'Reilly (1989) has argued, experience is essentially incoherent: it comes not with a particular, predetermined meaning, but rather with a multiplicity of meaning, an excess of meaning, the content of which can even be contradictory. But in the light of what we have considered here we might say that as we go about our lives acting in a particular occupational capacity a certain coherence is disclosed to us, a world of profoundly interconnected meanings and involvements inextricably related to our purposes, goals and values – purposes, goals and values which must be approximate in some sense to those of our fellow practitioners. As an engineer, a mother or an architect, not only is the world revealed differently but what we *are* is inseparable from the world which is disclosed to us; our being, our very identity, cannot be separated from the realm of concerns and meanings which our being able to act in that world necessitates. Our becoming vocationally capable is primarily about our gaining certain fundamental understandings and abilities relating to how that particular world works, how to cope in it and find our way around it – rather than necessarily being able to exhibit the secondary and derivative behavioural or propositional manifestations of those understandings. In becoming capable we learn to adopt a particular stance, a certain interested and purposeful viewpoint which in turn structures our consciousness and our experience. We thus come to be equipped with a certain kind of 'readiness'; we are able to see things *as* certain things, we are able to interpret what we experience and extrapolate from it in a way which is appropriate to the world in which we wish to operate. Importantly, it would seem that this is what is required for *all* occupations – without exception. We might note that to conceive of occupational capability in these terms makes it possible to account for the expertise of the maintenance technician in our earlier example – an expertise which, as we saw, could not be accounted for in terms of propositional knowledge or physical dexterity. And similarly with any other occupation: the mathematician, the racing driver, the opera singer, the supermarket shelf-filler, the surgeon, they all have this much in common.

Of course, this is not to suggest that such diverse occupations should in any way be regarded as equivalent; rather, it is simply to say that insofar as they are different then that difference should be *correctly* characterized. On the view presented here, any given occupation differs from another by virtue of the fact that it requires the agent to engage with a particular sphere of involvements – each occupation requires, in effect, the facility to operate in a different world. (We might note that this alone should be sufficient to make us treat with suspicion the viability and meaningfulness of such things as 'transferable skills'.) Different *levels* of occupation – for example, the crafts as against the professions – are properly distinguished not by assigning to each some spurious category of knowledge, or by allowing certain types of occupation to make exclusive claims on such things as judgement or imagination, but, rather, by simply acknowledging that the world of meanings within which each is required to operate may differ quite radically both in complexity and in level of abstraction.

Both Heidegger and Searle acknowledge, of course, that these contingent worlds, although Dasein-related or human-dependent, cannot result from the will of any one person. When we are confronted with questions about what it is that makes one artefact more skilfully made than another, or what constitutes the correct tool for the job, or what kind of actions might be regarded as competent or skilled, we know that these matters are far from arbitrary or open for any one person to decide. Such things, it would seem, entail some form of agreement or consensus. The question, then, is what form this consensus takes; or more precisely, whether, and in what sense, vocational capability might be said to be rule-governed.

Notes

32   The term 'intentionality' is used here in the technical sense of mental states being about or directed at the world. Perceptions, beliefs and desires are intentional in this sense, as are intentions, although there is no special connection between intentionality and intending (see Searle, 1983).

33   Harrison Hall (1993) sees Heidegger as employing 'at least three' notions of intentionality: first, that of the 'theoretical subject'; second, that of the practical subject; and third, 'a more primordial intentionality and world ... which precludes any use of the subject-object model and without which the understanding of the other two sorts of intentionality and world are necessarily misunderstandings' (p. 124). However, given the non-representational nature of this third kind of 'intentionality', it is perhaps more appropriate to follow Charles Taylor (1993) here and characterize this 'more primordial intentionality' as the background to the intentional.

34   Michael Inwood (1999) is here commenting on Heidegger's *Einführung in die phänomenologische Forschung*.

35   The term 'judgement' is used by Abercrombie in two different senses. First, in the ordinary sense such as, for example, when a radiologist after studying X-ray plates makes a judgement about whether a bone is fractured. Second, and more importantly here, she also uses the term 'judgement' to refer to the unconscious processes which determine how and what we perceive.

[36] One thing that distances Abercrombie's account from the Heideggerian perspective – and indicates some limitations of her account – is her mentalistic vocabulary evident, for example, in her references to a person's being able to 'select' information from past experience, as if the 'I' that does the selecting is something that can be meaningfully differentiated from the content of such mental states.

[37] Gerold Prauss (1999) has argued that there are two conflicting interpretations of Heidegger's account within *Being and Time* of knowing and doing, or theory and practice. First, there is the view that Heidegger seeks to establish the primacy of the 'ready-to hand' and hence practice over theory. Second, there is that which understands Heidegger as wishing to dissolve the distinction between theory and practice. This is not the place to develop these matters of interpretation in detail; suffice it to say that Prauss attempts to resolve these difficulties and demonstrate the 'real primacy of doing over knowing' by showing that knowing is not simply directed at the actual, but rather, 'knowing is instead nothing but the way in which doing directs itself toward what is already actual' (p. 41). (See also Zimmerman, 1990, pp. 142–3.)

[38] We might note that Argyris and Schön (1974) find it necessary to distinguish 'theories in use', i.e. the theory on which professional action is based, from the 'espoused theories' which we use to explain our actions.

[39] Michael Oakeshott (1991), in his essay 'Rational conduct', essentially makes the same important point when he emphasizes that 'The characteristic of the carpenter, the scientist, the painter, the judge, the cook, and of any man in the ordinary conduct of life, and in his relations with other people and with the world around him is a knowledge, not of certain propositions about themselves, their tools, and the materials in which they work, but a knowledge of how to decide certain questions; and this knowledge is the condition of the exercise of the power to construct such propositions' (p. 110).

[40] Macquarrie and Robinson's footnote to Heidegger reminds us that 'theory' derives from θεωρειν – originally meaning 'to see' (see Heidegger, 1962, p. 99, note 1).

[41] Wilson (1972) is rightly critical of those who are 'bewitched with the common idea that knowledge is like a physical object which can be broken down or built up into a hierarchy of component parts' (p. 106). Those who are lured down this path are prone to set about cataloguing the various manifestations in which someone's knowledge might become apparent. There is no shortage of such accounts in the literature: Norman (1985) distinguishes five ('technical skills', 'clinical skills', 'knowledge and understanding', 'interpersonal attributes' and 'problem solving and clinical judgement'). Eraut (1994) lists six ('knowledge of people', 'situational knowledge', 'knowledge of educational practices', 'conceptual knowledge', 'process knowledge' and 'control knowledge'). Others,

for example Dreyfus and Dreyfus (1986) and indeed the UK NVQ system (see NCVQ, 1991), distinguish five *levels* of skill or competence while Broudy distinguishes four modes of knowledge *use* (see Broudy, et al., 1964; also Broudy as cited by Eraut, 1994, pp. 26–7). The arbitrariness of such distinctions is highlighted by the fact that using the same logic it is possible to acknowledge almost any number of categories or 'modes' of knowledge, or 'levels' of capability. Generally, such distinctions are configured in such a way as to serve some wider purpose: most usually to provide a justification for discriminating between occupations (see, for example, Eraut, 1994, pp. 26–7).

[42] Claims to the effect that a vocational role requires negligible capabilities often play a part in the adversarial posturing between employers and employees. For instance, O'Reilly (1996) reports one employer as commenting that the requirement for the job of an operator was 'two arms and two legs' (p. 25); elsewhere it has been suggested that the idea of a 'skills gap' is merely a 'subjective notion', used 'to blame young people for not being employable' and that there are 'more skills involved in most young people's computer-based leisure activities that there are in the average job' (Hayes, 1996, pp. 45–6).

7

Working to Rules

It is possible to discern in the literature two very different viewpoints regarding the role of rules in relation to human capabilities. On the one hand there is the view that an important part of what it is to be skilled, capable or competent consists in being able to act effectively without recourse to rules. On this view, to be truly skilled or capable is to possess the kind of abilities or understandings which in Michael Oakeshott's (1973) words, are 'capable of carrying us across those wide open spaces, to be found in every ability, where no rule runs' (p. 168). Indeed, behaviour which is rule-governed might be thought of as the province of the novice, the very opposite of what it is to be competent or skilled, and to the extent that a person is guided in his or her actions by rules many would regard it as reasonable to judge that person less skilled or less capable. Michael Eraut (1994), for example, treats 'working with rules or procedures' (p. 48) as a feature of lower 'modes' of knowledge use. On the other hand, others would argue that for a person to be deemed skilled, capable or competent his or her actions must, of necessity, conform to rules. They would hold that in order for a person's actions be recognized as being skilled or competent there must be some conception of what *counts* as skilled or competent behaviour and this necessitates the existence of rules to which we are able to say his or her behaviour either does or does not conform.

The adoption of one or the other of these positions is implicit in much theorizing about vocational capability. Those who, in delineating an epistemology of professional practice, draw attention to such things as 'judgement' or 'reflection' can often be seen to implicitly adopt the first view. Those with bureaucratic or managerial inclinations invariably tend towards the second; the competence approach, for example, manifestly rests on the assumption that all competent behaviour conforms to identifiable and expressible rules, criteria, or standards.

While the latter position has the apparent virtue of being universally applicable to any kind of vocational capability, the former would appear to have unavoidably divisive repercussions. For it is not (and could not be) denied that *some* kinds of work are rule-governed or even that *some* of the tasks carried out by 'professionals' are rule-governed. The assumption, then, is that there exist two fundamentally different kinds of activities: those which are rule-governed and those which are not. The corollary of the claim that the professions are distinguished by the extent of non-rule-governed practices is that the more menial occupations are epistemologically distinctive precisely by virtue of their being rule-governed. While many would instinctively concur with this view, we shall see that this viewpoint derives in large part from an oversimplistic understanding of the notion of rules.

Insofar as these two positions have *philosophical* counterparts, nowhere are they more explicitly and cogently represented than in the respective work of Michael Oakeshott and Peter Winch. In his essay 'The Tower of Babel'[43] Oakeshott argues that in the majority of our activities we are guided not so much by the application of rules as by certain habits or customs: 'The current situations of a normal life are met not by consciously applying to ourselves a rule of behaviour ... but by acting in accordance with a certain habit of behaviour' (1991, p. 467). Now there are two crucial points to be made here, the importance of which will subsequently become clear. First, Oakeshott expressly takes rules to mean something which we *consciously* apply. Second, as is made apparent in the following passage, the notion of 'habit' Oakeshott has in mind here is not at all the kind of involuntary response to a stimulus that a behaviourist might conceive of; it is not merely a blind habit or compulsive repetition of antecedent behaviour. Indeed, Oakeshott's explication of the notion of custom is noticeably reminiscent of Heidegger's point that the 'atheoretical' nature of practical behaviour should not be equated to 'sightlessness':

> Custom is always adaptable and susceptible to the *nuance* of the situation. This may appear a paradoxical assertion; custom, we have been taught, is blind. It is however, an insidious piece of misobservation; custom is not blind, it is only 'blind as a bat'. And anyone who has studied a tradition of customary behaviour (or a tradition of any other sort) knows that both rigidity and instability are foreign to its character ... Indeed, no traditional way of behaviour, no traditional skill, ever remains fixed; its history is one of continuous change. (Original emphasis; *ibid.*, p. 471)

Of course, one argument against the idea that intelligent behaviour is essentially rule-guided is that famously given by Wittgenstein (1968) when he considers the sense in which language use might be thought of as a rule-governed activity. How might a shopkeeper understand and act on the words 'five red apples' on a shopping list? Perhaps, Wittgenstein hypothesizes (§1, pp. 2–3), the shopkeeper goes to the drawer marked 'apples', looks up the word 'red' on a colour chart or table, takes out apples as he runs through the cardinal numbers in his head until he gets to the number five. But the problem with assuming that the shopkeeper's actions are based on rules is that there seems to be no end to them – we require rules to tell us how to use rules; for example, how does the shopkeeper know where and how he is to look up the word 'red', or what he is to do with the word 'five'? How does he know how to use a chart or table; is he acting on a rule that says he must trace a line with his finger from left to right? And if this is so, can we not 'imagine further rules to explain this one?' (*ibid.*, §86, p. 40). It would seem that in accepting that our actions are rule-governed we are inexorably drawn into an infinite regress of rules; yet explanations, as Wittgenstein says, must 'come to an end somewhere' (*ibid.*, §i, p. 3).[44]

However much this argument may cause us to treat with scepticism the suggestion that behaviour is essentially rule-guided – we might recall that Ryle employs the very same strategy against the 'intellectualist legend' – it is not the one adopted by Oakeshott. If we think of the infinite regress argument as a complaint which arises from a frustrated expectation that rules might somehow be semantically self-sufficient, Oakeshott can be seen to take entirely the opposite approach – effectively arguing that rules are in themselves inert and essentially devoid of meaning. In 'The Tower of Babel' Oakeshott sets rules in contradistinction to the notion of habit or custom, but in his later 'Learning and Teaching' Oakeshott approaches the issue from a different perspective when considering how rules might relate to his conception of knowledge as a manifold of abilities – we will recall that he conceives of abilities, in turn, as a synthesis of judgement and information. On Oakeshott's view, the importance of information lies precisely in its capacity to function as rules or rule-like propositions whether it consists of mathematical equations, recipes, chemical formulae or statements such as 'glass is brittle'. However, he is keen to emphasize that the rules, propositions and facts which constitute information cannot on their own provide us with the ability to do, make, understand or explain anything.

> For rules are always disjunctive. They specify only an act or a conclusion of a certain general kind and they never relieve us of the necessity of choice. And they never yield more than partial explanations: to understand anything as an example of the operation of a rule is to understand it very imperfectly. (Oakeshott, 1973, p. 168)

In order that we might be said to have an ability, then – and here we can recognize striking parallels with Abercrombie's account of perception – information in the form of rules or rule-like propositions has to be selected and interpreted; we have to be able to discern when and where to use it. It is only by the application of 'judgement' that, on Oakeshott's view, we are able to act.

Nowhere is the opposition between Oakeshott and Winch more apparent than in their diverse approach to the question of literary 'style'. Of course, both would acknowledge the role of rules in determining such things as correct grammar but beyond this point they part company. Winch concedes that stylistic canons 'do not *dictate* that one should write in one way rather than another' (original emphasis; p. 53) but nevertheless insists that it would plainly be mistaken to conclude from this that literary style is not governed by any rules at all: it is something that can be learned, something that can be discussed, and the fact that it can be learned and discussed is essential to our conception of it. (Winch, 1965, pp. 53–4)

In contrast, Oakeshott is equally insistent that

every significant act or utterance has a style of its own, a personal idiom, an individual manner of thinking of which it is a reflection. This, what I have called style, is the choice made, not according to the rules, but within the area of freedom left by the negative operation of rules. (Oakeshott, 1973, pp. 174–5)

While Oakeshott's deprecation of rule-governed behaviour is consistent with his opposition to a rationalist conception of human action, Peter Winch's discussion of rules in *The Idea of a Social Science* (1965) forms part of his wider argument about the logical nature of the social sciences and their relation to the natural sciences. It will be useful here to note very briefly some of the main features of this argument since it will turn out later that some of them are particularly relevant to our concerns.

Winch's main purpose is to counter the empiricist assumption[45] that all kinds of explanation have the same logical structure and that the social sciences should proceed by discovering regularities and formulating empirical generalizations in exactly the same way as do the natural sciences. He points out that since regularities consist in the 'same kind of event on the same kind of occasion' (*ibid.*, p. 83) their discovery is dependent upon our being able to make 'judgements of identity' (*ibid.*), i.e. we have to determine what counts as being the 'same'.

So to investigate the type of regularity studied in a given enquiry is to examine the nature of the rule according to which judgements of identity are made in that enquiry. Such judgements are intelligible only relatively to a given mode of human behaviour, governed by its own rules. (*Ibid.*, pp. 83–4)

It follows, then, that while it is appropriate for the natural scientist to make judgements of identity according to the rules which generally govern the activities of natural scientists, the social scientist in contrast, must make such judgements in accordance with the rules which govern the behaviour of the persons studied. No matter how valid causal explanations may be for natural science, social phenomena, on Winch's view, must be explained in terms of the rules which give rise to the agent's reasons and motives for acting, for it is only in relation to these rules that such reasons and motives become intelligible. Consequently, according to Winch, not only is it profoundly mistaken to assume that sociological study can satisfactorily proceed by the use of statistics, causal laws and quasi-causal explanations such as the notion of function[46], but also it is clear that the notion of a rule is of central importance in explaining *any* purposeful behaviour. It is thus that Winch makes the bold assertion that 'all behaviour which is meaningful (therefore all specifically human behaviour) is *ipso facto* rule-governed' (*ibid.*, p. 52).

Needless to say, this would appear to be diametrically opposed to Oakeshott's stated view that most human behaviour should more properly be conceived of as 'acting in accordance with a certain habit' rather than in accordance with a rule. Indeed, Winch specifically draws attention to this opposition and sets about showing why in his view Oakeshott is mistaken. Now I want to suggest that what Winch goes on to say about rules, and the distinction he draws between his understanding of rules and Oakeshott's, is vitally important not because it shows Oakeshott to be mistaken, but because it provides an insight into the disparate nature of rules and the different ways in which they can be seen to relate to human capabilities. It seems to me that taken together, these two apparently irreconcilable accounts serve to indicate the important sense in which there might be said to be different *kinds* of rules and when the implications of this are more fully worked out these prima facie contrary positions may turn out to be substantially consistent with each other. If this is correct, then not only does it testify to a far more complex conception of rule-governed behaviour than is generally assumed, but it also indicates the profound inadequacy of both of the conventional viewpoints regarding the relation of rules to vocational capability.

Different kinds of rules

The sceptic's first response to the claim that all meaningful behaviour is rule-governed will be to think of instances of behaviour where this cannot be the case. Of course, because we are expressly concerned with *meaningful* behaviour the 'pointless behaviour of a berserk lunatic' (Winch, 1965, p. 53) is not a case in point. But the sceptic may, for example, point to instances where a person purposefully takes steps to avoid conforming to rules; how can we admit of behaviour in these cases being rule-governed? Pre-empting this line of thought Winch considers the behaviour of an anarchist. He concedes that the behaviour of the anarchist is rule-governed in a different sense from, say, that of a monk. Nevertheless, Winch insists, it would be a mistake to assume that the notion of a rule has no relation to the anarchist's behaviour; for the crucial point is that 'the anarchist's way of life is a *way of life*' (original emphasis; *ibid.*). Behind the truism lies a profound insight:

> The anarchist has reasons for acting as he does; he *makes a point* of not being governed by explicit, rigid norms. Although he retains his freedom of

choice, yet they are still significant choices that he makes: they are guided
by considerations, and he may have good reasons for choosing one course
rather than another. And these notions, which are essential in describing
the anarchist's mode of behaviour, presuppose the notion of a rule.
(Original emphasis; *ibid.*)

On Winch's view, then, the difference between the monk and the anarchist
consists not in the fact that one follows rules and the other does not; rather, 'it
lies in the diverse *kinds* of rule which each respectively follows' (original
emphasis; *ibid.*, p. 52). Unfortunately, Winch says little about the sense in
which there are different kinds of rules, except to say that we would expect the
rules observed by the monk – in contrast to the rules which describe the
anarchist's behaviour – to be 'explicit and tightly drawn' (*ibid.*) and provide
little scope for individual choice.

Now it might be objected that in using the term 'rule' in connection with
the anarchist's behaviour Winch is employing the term in a way which is so
far removed from its normal usage as to bear no resemblance to rules as they
are normally conceived. Certainly, we might judge this to be the case if, like
Oakeshott, we were to conceive of rules as more properly consisting in
something which we *consciously* apply; that is, if we were to take it that in order
for us to say that a person's behaviour is rule-governed that person must be
explicitly aware of applying or behaving in accordance with rules. But Winch
has in mind a very different idea from Oakeshott about what it is that
determines whether someone's behaviour is rule-governed:

> In opposition to this I want to say that the test of whether a man's actions
> are the application of a rule is not whether he can *formulate* it but whether it
> makes sense to distinguish a right and a wrong way of doing things in
> connection with what he does. Where that makes sense, then it must also
> make sense to say that he is applying a criterion in what he does even
> though he does not, and perhaps cannot, formulate it. (Original emphasis;
> *ibid.*, p. 58)

The logical interdependence between the notions of right and wrong on the
one hand, and the concept of a rule on the other, make this a compelling
argument.[47] But while it allows us to infer the existence of one from the other,
it does little to clarify what might be meant by 'diverse *kinds* of rules' except to
imply that diverse kinds of rules give rise to diverse kinds of right and wrong
ways of acting. Without a clearer indication of what might be meant by
diverse kinds of rules the doubts remain, as evidenced by Alasdair
MacIntyre's response to Winch:[48]

> If I go for a walk, or smoke a cigarette, are my actions rule-governed in the
> sense in which my actions in playing chess are rule-governed? ... What is

the wrong way of going for a walk? And, if there is no wrong way, is my action in any sense rule-governed? (MacIntyre, 1973, p. 21)

MacIntyre's complaint is not so much that Winch is using 'rule' where it should not be used, but rather that he is applying the notion of a rule 'so widely that quite different senses of *rule-governed* are being confused' (original emphasis; *ibid.*) and he emphasizes – as if Winch had failed to recognize it – that 'rules may govern activity in quite different ways' (*ibid.*). Yet it is surely this last point which ultimately lends weight to Winch's case; for if there *are* different ways in which rules can be said to govern behaviour then we are not obliged to conceive of, say, the anarchist's behaviour, or the act of taking a walk, as being rule-governed in the same way that playing chess is rule-governed. Far from detracting from Winch's argument, our being open to the possibility that there are different senses of rule-governed, and that different activities might be governed in different ways, would presumably be the only way we could possibly accede to Winch's suggestion that for any (meaningful) behaviour there is a right and a wrong way of acting. Intuitively, we know that if there is a sense in which there is a right and a wrong way of going for a walk it must be one which is vastly different from the sense in which there is a right and a wrong way of moving a chess piece, and because it is only in relation to a rule that the notions of right and wrong are intelligible, this would seem to require the operation of different kinds of rules.

Again it is to be regretted that MacIntyre, like Winch, reveals little about the different senses in which activities might be said to be governed by rules. But for a clearer picture of how each of these rules might be defined and distinguished from each other we might usefully draw on the work of a range of other commentators such as John Rawls, Michael Polanyi, Hubert Dreyfus and particularly John Searle, who makes one particular kind of rule one of the 'building blocks' of his constructed social reality.[49] Each makes a distinction between two different kinds of rule, or different ways in which a person's behaviour might be said to be rule-governed. Although there is some correspondence between these various accounts there is little which could count for a consensus. Nevertheless, when we glean the most cohesive elements from each, a discernible pattern begins to emerge whereby it becomes practicable to distinguish three different kinds of rules. Adopting Searle's terminology we might refer to *regulative rules* and *constitutive rules* (see Searle, 1969, p. 33ff.; 1995 *passim*), and to these I will add a third kind which I will refer to as *explanatory rules*.

Let us begin our examination of rule types with Wittgenstein's (1968) consideration of the problems associated with assuming that a person who uses language is 'operating a calculus according to definite rules' (p. 38):

What do I call 'the rule by which he proceeds'? – The hypothesis that satisfactorily describes his use of words, which we observe; or the rule

which he looks up when he uses signs; or the one which he gives us in reply
if we ask him what his rule is? (Wittgenstein, 1968, §82, pp. 38–9)

At a stroke Wittgenstein not only reveals the extent of the problem we face
when we attempt to provide an account of behaviour as rule-governed, but he
also provides an insight into how different kinds of rules might relate to
behaviour in very different ways. First, there is the rule which consists of *our*
description of what a person does, an *explanation* based on our describing that
'which we observe'. Second, there is 'the rule which he looks up'; the explicit,
prescriptive rule to which his behaviour conforms and which thus might be
said to *regulate* his activity. Third, there is the rule which, presuming the
person is able,[50] he 'gives us in reply'; the rule which recalling Winch's main
thesis, we might regard as being related to the agent's reasons and motives for
acting in a particular way and which determines what it is for that person that
constitutes a right and a wrong way of doing things. Wittgenstein's example
thus provides a preliminary indication of what I want to suggest are three
basic rule types: explanatory, regulative and constitutive.

From even the most cursory consideration of these different kinds of rule it
is possible to recognize certain fundamental differences in form. While
explanatory rules are essentially *descriptive*, such as the kind of 'law' employed
in the natural sciences to describe observed regularities and causal relations,
regulative rules have a *prescriptive* form intended to specify what should or
should not be done. Importantly, the structure of constitutive rules is neither
prescriptive nor descriptive but seems to be related more to their apparent
constructivist function; the implications of this will become more apparent as we
begin to explore how these different kinds of rule work.

By way of a preliminary explication, and at the risk of belying their
complexity, we might illustrate how these different types of rule operate by
considering how each might be related to the behaviour of drivers at traffic
signals.

Regulative rule (prescriptive): 'Vehicles must stop at red lights'.
(Regulation in highway code)

Explanatory rule (descriptive): 'Vehicles stop at red lights'.
(Derived from observations of driver behaviour at road junctions)

Constitutive rule (constructive): 'Stopping at red lights is constitutive of competent driving'.
(Rule related to the driver's reasons and motives for acting in one way
rather than another)

Before examining how each of these rule types might relate to vocational
capability it will be helpful to get a little clearer about some of their basic

features, in particular the distinction between regulative and constitutive rules.

We noted earlier that on Searle's (1995) view constitutive rules are one of the three 'building blocks' of social reality and that they thus partly constitute the means by which it is possible for there to be 'objective' features of the world which exist entirely by virtue of human agreement. Searle elucidates his notion of constitutive rules by contrasting them with regulative rules; the important distinction between the two is that while regulative rules regulate *antecedently existing* activities, constitutive rules actually *create* the possibility of certain activities.[51]

Examples of regulative rules would include such things as the highway code or planning regulations. The driving of vehicles and the erecting of buildings can logically (and historically did) exist prior to the existence of rules about which side of the road we should drive on, or where buildings may be situated; in other words, such rules regulate antecedently existing activities. In contrast, constitutive rules are *constitutive* of the activity. The rules of the game of chess, for example, are constitutive of the game in the sense that if we didn't follow the rules we would not be playing chess. Although constitutive rules are entirely human inventions Searle emphasizes that they are not arbitrary in the way that 'conventions' are. For example, we can acknowledge that it is a convention that the king is larger that the pawn, but the game of chess is not reliant on this; we could still play chess if it was otherwise.

There are other accounts in the literature which corroborate the kind of distinction Searle is making here, and also his suggestion that some kinds of rules are constitutive of the practices to which they relate. For example, Michael Oakeshott (1973) might be seen going some way to differentiating between regulative and constitutive rules when he contrasts the rules of grammar with the rules of Morse code, characterizing the latter as the kind of rules which must be known 'as a condition of being able to perform' (p. 165).[52]

But perhaps the best precedent is John Rawls's (1967) distinction between what he calls the 'summary view of rules' and the 'practice conception of rules'. According to Rawls, we can conceive of rules as either 'summaries of past decisions' (p. 158) – as guides to what works best based on past experience of existing practices – or alternatively as rules which are capable of 'defining a practice' (p. 162); that is to say, we can use them to specify and effectively create 'a new form of activity' (*ibid.*). The important thing here is that Rawls's distinction, like Searle's, draws attention to the way in which we may differentiate between rules which regulate pre-existing activities and those which are constitutive *of* activities. Now that we have mapped out some of these basic characteristics of these rule types we can turn to the matter of how each can be seen to relate to vocational capability.

Regulative rules

Regulative rules either explicitly or implicitly impose a requirement or prescription to carry out a particular action and thus typically have the form 'Do X' or 'If Y do X' (Searle, 1969, p. 34); accordingly, they are sometimes referred to as 'If–then rules' (see, for example, Eraut, 1994). All occupations employ regulative rules of some kind whether they consist in the simple and informal do's and don'ts of a job, or are set down in more formal standards, specifications, regulations, statutes, etc. From one perspective the structure of regulative rules can be seen as an expression of the hegemonic relations which exist within the sphere of employment; their prescriptions effectively provide a subtext to the contractual arrangements which exist between employer and employee. It is easy to move from this to the idea that all rule-governed behaviour consists in the agent's passive response to a demand from another to act in a predetermined way. Some instances of regulative rules do seem to work like this; for example, the actions of an employee who manufactures chess pieces to dimensions carefully specified by his employer are clearly governed by rules which can only be related to the employer's reasons and motives for requiring that specification. Those who are adverse to the idea that all meaningful behaviour is rule-governed will often portray the agent who is acting according to rules as someone who, by definition, is dispossessed of the opportunity to determine the nature of what he is doing, where this has been determined by someone else. They contrast this with cases where the agent is required to be instrumental in determining *what* is to be done, instances where the agent is required to make decisions by applying judgement, reflecting on past events, etc.; such a person, they would stress, far from being rule-governed, is required to 'go beyond the rules'.

Yet one of the most useful functions of regulative rules is precisely their capacity to assist decision-making by providing, as Rawls would put it, 'summaries of past decisions'. In this guise regulative rules can be thought of as a distillation of accumulated experience of similar cases in which relevant factors have been identified, empirical evidence obtained and causal relationships proven.[53]

One of the benefits of using such rules is that they greatly reduce the extent of the procedures involved in reaching a decision whenever cases of the same type arise; the use of the rule eliminates the need for a constant repetition of the same investigations on each and every occasion. Moreover, such rules also free users from the need to base their decisions on *their* experience; by using such a rule they can come to a satisfactory decision without having to have personally carried out extensive research. Indeed, the expertise which allows the formulation of this kind of rule will often more properly belong to a different occupational group. We might say, then, that one function of regulative rules is that they allow one occupational group to be informed by the accomplishments of another without having to assimilate the same level of expertise. Perhaps a chef, for instance, knows that if he wishes to achieve a certain result then he should use a pan made from a certain alloy formulation and he chooses one accordingly, but his knowledge of this fact and the decision he makes is none the worse for his not having a knowledge of metallurgy. Seen thus we might say that regulative rules are one way in which we can admit of the profound interconnectedness of knowledge while keeping the knowledge base of an occupation within reasonable bounds. But the main point to be made here is that the use, or indeed, reliance upon these kinds of rules does not necessarily detract from the value or nature of the decisions made.

However, none of this is to say that in cases where regulative rules are employed they can be regarded as the *only* rules in operation or that all meaningful behaviour is necessarily governed by this kind of rule. It does not, for example, follow from the fact that regulative rules can be seen to have a role to play in some kinds of decision-making that all decision-making must therefore be reducible to this kind of rule. Yet some do aspire to this kind of ambition and set about scrutinizing professional decision-making with the aim of reducing it to a 'decision system' of regulative rules. Boreham's analysis of the expertise involved in making complex decisions about optimum drug dosages in the treatment of epilepsy is one such attempt to reduce the decision-making process into the If–then format of regulative rules:

If (10mg/l < serum concentration)
Then (add 25mg to present daily dose *and* reassess after several weeks)

If (7mg/l < serum concentration > 10mg/l)
Then (add 50mg to present daily dose *and* reassess after several weeks)

If (serum concentration < 7mg/l)
Then (add 100mg to present daily dose *and* reassess after several weeks)
(Original emphasis; Boreham, 1989, p. 172;
cited in Eraut, 1994, p. 135)

But attempts such as this are invariably fraught with difficulties and in practice such rules tend to be of limited value, with practitioners often finding it necessary to abandon them in order to apply their own judgements to a particular case (see Eraut, 1994, p. 136). The most obvious difficulty is that while decision systems of this kind can be effective when applied to a perfectly 'closed' system, i.e. one where there exists a finite number of possibilities which are all covered by the rule, they become less useful when applied to situations where it is difficult to determine in advance all the factors relevant to the decision. Some games are good examples of closed systems – noughts and crosses, for example, has few permutations and it is easy to compile a list of If–then rules to cover all eventualities. Chess, too, is a closed system with a finite, albeit huge, number of possible permutations. But most instances of occupational decision-making are far from being closed in this sense and the efficacy of regulative rules in the majority of cases is thus not only dependent on the *proportion* of relevant variables covered by the rule, but is also related to the *probability* of factors not covered by the rule becoming significant.

While this will suffice as an explanation of why regulative rules are not always as effective or reliable as might be hoped, or why they are less useful in relation to some activities than others, the claim that all professional knowledge, decision-making, problem-solving, etc. can be analysed entirely in terms of such rules is something which warrants an altogether more critical response.

The assumption that a precise and complete account of human action can be couched entirely in terms of rules of this kind is highly problematical for a number of reasons. We might begin by noting that there are instances in which compliance with rules of this kind is evidently not a sufficient condition for a performance to be deemed skilled, competent, intelligent, etc. Ryle (1949) made the point that the performance of a 'well-regulated clock' or 'well-drilled circus seal' might be said to comply perfectly with certain criteria but this does not constitute an intelligent performance; he concluded that it is *how* criteria are applied, not simply the satisfaction of them, that determines whether a performance is intelligent or not. Wittgenstein made a similar point when he considered the example of a pupil learning about numbers and being required to write out the numbers in the manner of the teacher. We might imagine, he suggests, that eventually the pupil begins to write correctly formed numbers on his own ...

> but not in the right order: he writes sometimes one sometimes another at random. And then communication stops at *that* point. – Or again, he makes *mistakes* in the order. – The difference between this and the first case will of course be one of frequency. – Or he makes a systematic mistake; for example he copies every other number, or he copies the series 0, 1, 2, 3, 4, 5 ... like this: 1, 0, 3, 2, 5, 4 ... Here we shall almost be tempted to say he has understood *wrong*. (Original emphasis; Wittgenstein, 1968, §143, pp. 56–7)

The point here, again, is that in teaching or learning skills we have an interest not just in whether a criterion or rule is being adhered to, or whether an example is being followed, but in the *way* in which the criterion or rule is applied. As Winch (1965) says, the pupil 'has to learn not merely to do things in the same way as his teacher, but also *what counts* as the same way' (original emphasis; p. 59). To learn the series of natural numbers is not merely to repeat what has been shown – 'it involves *being able to go on*' (original emphasis; *ibid.*). Importantly, such shortcomings are not remedied by simply adding further rules; here we might recall the point made earlier – one corroborated by Wittgenstein, Ryle and Winch – that attempts to provide an account of behaviour as rule-governed (and I would stress that here we are talking of *regulative* rules) inevitably leads us into an infinite regression where each and every rule used would require a further rule to guide its use.

But there are other difficulties with the assumption that when we make decisions we are simply involved in the manipulation of sequences of If–then rules. Analysing decision-making from a neurological perspective, Antonio Damasio (1996) has recently argued that this kind of calculative model of decision-making is flawed not least because of the brain's limited memory capacity – given the speed with which we make decisions, the human brain is simply not capable of holding in view and manipulating the enormous number of factors and variables involved in even the most ordinary day-to-day decisions – and there is also the matter of the obvious inability of most humans to deal with such things as probabilities, statistics, etc. For example, if we are trying to decide whether to do potentially lucrative business with a client who happens to be the arch-enemy of our best friend, then as Damasio says, we manifestly do not run through an extensive cost/benefit analysis of all the possible outcomes and their related probabilities. Indeed, this model of mental processing, according to Damasio (and we might recall the similar point made by Oliver Sacks), 'has more to do with the way which patients with prefrontal damage go about deciding than with how normals usually operate' (p. 172). Damasio rejects this 'high-reason' view of decision-making – the prevailing common-sense view of the rational as operating according to the rules of formal logic – in favour of what he calls the 'somatic-marker hypothesis'. He argues that when approaching a situation which requires a decision to be made, far from being blank at the beginning of the reasoning process, the mind is

> replete with a diverse repertoire of images, generated to the tune of the situation you are facing, entering and exciting your consciousness in a show too rich for you to encompass fully. (*Ibid.*, p. 170)

According to Damasio, *before* any cost/benefit analysis takes place we automatically reduce the number of options by 'marking' an image with a particular gut feeling or sensation which 'forces attention on the negative (or positive) outcome to which a given action may lead' (my text in parentheses; *ibid.*, p. 173). The connection between a particular outcome or scenario on the one hand and certain emotions and feelings on the other is something which is learned; we learn to associate certain events with particular body states and it is thus that the somatic-marker system 'acquires the hidden, dispositional representation of this experience-driven, noninherited, arbitrary connection' (*ibid.*, p. 180). This is not merely to express the commonplace that our decisions are affected by our past experience; rather, it is to say that rational decisions are not the product of logic alone but necessarily require the involvement of *emotions*. Indeed, Damasio points to clinical evidence which indicates that the capacity for rational decision-making is impaired when the emotional capacities of the brain are defective. We might say that, just as the processes of perception are dependent upon our being primed by experience and upon the schemata we consequently adopt, so too, on this view, are we always *emotionally* predisposed to the act of decision-making by the juxtaposition of somatic-markers to our mental representations of possible outcomes. The somatic-marker hypothesis thus seems to undermine the idea that it is possible to specify what it is to be vocationally capable by providing an account of regulative rules.

But perhaps more to the point here is that this idea – that intelligent capability consists in exercising sequences of If–then rules, or that such capability might be sufficiently specified in terms of such rules – is fundamentally at odds with the conception of vocational capability which has emerged from the present account. Later we shall see why it is more appropriate to regard the structure of such capabilities as a structure of *constitutive* rather than regulative rules, but it is significant that the kind of argument with which we might counter the suggestion that intelligent human behaviour consists in the application of regulative rules closely corresponds to the kind of argument which might be levelled against proponents of artificial intelligence (AI) who similarly assume 'that all human behaviour must be analyzable in terms of rules relating to atomic facts' (Dreyfus, 1992, p. 226). The structure of a rule in the context of computer programming is precisely that of a regulative rule. No matter how complex the various heuristic, fuzzy logic or neural net configurations become, ultimately just as with simple algorithms, they can be seen to conform to the If–then format of regulative rules. In his comprehensive critique of artificial reason Hubert Dreyfus (1992) argues cogently that disembodied machines are inherently incapable of simulating higher mental functions. Adopting what is for the most part an Heideggerian conception of human agency, he outlines three important aspects of intelligent behaviour neglected by the AI lobby:

> the role of the body in organizing and unifying our experience of objects, the role of the situation in providing a background against which behaviour can be orderly without being rulelike, and finally the role of human purposes and needs in organizing the situation so that objects are recognized as relevant and accessible. (*Ibid.*, p. 234)

Of course, all of this is at one with the account of vocational capability we have been developing here – the embodied nature of human agency, the idea that the meaning we ascribe to any particular feature of the world is profoundly context dependent, inextricably part of a wider sphere of signification, together with the idea that such meaning is inseparable from the priorities we unavoidably bring to our understanding of the world. Just as human engagement conceived of in these terms undermines the aspirations of the AI lobby, so too does it belie claims to the effect that vocational capability can be reduced to a 'decision system' of regulative rules. The only qualification we might add to Dreyfus' argument is that while he appears to militate against rules per se, it should be *regulative* rules which should be identified as the substantive target – something which perhaps becomes more clear in the following passage by Wittgenstein:

> The regulation of traffic in the streets permits and forbids certain actions on the part of drivers and pedestrians; but it does not attempt to guide the totality of their movements by prescription. And it would be senseless to talk of an 'ideal' ordering of traffic which would do that; in the first place we should have no idea what to imagine as this ideal. If someone wants to make traffic regulations stricter on some point or other, that does not mean that he wants to approximate to such an ideal. (Wittgenstein, 1967, p. 78)

This is not to say that actions which are not governed by regulative rules must therefore be entirely arbitrary or random: the point here is that behaviour can be orderly without recourse to regulative rules. The distance between stationary cars in a queue at traffic signals, for instance, is something which is not governed by any regulative rule, but that is not to say that it is an entirely aimless or haphazard affair. A car driven within centimetres of the vehicle in front, or alternatively, stopped some tens of metres away from it, might intimidate the driver in front, or irritate the one behind. There is clearly something which counts as an appropriate distance which most drivers are able to adopt most of the time. Here we might recall the point made earlier about how our Background capacities or the mental schemata we adopt, dispose us to certain kinds of behaviour, for example speaking at certain levels of loudness, gender-specific ways of walking, standing at a certain 'comfortable' distance from other people. None of these things are governed by regulative rules but that is not to say that there is not a right or wrong way of doing these things; as Winch would say, if there is a right and a wrong way of doing something then there must be a sense in which that action is rule-governed.

The inescapable realization that so much meaningful human behaviour is manifestly not governed by regulative rules has a curious effect upon those who are determined to construct precise and unequivocal accounts of that behaviour. For it induces them to shift almost imperceptibly and apparently unwittingly from a prescriptive to a *descriptive* account. Thus a person who is determined to provide a more precise account of driver behaviour might set about observing, measuring and compiling statistical data which describes the distance between vehicles. Someone might, for example, calculate that for a given sample the average distance between stationary vehicles at traffic signals was precisely N metres, and might also express the standard deviation across the sample, and so on. Modern science knows few bounds in the precision with which such features may be described – down to the last nanometre if need be – and using modern technology vast quantities of such data can be amassed. For those who are captivated by the promise of such precise specifications the idea that vocational capability can be analysed in terms of regulative rules thus comes to be supplemented if not supplanted by the assumption that it is possible to specify the rules which *explain* that behaviour.

Explanatory rules

As with regulative rules, we can recognize that there are many instances where explanatory rules, or a knowledge of them, can be seen to be relevant to the notion of vocational capability. Whereas regulative rules might often be regarded as a distillation of accumulated experience in the form of a prescription, explanatory rules might be thought of as the explicit description of that experience. The rules or laws formulated by the scientist to describe observed regularities and causal relationships are a case in point. This feature of explanatory rules is fairly self-evident, but the more pertinent issue here is whether, or to what extent, explanatory rules can be used to specify precisely what is involved in being skilled, capable or competent.

In his discussion of skills in *Personal Knowledge* (1962), Polanyi makes the point that the rule which *explains* a skill is not at all the same as the rule which is *used* in the performance of that skill. For example, the rules which describe what happens when someone rides a bicycle are not the rules or criteria employed by the cyclist in the act of riding. Polanyi's argument here is worth quoting at length:

> The rule observed by the cyclist is this. When he starts falling to the right he turns the handlebars to the right, so that the course of the bicycle is deflected along a curve towards the right. This results in a centrifugal force pushing the cyclist to the left and offsets the gravitational force dragging him down to the right. This manoeuvre presently throws the cyclist out of balance to the left, which he counteracts by turning the handlebars to the left; and so he continues to keep himself in balance by winding along a series of appropriate curvatures. A simple analysis shows that for a given angle of unbalance the curvature of each winding is inversely proportional to the square of the speed at which the cyclist is proceeding.
>
> But does this tell us exactly how to ride a bicycle? No. You obviously cannot adjust the curvature of your bicycle's path in proportion to the ratio of your unbalance over the square of your speed; and if you could you

would fall off the machine, for there are a number of other factors to be taken into account in practice which are left out in the formulation of this rule. (Polanyi, 1962, pp. 49–50)

The same point is made by Oakeshott (1973): again using the example of riding a bicycle, he notes that the 'principles' which supply an 'underlying rationale' (p. 166) to the performance do not constitute any part of the knowledge needed for the performance:

> these principles are utterly unknown to even the most successful cyclist, and being able to recite them would not help to be more proficient. They do not constitute a criterion. Their sole value is in the contribution they make to our understanding of what is going on. In short, they are unrelated either to learning or to practising the skill. They belong to a separate performance, the performance of explaining. (*Ibid.*)

Similarly, Hubert Dreyfus (1992) notes that 'although *science* requires that the skilled performance be *described* according to rules, these rules need in no way be *involved* in producing the performance' (original emphasis; p. 253). As Dreyfus says, my randomly waving my hand in the air *could* be described in terms of precise spatial coordinates but such a description is not part of my performance; if I happened to touch something I could easily do so again – and I could repeat whatever it was I did without recourse to any of the rules or laws which might describe that performance.

Polanyi, Oakeshott and Dreyfus are surely correct: there is a fundamental distinction to be made between the kind of explanatory rule which might be used to *describe* the outward manifestations of a skill and the kind of rule or criterion used in the performance of that skill.[54] It is clearly a mistake to take the former for the latter; yet there is currently a pervasive tendency in VET to do just this, as we shall see when we return to our consideration of 'competence-based' and 'outcomes' approaches to VET.

Undoubtedly, one reason why, in attempting to describe skills, many are compelled to give descriptions in terms of explanatory rules is just simply because these rules are easier to articulate than those used in the performance. With the help of modern scientific techniques our capacity to give an accurate account of the forces, angles and curves related to the cyclist's performance is infinitely greater than our ability to describe, say, the kind of 'feel' which enables the cyclist to adopt an 'appropriate' position when going into a tight corner. It would seem that the greater the emphasis on the need for *precise* rules, the more likely it is that the analysis will resort to those of an explanatory kind. But perhaps another reason why many resort to accounts couched in terms of explanatory rules is that, apart from regulative rules, they find it difficult to see what alternative there might be. Even Polanyi (1962) can say only that 'the aim of a skilful performance is achieved by the observance of a set of rules which are not known as such to the person following them' (p. 49).

Against this background many might take the view that even if the resort to explanatory rules is not entirely ideal, it is necessitated by the sheer impracticality of representing a skilful performance in any other terms. That said, given the quite radical distinction between explanatory rules and the kind of rules or criteria used in the performance of a skill, the blatant substitution of one for the other stands in need of some justification; moreover, it would seem that the only possible justification for such a substitution is that it is warranted by virtue of there being a causal connection between the having of a skill and the more tangible manifestations of that skill in artefacts and behaviours. Of course, the standard retort to this – a perennial theme in the context of assessment – is to cast doubt on the validity and reliability of this connection. It would be noted that validity is effectively sacrificed in the act of substitution, and any claim to reliability is dependent at the very least on the sufficiency of evidence.

When the debate is framed in these terms it looks as though we are simply covering old ground where, yet again, we are required to recite the reasons why descriptions of behaviour are not sufficient to describe what it is to be skilled or capable. But note how easily we have slid into talking of *descriptions* and the idea that the dispute is essentially about the kind of descriptions to which we are prepared to give credence. It is important not to lose sight of the fact that what we are concerned with here is not competing descriptions but rather different kinds of *rules*, for it is this which gives the kind of point made by Polanyi and Oakeshott its force.

In order to see why, it will be helpful to return to Peter Winch's account of rule-governed behaviour. Adopting his way of speaking we might say that what we are interested in is a particular kind of regularity or recurrence: we are interested in what it is that makes the *same* kind of action skilled, capable or competent each time it occurs. Now, according to Winch, in order to count as the 'same kind of event on the same kind of occasion' (Winch, 1965, p. 83) a judgement of identity must be made, and crucially such judgements are only intelligible in relation to a particular form of life governed by its own rules. As we saw earlier, Winch's main purpose is somewhat at variance with ours in that he is trying to show that the study of social phenomena cannot proceed by the same rules and the same judgements of identity as the natural sciences do; nevertheless, the following passage could hardly be more relevant to our present purposes:

> it is quite mistaken in principle to compare the activity of a student of a form of social behaviour with that of, say, an engineer studying the workings of a machine; and one does not advance matters by saying, with Mill, that the machine in question is of course immensely more complicated than any physical machine. If we are going to compare the

social student to an engineer, we shall do better to compare him to an apprentice engineer who is studying what engineering – that is, the activity of engineering – is all about. (*Ibid.*, p. 88)

It is clear that the distinction here between studying 'what engineering is' and studying 'the workings of a machine' is of some importance. What makes it particularly interesting for our purposes is that in vocational education and training – particularly under present arrangements – such a distinction would be largely incomprehensible: according to the orthodoxy, to study engineering is precisely to study such things as 'the workings of a machine' – the two would be regarded as synonymous. Now it would seem that this distinction, one which is clearly important for Winch, is to be understood at least in part by the two very different kinds of relations which are involved in the engineer's ability to recognize regularities or instances of something being the same sort of thing on the same sort of occasion: first, his relation to the machine; and second, his relation to the wider community of engineers. Following Winch we might say that any attempt to understand how someone in a particular vocational role is able to make judgements of identity, and thus discern regularities appropriate to that particular occupation, must take due account of *both* of these relations, and this is something which is equally the case whether the area of activity is engineering, sociology or natural science.

to understand the activities of an individual scientific investigator we must take account of two sets of relations: first, his relation to the phenomenon which he investigates; second, his relation to his fellow scientists. Both of these are essential to the sense of saying that he is 'detecting regularities' or 'discovering uniformities'; but writers on scientific methodology too often concentrate on the first and overlook the importance of the second. (*Ibid.*, pp. 84–5)

Of course, it is not only 'writers on scientific methodology' who overlook the relation of the practitioner to his fellow practitioners – we might say that this is an oversight which is endemic in VET whenever the orthodox conceptions of skill and training are adopted. Missing from Winch's account is an explanation of how these two sets of relations have a bearing on the sense in which we may say an individual's behaviour is rule-governed. This is not really surprising because in order to convey something of this it becomes necessary to distinguish between different kinds of rules – something which Winch stops short of. But in the light of what we have said about rule types we can see how these different 'relations' might be related to different kinds of rules. For example, we can say that in studying the machine an engineer seeks to provide a description of it using explanatory rules to describe the regularities he discerns in the machine's physiognomies or workings. However, the rules in relation to which the engineer's judgements of identity are intelligible derive not from his observations of the machine, but from his form of life. The engineer must have some conception, in common with his fellow engineers, about what *counts as* a particular kind of regularity or uniformity and this indicates the existence of some form of rule.

We can now see a little more clearly what it is that separates the engineer who is studying a machine from the apprentice who is studying what engineering is. The engineer, by virtue of being an engineer, will already have an understanding of the rules which enable him to make appropriate judgements of identity; indeed, his 'studying the machine' and his being able to formulate the explanatory rules which describe the machine presupposes the implicit use of such judgements. For the apprentice, however, it is precisely this understanding which is at issue. To use Winch's words we might say that the apprentice must come to understand 'what is to count as "doing the same kind of thing" in relation to that kind of activity' (*ibid.*, p. 87); indeed, much of what is involved in his becoming an engineer would seem to be about his learning the rules according to which such judgements of identity can be made. It is *these* rules which are more fundamentally related to the engineer's capabilities *as an engineer* rather than those which, as Polanyi and Oakeshott saw, belong to the very different activity of 'explaining'. Given the way in which these rules determine what is to count as a regularity or a uniformity, it would appear that these rules have a particularly distinctive structure, one which indicates their *constitutive* rather than explanatory function.

It would seem, then, that neither regulative nor explanatory rules are sufficient to provide a complete or sufficient account of human behaviour or capabilities. To return to Wittgenstein's example, we might say that, as a product of human involvement, the movement of traffic in the street can no more be satisfactorily explained by reference to explanatory rules than regulative rules – a point corroborated by H. L. A. Hart (1961) in *The Concept of Law*, when he notes that although it would be possible for an observer who knew nothing of traffic regulations to discern regularities in the behaviour of drivers at traffic lights, nevertheless, a more complete understanding of such regularities could only come from considering the way in which drivers conform their behaviour to rules which give them reasons for acting as they do. Of course, we can now see that we have been here before – for this amounts to much the same thing as Searle's claim that there are so many aspects of human life which cannot be accounted for in terms of the 'brute' facts of empirical science – facts which ultimately derive from rules or laws of an explanatory kind. With Searle, we can recognize that in order to account for many kinds of human involvement – including those relating to vocational and professional capability – we must resort not only to a different kind of fact but also to a different kind of rule. It is with this in mind that we now turn to consider the notion of constitutive rules.

Notes

43 In Oakeshott, 1991, pp. 465–87; I should point out that Oakeshott's specific concern here is with *moral* behaviour; nevertheless, with Winch (1965) we can take it that there is nothing which limits Oakeshott's argument to moral matters, for what he says is applicable to human activities generally.

44 Peter Winch, too, acknowledges this problem of regression of rules and invokes Lewis Carroll's story 'What the Tortoise Said to Achilles' by way of illustration (see Winch, 1965, pp. 55–7). Achilles and the Tortoise discuss three propositions A, B and Z which are logically related in such a way that Z follows from A and B. The Tortoise accepts the truth of A and B but not the hypothetical proposition (C) 'If A and B are true, Z must be true'; eventually Achilles succeeds in persuading the Tortoise of the truth of C and this is added to make (D) 'If A and B and C are true, Z must be true'; but the Tortoise then demands to be persuaded of the truth of *this* proposition, hence the argument becomes (E) 'If A and B and C and D are true then Z is true', which, again, is a proposition the truth of which the Tortoise must be persuaded, and so on and so forth. Winch rightly says that the real issue here is that the act of drawing an inference is not itself something which can be demonstrated within the formula; rather, it is achieved by our 'learning *to do* something' (original emphasis; *ibid.*, p. 57). What Winch omits to show is how this sits with his claim that all meaningful behaviour is *ipso facto* rule-governed. As we shall see, there is no inconsistency on Winch's part once we recognize that the kind of rule by which it is possible to determine what counts as drawing an inference is fundamentally different from the kind of rule which governs explicit logical relations.

45 One of the classic formulations of which is that given by J. S. Mill in *A System of Logic*; see Mill (1876), pp. 630–43.

46 That is, explanations couched in terms of the function of roles, institutions, etc. in society. It is appropriate here to recall our earlier discussion of the imposition of function and note that Winch's thesis is supported by Searle's (1995) claim that function is not an intrinsic feature of the world but an observer-relative feature imposed within a context of previously determined interests, values or purposes.

47 Winch is surely correct when he says that 'the notion of following a rule is logically inseparable from the notion of *making a mistake*' (original emphasis; *ibid.*, p. 32).

48 We might note that Wittgenstein (1968) raises similar questions when considering the sense in which language use or ball games might be said to be rule-governed. He imagines people casually playing with a ball, sometimes playing parts of a game but not finishing it, joking, chasing each other with the ball, and so on; the difficulty, as Wittgenstein rightly

says, is when someone wants to say: 'The whole time they are playing a ball-game and following definite rules at every throw' (§83, p. 39). Moreover, with Wittgenstein, we might also wonder what exactly is happening when we make up the rules of a game as we go along.

49 While many commentators are content to contrast two kinds of rules, Wittgenstein and Oakeshott each indicate three different senses in which an activity can be said to be rule-governed. Oakeshott's clearest statement on the three rule types appears in his later essay 'Learning and Teaching', which, it should be emphasized, appeared after the publication of Winch's *The Idea of a Social Science*.

50 I have in mind here Polanyi's point about our inability to articulate such things.

51 Anthony Giddens (1984) has questioned the validity of Searle's distinction between regulative and constitutive rules on the grounds that constitutive rules can be seen to have regulating properties (e.g. the rules of chess 'regulate' the activities of chess players) and regulative rules can be seen to have 'constitutive aspects' (p. 20). However, Giddens' largely semantic and etymological objections were directed at Searle's earlier formulation of the distinction (1969, p. 33ff.) and seem to be more than adequately countered by Searle's later (1995) clarification of the distinction in terms of the nature of the activities in relation to which the two rules stand, i.e. either antecedently existing activities or activities made possible by the rules.

52 Oakeshott's grounds for the distinction are far less convincing than Searle's and at the very least open to the kind of objections which Giddens raises against Searle's early formulation (see above). While it is true that there is an important sense in which ordinary language use does not presuppose a knowledge of the formal rules of grammar, nevertheless, it is possible to conceive of some uses of language which *do* require such knowledge 'as a condition of being able to perform'; clearly, it depends on what one is trying to do. One difficulty in adopting Oakeshott's view of rules is that it is difficult to see how we would draw a line between where one would, or would not, require such knowledge. But the more immediate point here is that this way of characterizing the (constitutive) rules of Morse code fails as a means of distinguishing them from other (regulative) rules. Similarly unsuccessful is Oakeshott's characterization of the 'rules of grammar' as the kind of rules which 'constitute the criterion by which a performance may be known to be incorrect' (p. 165). Again, we can acknowledge that there is a sense in which this is often the case, but it will not suffice as a defining feature of regulative rules. First, because, as we shall see, regulative rules are *not* always sufficient to determine the correctness or even incorrectness of a performance; and second, because it will turn out that regulative rules are not the only rules by which the correctness of a performance might be judged.

53   It may be useful here to consider one such practical application of a regulative rule. When an electrical engineer is required to determine the appropriate size of a protective (earth) conductor to be installed in a building, one of his main concerns will be to ensure that in the event of a fault the conductor will be of sufficient size so as not to overheat and possibly cause a fire. Now empirical research has shown that for a given size of conductor its temperature under fault conditions is related to three things: the level of the prospective fault current (I), the time it takes for the protective device (e.g. fuse) to operate (t), and the adiabatic characteristics of the materials from which the conductor is made (represented by a factor k). But there is no need for the engineer to carry out such experiments himself for, by carrying out appropriate calculations and consulting relevant tables, he can determine the minimum cross-sectional area (S) of the conductor by applying the following rule laid down in the UK Wiring Regulations (IEE, 1997, p. 102.):

$$S = \frac{\sqrt{I^2\,t}}{k}$$

This equation is essentially an If–then rule, for it amounts to saying that *if* presented with a certain state of affairs *then* the conductor should be of a particular size in order to ensure safety.

54   Argyris and Schön (1974) make much the same distinction when they make the point – raised earlier – that we should distinguish 'theories in use', i.e. the theory on which professional action is based, from the 'espoused theories' which we use to explain our actions.

8

Constitutive Rules and the Problem of Structure

Since the notion of constitutive rules I will develop here will be somewhat at variance with the account given by Searle (1995) I should stress at the outset that Searle would not necessarily concur with my use of the term. The difference between our accounts arises from the fact that while Searle is primarily interested in how constitutive rules allow the creation of 'objective' institutional facts relating to such things as money, presidencies, marriages, games of chess, etc., I want to suggest that in addition to this, there is also a sense in which these kinds of rules can be seen to be constitutive of what it is to act skilfully or perform competently. More precisely, I want to say that all human capabilities necessarily have a rule-governed structure and that that structure is essentially a structure of constitutive rules. It is far from clear from Searle's work whether or how far he would be prepared to agree with this, but since my version is based very much on his it is appropriate to begin by examining how he understands constitutive rules.

We have seen that on Searle's view, constitutive rules are one of the three 'building blocks' of social reality: they partly constitute the means by which it is possible for there to be 'objective' features of the world which exist entirely by virtue of human agreement. We have also seen that, unlike regulative rules which regulate antecedently existing activities, constitutive rules can create the very possibility of an activity. Now according to Searle, constitutive rules, either individually or collectively as a system of rules, characteristically have the form:

'X counts as Y' or 'X counts as Y in context C'

For example, the institution of money or, more to the point, the institutional facts relating to money (e.g. the 'objective' fact that I have a five-pound note in my pocket) are created in part by the constitutive rule that a piece of paper of a certain kind (X) counts as having a certain value (Y) in the United Kingdom (C). On Searle's view, such rules provide the means by which a social group may collectively assign to a particular class of object (X) a function (Y) which it does not have by virtue of its physical characteristics.

It is clear that in order for constitutive rules to work, some form of human agreement is required. In the same way that it would be nonsense for one person to decide to use an object of no inherent value (or more precisely, no value recognizable by others) as money, for one individual to decide in the absence of potentially like recognition from others, that something or someone was skilful or competent is similarly unintelligible. In order that artefacts be deemed skilfully made, or behaviour or persons competent or capable, it would seem necessary for there to be some kind of consensus – either as a group, a profession, or as a society.

Searle's approach to this issue of social or collective agreement is to introduce his third 'building block' of social reality in the shape of 'collective intentionality' – the shared beliefs, desires, intentions, etc. which in his view constitute the necessary agreement to apply constitutive rules. Searle describes collective intentionality as a 'We Consciousness' (*ibid.*, p. 24) in the sense that *I* do something only as part of *our* doing something. He tells us that whenever we take part in collective behaviour, collective intentionality takes the form of 'we intend' or 'we are doing this', etc., in contrast to the singular 'I' intentionality. He points out that collective intentionality exists as a primitive and fundamental form of mental life – a form exhibited by wild animals when hunting in a pack. This 'biologically primitive phenomenon' (*ibid.*), according to Searle, is fundamental to explaining variously the collective activities of primitive hunters, football players or musicians in an orchestra:

> if I am an offensive linesman playing in a football game, I might be blocking the defensive end, but I am blocking only as part of *our* executing a pass play. If I am a violinist in an orchestra I play *my* part in *our* performance of the symphony. (Original emphasis; *ibid.*, p. 23)

The notion of collective intentionality is important for Searle's account because it is only while there is some form of continued collective acceptance of an assigned function that constitutive rules enable a new status to be assigned to a phenomenon:

> the 'counts as' locution names a feature of the imposition of a status to which a function is attached by way of collective intentionality, where the status and its accompanying function go beyond the sheer brute physical functions which can be assigned to physical objects. (*Ibid.*, p. 44)

This, on Searle's view, is how institutional facts are created – how the three 'building blocks' fit together to create social reality. Provided that there is the necessary agreement, constitutive rules are the means by which we are able to assign a function and/or status to something which, without that agreement, it would not have. Despite the prima facie plausibility of this account it will turn out that there are certain difficulties with the notion of constitutive rules as

Searle conceives of them, difficulties which start to surface when we begin to scrutinize his account a little more closely. Certainly, in order that we will be able to acknowledge that such things as skilful acts are governed by constitutive rules, it will be necessary to substantially modify the account of constitutive rules as it is implied here.

At first sight Searle might be taken merely to be stating the commonplace that – if we take the example of money – the paper from which money is made would be of little value were it not for the status and value contingently imposed upon it by way of common agreement. This much is fairly uncontroversial. But he also seems to be suggesting that a *necessary* feature of constitutive rules is that they impose functions which 'go beyond the sheer brute physical functions'; in other words, the function which the 'counts as' locution allows us to assign to certain pieces of paper is to be contrasted with the kind of function which is related more to their intrinsic, 'brute physical' characteristics whereby these same pieces of paper might be deemed to be useful for, say, writing on, but of negligible monetary value. Searle might thus be understood as suggesting that although constitutive rules have a role in ascribing a certain status and function to money, they would not be involved in ascribing the function of, say, a hammer because that function is somehow related to the hammer's 'brute' physics.

Now because Searle is concerned first and foremost with how it is possible for there to be 'objective' facts in the world which are entirely dependent upon human agreement, he purposefully attends to the kind of cases (e.g. money, games) where this dependency is both patently manifest and widely acknowledged. But I want to suggest that the kind of cases we are concerned with (e.g. competent performances, skilfully made artefacts) are similarly dependent upon human agreement; however – and this is what makes them more problematical – in *these* cases the extent of the dependency upon human agreement is *not* generally acknowledged. What makes the dependency so apparent in the kind of cases considered by Searle is the conspicuous lack of any 'brute' ontology which might otherwise be identified as grounds for claims to objectivity. At times, as in the above passage where he explains the role of the 'counts as locution', Searle seems to imply that constitutive rules *only* operate in cases of this kind. In contrast, I want to say that although the operation of constitutive rules is certainly *more evident* in these cases, this form of rule can nevertheless be seen to play a part in *any* meaningful human activity.

If we turn again to the Searle passage cited above, we can see that much hangs on the distinction he makes between 'sheer brute physical functions' and those functions which are imposed by means of constitutive rules. However, this distinction is not at all as straightforward as it seems and perhaps reveals something of an inconsistency in Searle's account. We might recall Searle's crucially important (and to my mind correct) point that 'functions are never intrinsic to the physics of a phenomenon but are assigned from outside by conscious observers and users' (*ibid.*, p. 14), hence the distinction here cannot be between intrinsic and imposed functions because *all* functions are imposed. The question, then, is whether among the functions we impose some are somehow related to the 'brute physical' nature of the objects they are imposed on and others not. It seems to me that if there is a distinction to be made it can only be a matter of degree. First, because as Searle himself acknowledges, 'brute facts' *always* have a logical priority over 'institutional facts'; money, for example, 'has to exist in some physical form or other' (*ibid.*, p. 34), so social or institutional facts are never entirely detached from some brute physical ontology. For argument's sake we might say that there would be little point in having currency which consisted in physical objects so fragile that they disintegrated on contact, or were so minute that different denominations could only be distinguished with the aid of a microscope. So even with money it seems reasonable to suggest that there is *some* relation between the imposed function and what Searle would regard as the brute physical characteristics of the phenomenon. Second, because, again by Searle's own account, function is never equivalent to a causal relation: Searle tells us that 'what the vocabulary of "functions" adds to the vocabulary of "causes" is a set of values (including purposes and teleology generally)' (*ibid.*, p. 16). Accordingly, even in those cases where certain causal effects might be associated with the 'brute physical' characteristics of a phenomenon (e.g. the mass of the hammer head is causally related to the driving in of nails), the function of the phenomenon remains more fundamentally related to our own purposes and values than to those effects.

The upshot of all this is that it would be a mistake (if this is what Searle is suggesting) to assume that we can distinguish between two kinds of functions, those which are 'sheer brute physical functions' and those which are not, and that it is the latter, and only the latter, which are created by constitutive rules. This is important because one issue on which I might be said to depart from Searle's account is in relation to the extent of human activities where people might be said to act according to constitutive rules. While Searle seems to want to restrict this to more formal social institutions such as money, games, etc., I want to say that there is a fundamental sense in which *all* human behaviour might be said to relate to constitutive rules and that it is in this sense that we can endorse Peter Winch's claim that all meaningful behaviour is *ipso facto* rule-governed.

More specifically, I want to say that there is an important sense in which such matters as whether or not a performance is competent, an act skilful or an artefact skilfully made, must ultimately be judged by reference to rules of a constitutive as opposed to a regulative or an explanatory kind. While it can be acknowledged that regulative and explanatory rules have certain applications in relation to many occupational activities, it seems to me that it is constitutive rules which are more fundamental to any conception of vocational capability as something which is rule-governed. When we make judgements about such things, either as performers or as observers, we implicitly and necessarily appeal to some notion of what 'counts as' a competent performance or a skilful act – or in other words, what 'counts as' the kind of regularity or recurrence we have an interest in. And, of course, because such things are invariably context dependent – i.e. what counts as a competent performance in one set of circumstances may not in another – such judgements are generally required to be sensitive to the particular context in which the performance or act occurs. It seems to me that this indicates the essentially constitutive nature of the rules according to which we make such judgements, but as we shall see it will turn out to be a quite different kind of 'rule' to the formal, explicit rules Searle has in mind.

The constitutive nature of the Background

One of the important features of constitutive rules, according to Searle, is the way in which their application, like the assigning of function, is to a large extent invisible. We do not have to think about the existence of the rule that a certain kind of paper 'counts as' having a particular value whenever we buy something – we just hand over the note in exchange for goods. Similarly, we might say that the craftsman does not have to consciously or explicitly bring to mind the rule that determines what it is that constitutes a skilful performance or determines whether or not something is 'correctly' made. He just sees these things *as* such. At a glance he is able to recognize what it is that counts as the 'correct' way to hold a tool, or what counts as a 'suitable' blow of the mallet to the chisel, or whether the cut of the tool is to an 'appropriate' depth, etc. Moreover, from instant to instant the craftsman is continually reviewing what he does against what 'counts as' appropriate given the circumstances in which he is operating; at every cut of the tool he assesses his previous action and re-evaluates what will be appropriate for his next move. He is also – and this is a point we shall return to – continually and implicitly measuring his own behaviour against those of his fellow practitioners; he has a vital interest in how his actions accord with theirs. The crucial point here is that it is only by appeal to some notion of a rule that we can make sense of these notions of 'correct', 'suitable' or 'appropriate'; as Winch would say, where it makes sense to speak of a right and a wrong way of doing something then it must also make sense to say that we are acting in accordance with some kind of rule.

It would seem that the same can be said of any meaningful behaviour, and in response to the question posed by MacIntyre earlier, we can now say that there really *is* a right and a wrong way of doing such things as going for a walk or smoking a cigarette. Odd though this may sound, once we are alert to the structure of constitutive rules it seems indisputable. If, for example, someone announced that they were going for a walk but then set off and did not return for several years, or perhaps they took just a few strides before getting into their car, we would insist that their actions did not constitute 'going for a walk'. Furthermore, it is entirely feasible that we could acknowledge certain 'correct' or 'appropriate' styles of walking, styles which are perhaps gender, age or culture specific, or perhaps appropriate to certain contexts – the way one saunters down the street would not be appropriate if one was walking up the aisle of a church during a ceremony. We might say that the comedic notion of a 'silly walk' would be incomprehensible unless there were something which counted as a 'normal' or 'correct' walk. Again, if it makes sense to speak of a right and a wrong way of doing something then it must also make sense to say that it is being done in accordance with some kind of rule, and in such cases it is a rule which has the characteristic structure: 'X counts as Y in context C'.

But the main point here, as Searle himself would say, is that we need not be aware of applying rules as such – it would seem that as we develop skills and capabilities they become absorbed into the Background *as* rule-governed abilities:

> The key to understanding the causal relations between the structure of the Background and the structure of social institutions is to see that the Background can be causally sensitive to the specific forms of the constitutive rules of the institutions without actually containing any beliefs or desires or representations of those rules ... One develops skills and abilities that are, so to speak, functionally equivalent to the system of rules, without actually containing any representations or internalizations of those rules. (*Ibid.*, pp. 141–2)

As far as it goes, I think Searle is largely correct in what he is saying here. Another way of putting it would be to say that we have the ability to develop skills and abilities which are 'functionally equivalent' to rules but which are not dependent upon our having intentional states directed at those rules.

But let us examine a little more closely how Searle understands 'rules' here. If we consider the rules relating to the kind of cases he deals with – money, marriages, presidencies, games of chess, etc. – we can see that what they all have in common is that they are all formal and explicit. If anyone wished, they could examine these rules by consulting the relevant statutes, or in the case of chess, by looking them up in a book of rules for the game. In contrast, there are no rules of this kind relating to the correct way to walk up the aisle of a church, or how to use a tool correctly, and importantly, if we tried to formulate such rules they would be *derivative rather than constitutive of* the practices to which they relate. While the formal, explicit rules Searle has in mind create the possibility of certain practices, the rule we might formulate to, say, *describe* how a tool should be used would be derivative of the practice – and the language here indicates how any such attempt would be likely to slide into an account of descriptive, *explanatory* rules. Clearly, there is need for some clarification here if we want to be able to say that all meaningful behaviour is governed by constitutive rules.

The key to this, I want to suggest, is to recognize that the phenomenon described by Searle – our ability to evolve practices which are 'functionally equivalent' to certain explicit, formal rules – is a manifestation of a more fundamental phenomenon whereby we are able to develop practices which are functionally equivalent to rules of a kind which, while being neither explicit nor formal, are nevertheless constitutive of those practices. More precisely, I want to suggest that the fact that we are able to develop skills which are functionally equivalent to systems of formal constitutive rules is indicative of the profoundly *constitutive structure of the Background*.

One way of getting clearer about this is to consider the kind of priority that might be attached to different kinds of rules. According to Searle, an 'institutional fact' such as 'X is a criminal' is constituted in part by certain rules relating to crimes, punishments, etc., and these constitutive rules can be generated by regulative rules: he tells us, for example, that

> the regulative 'Thou shalt not kill' generates the appropriate constitutive 'Killing under certain circumstances, counts as murder, and murder counts as a crime punishable by death or imprisonment.' (*Ibid.*, p. 50)

On this view, then, regulative rules appear to be logically prior to constitutive rules. But we might say that if there is one rule type which is ultimately more fundamental or logically prior, it *must* be those of a constitutive kind; what I have in mind here, however, is not the kind of formal, explicit, institutional rules that Searle means when he refers to constitutive rules. The point is that for any formal rule to work, we must have some fundamental understanding of how the world works; we must have certain Background capacities. In order to apply any regulative rule, whether it be 'Thou shalt not kill' or 'Vehicles must stop at red lights', we must have some understanding of what it is that constitutes 'kill', 'vehicle', 'red', and so on. This is not simply to say that we need to be equipped with definitions but rather that we require an appropriate understanding of what it is that constitutes these things, and this is a function of the Background.

As Searle himself says, 'the Background structures consciousness' (*ibid.*, p. 133); it allows us to interpret and perceive things in particular ways: 'we are able to see things as certain sorts of things' (*ibid.*) – in other words, things *count as* certain things and certain features of the world come to matter to us. The interpretative and constitutive nature of human being is corroborated not only in Searle's account of Background but also, as we have seen, in the work of Heidegger, Wittgenstein and Abercrombie. Accordingly, rather than simply acknowledging Searle's point that the Background is 'causally sensitive' to formal constitutive rules, it would perhaps be more appropriate to say that the Background itself has a structure which is essentially constitutive. We might say our understanding of the world comes *as* rule-governed because the operating structure of the Background *is a constitutive structure*.

We can thus recognize that any kind of rule, in the formal explicit sense, is derivative of, and ultimately dependent for its operation upon, the innate constitutive structure of the Background. We do not learn to see a certain kind of paper as a five-pound note, as something of value, by studying some formal edict from the Bank of England – indeed, most people never have sight of the formal rules which Searle refers to as constitutive; we learn to see it in exactly the same way that we learn to see a certain kind of thing as a hammer, or a skilfully made artefact, or a competent performance. Indeed, we might note that without the innate constitutive structure of the Background, Searle's formal constitutive rules would not be constitutive at all – if it was possible for them to function without the constitutive structure of the Background they could only function as *regulative* rules. The exchange of certain pieces of paper in certain transactions would occur solely because that was what we had been instructed to do – the 'counts as' locution would become merely a prescription for us to treat certain things as if they were certain other things; we wouldn't actually *see* them as such. In fact, it is unlikely that this state of affairs could ever arise, because the constitutive Background is so fundamental that without it we would almost certainly be incapable of acting – even to regulative rules. We might say that this, at root, is what separates human beings from machines – for machines *can* act according to regulative rules without employing a constitutive Background, and it is this which ultimately precludes them from being deemed intelligent or conscious.

All this, of course, is of a piece with Heidegger's account of human being. For Heidegger (1962), Being-in-the-world *is* a 'constitutive state' (p. 78). The craftsman in his workshop inhabits a world which is constituted in relation to his ends and purposes: things are within reach or out of reach, serviceable or not, too heavy or just right. As Heidegger understood, to attempt to specify the world in terms of abstract, formal rules, as with theoretical propositions generally, requires an abstraction, a 'deficiency' (*ibid.*, p. 88) in our dealings with the ready-to-hand.

There are several important points to be extricated from all this. Certainly, we can recognize that the notion of 'rule-governed' indicated here is very different from the formal constitutive rules that Searle has in mind – the rules which are purposefully contrived in order to bring about some preconceived social or institutional end. Moreover, we can see that any attempt to articulate this Background structure and express it in precise formal terms is, as Polanyi in effect recognized, inherently problematical. So not only does much of the craftsman's understanding of what 'counts as' correct or appropriate within a particular context, not come from following any *formal* rule, but the constitutive rule he *is* following cannot be readily communicated in explicit terms. In the following passage Heidegger gives a profound insight into the nature of this difficulty.

> Every phenomenological proposition, though drawn from original sources, is subject to the possibility of concealment when it is communicated as an assertion. Transmitted in an empty and predisposed way of understanding it, it loses its roots in its native soil and becomes a free-floating naming. (Heidegger, 1992b, p. 87)

Yet however incomplete or indistinct our attempts to articulate this Background might be, we can nevertheless recognize its essentially constitutive structure. Whenever we try to communicate the nature of a skill or a capability the *form* our account takes is invariably that of a constitutive rule: we invariably strive to depict what it is that *counts as* correct, appropriate or suitable given a particular *context*. It is not insignificant, for example, that CBET's attempts to describe vocational practice consists of such things as performance criteria (X counts as Y) and range statements (in context C). We can also see that it is a structure which creates the possibility of activities, rather than merely regulating pre-existing ones. As Heidegger showed, the craftsman's capacity to use a tool is ultimately dependent upon his wider understanding of the world he inhabits and his interpretation of that world in a way which is appropriate to his wider purposes. This understanding opens up possibilities; it is what enables us, and creates the possibility of action.

Once we acknowledge the constitutive structure of the Background we can begin to see how it is possible for us to acknowledge our practices to be rule-governed without the problem of the infinite regress of rules which besets any account couched in terms of regulative rules. For there is no regress with constitutive rules – we just see what it is that *counts as* the 'correct' way to hold a tool, or what *counts as* an 'appropriate' way of walking – there the explanation comes to an end. Indeed, as we have seen, our use of regulative rules is only possible by virtue of their ultimately terminating in 'rules' of this form. Michael Polanyi communicates something of this while again emphasizing the essentially tacit nature of rules of this kind:

> we cannot go on having specific rules for the application of specific rules for the application of specific rules ad infinitum. At some point we must have 'rules' of application (if we can call them that) which we cannot specify, because we must simply dwell in them in a subsidiary way. They are part of our deepest commitments. But for this reason they are not specifiable. (Polanyi and Prosch, 1975, p. 61)

It is understandable that Polanyi is hesitant to speak of 'rules', because what we are concerned with here is far removed, not only from rules of a regulative or explanatory kind, but also from the sort of explicit and formal constitutive rules which Searle attends to. It would be entirely reasonable if we were to prefer, with Oakeshott, to reserve the term 'rule' for those which are explicitly and consciously applied, and refer to this constitutive Background as a kind of custom or habit – for this, *pace* Winch, is perhaps how we should best read Oakeshott. Yet it seems to me that this use of the term is warranted because, as Peter Winch would say, what we are concerned with is something which gives coherence to the idea of a right and a wrong way of doing something. Recalling Winch's point about the logical interdependence between following a rule and the idea of making a mistake, it is of particular consequence to retain the notion of 'rule' in connection with vocational capability where this interdependence is invariably at the forefront of concerns. Given this interdependence, and conceding – as our previous discussion has indicated we must – that in this sense at least, all meaningful behaviour is rule-governed, to relinquish the term 'rule' would be to leave the way open to those who mistakenly set out to delineate vocational practice as a system of regulative or explanatory rules. As Rawls indicates, the very idea of a practice evokes the notion of a rule, but he too alludes to the need to distinguish the substantive rules of practice from those of an explanatory or regulative kind:

> It is the mark of a practice that being taught how to engage in it involves being instructed in the rules which define it, and that appeal is made to those rules to correct the behaviour of those engaged in it. Those engaged in a practice recognise the rules as defining it. The rules cannot be taken as simply describing how those engaged in the practice in fact behave: it is not simply that they act as if they were obeying the rules. (Rawls, 1967, pp. 162–3)

Ultimately, it would seem that the idea of a rule is inseparable from any conception of practices, skills or capabilities. As Winch (1965) recognized, the notion of rules or principles and the notion of a meaningful action are profoundly interconnected, but as is clear in the following passage, Winch does not mean by this that 'meaningful behaviour is simply a putting into effect of pre-existing reflective principles' (p. 63); rather, the 'principles' or rules he has in mind are such as

> arise in the course of conduct and are only intelligible in relation to the conduct out of which they arise. But equally, the nature of the conduct out of which they arise can only be grasped as an embodiment of those principles. (Winch, 1965, p. 63)

Together, Rawls and Winch might here be seen to corroborate what we have discovered through our consideration of different rule types. Both acknowledge the essentially rule-governed nature of human practices. And while Rawls intimates that the nature of these rules is such that they should be

differentiated from the kinds of rules associated with 'describing' (explanatory) or 'obeying' (regulative), and thus we might say implicitly attests to the
constitutive structure of such rules, Winch, for his part, lends support to the
idea that the rules which relate most directly to human conduct are such as to
be distinguished from the kind of 'pre-existing reflective principles' which
Searle has in mind when referring to constitutive rules.

The difficulty with assimilating the notions of 'meaningful behaviour' and
'rule-governed' as we have attempted to do here, is that it generally leaves us,
as Anthony Giddens (1993) has been at pains to point out, in need of an
explanation as to, first, the origins of the rules in question, and second, how it
is that the rules come to have the quality of being *sanctioned* – in other words,
how it is that one individual's rule-governed behaviour might be said to be
somehow in accord with that of fellow practitioners – and regarded by them
as such. From our previous discussion it should be clear that what we are after
here is not simply a description of this correspondence couched in terms of
explanatory rules; rather, what we are interested in is what it is about the
rules *followed* by each practitioner that allows these regularities to occur.
While our account of the constitutive structure of the Background and the
interpretative nature of understanding goes some way towards answering the
first question, we remain in need of an answer to the second.

As Peter Winch recognized, rules of any kind unavoidably have a 'social
setting' (1965, p. 33), yet I am not at all convinced that Searle's notion of
collective intentionality is sufficient to explain how it comes about that in
adopting the role of, say, architect, engineer or teacher, an individual is
somehow able to adopt the same priorities and perceptions as his or her fellow
practitioners. The question facing us now is how is it possible for the
conception of rule-governed practice we have outlined here – particularly
given the essentially tacit nature of its rules – to be a *social* phenomenon. How
is it possible for the constitutive Backgrounds of individual members of an
occupational group to become collectively aligned so that there exists the
requisite degree of commonality in their perceptions, priorities and purposes?
By way of an answer to this we will shortly turn to examine the important
sense in which vocational capability might be said to be *socially constructed*. But
in employing this term a more immediate difficulty arises, for the notion of
'social construct' has already been appropriated in relation to certain claims
about vocational capability and it thus becomes necessary first to determine
what kind of claims these are and whether they add to our understanding of
how such capabilities come to be a social phenomenon.

A misappropriation of the term 'social construct'

Something of a caveat is required to be added to the suggestion that we should
think of vocational capability as being in some sense 'socially constructed'.

For it turns out that there are numerous claims in the literature to the effect that notions such as skill are 'social constructs', claims which differ markedly from the sort of position which will be developed here. So before we begin our discussion of social construction proper it will be useful for us to examine the general thrust of these claims if only to be clear about what is *not* being suggested here.

Ian Hacking (1999) has criticized the plethora of works which claim to be about 'social construction' – works with titles characteristically of the form *The Social Construction of X*, where X could be anything from 'The child viewer of television' to 'Zulu Nationalism' (see Hacking, 1999, p. 1). Hacking remonstrates that the majority of these works employ the notion of social construction merely as a device to attack the status quo. He notes that they invariably amount to an argument along the lines of:

> X need not have existed, or need not be at all as it is. X, or X as it is at present, is not determined by the nature of things; it is not inevitable. (*Ibid.*, p. 6)

These arguments often progress further to conclude that X should thus be changed or perhaps eliminated altogether. Now it is important to make a clear distinction between these kinds of argument and the constructivist position developed here, one which has thus far been based, in part, on Searle's account of how social reality is 'constructed'. Indeed, Hacking himself has elsewhere (1997) purposefully singled out Searle's (1995) work as an approach to be distinguished from so-called 'social constructionist' work of which he is critical. In much the same vein I want to differentiate the present argument from certain other ways in which skill has been said to be a 'social construct'.

Those who make claims to the effect that 'skill is a social construct' (Blackmore, 1992, p. 351) usually seek to draw attention to the way in which notions such as 'skill' are socially and historically 'constructed' to the advantage of particular sections of society (see, for example, Attewell, 1990). They argue that the concept is used to differentiate between different groups of workers and different kinds of work, determining hegemonic and discriminatory relations between male and female, white and non-white, and young and old (Jackson, 1991). The idea of skill as a 'social construct' has, for example, become part of a feminist polemic where it has come to be seen as an 'ideological category imposed upon certain types of work by virtue of the sex and power of the workers who perform it' (Phillips and Taylor, 1980). Blackmore (1992) has demonstrated how the 'language of skill' has been used by the state, employers and workers in a variety of complex ways in order to defend their own particular interests at critical points in time. In this way skill differentials – the relative value attached to skills and hence the status and remuneration they attract – are substantively linked to gender

rather than the actual content or demands of the work. Similarly, Cockburn
(1983) notes how male trade unionists may actively resist changes in the way
skills are defined or changes to the boundaries between skills in order to
protect not just their remunerative advantage but also their gendered
identity. On this view, then, the prevailing conceptions of skill are
inextricably bound to the social context in which skills are found: skills are
judged differently according to how they are acquired, who possesses them
and in which context they are used. Indeed, it has been suggested that the
association of men with skilled work and women with unskilled work can be so
strong that the mere identification of a particular job with women may
require it to be downgraded (Phillips and Taylor, 1980; Blackmore, 1992).

These, then, are the kind of arguments that tend to accompany the claim
that skill is a 'social construct'. What they all have in common is that they all
seek to undermine certain historically developed hegemonies by denying that
'the concept of skill' constitutes an objective criteria for job evaluation. Yet
somewhat curiously, according to this way of thinking, skill is not *just* a 'social
construct', for it is acknowledged that some estimation of what a skill consists
of might also derive from material differences between what people do, or it
might be linked to such things as the relative supply and demand of particular
skills, as, for example, when professionals restrict access to a profession thereby
making their own skills more valuable. It becomes clear, then, that in parts of
the literature the phrase 'social construction' when used in connection with
notions such as 'skill' has come to be employed as a euphemism for 'public
estimation', and this generally accompanies the view that such estimation is
somehow to be regarded as a significant part of what it is to be 'skilled'. It is a
view exemplified by Pat Ainley when he claims that:

> There is always a triangular definition of skill that comprises not only the
> person performing the task and the social estimation of the skill involved in
> it but also the task itself. (Ainley, 1993, p. 21)

Now much as we might share the concerns of those who seek to highlight
the social injustices incorporated in the de facto ordering of occupations in
society, and much as we would similarly denounce differentiation on the
grounds of race, gender, age, etc., nevertheless we need to be clear that the
idea of 'social estimation' is not something which will help us to arrive at a
'definition' of skill. While we can acknowledge that the attitudinal
inclinations of different social groups is of undoubted sociological interest,
there is little to be gained for our purposes by scrutinizing the vagaries of
public opinion or the interested claims of employers, trade unions, and the
like. The fact that a trade union, for example, might choose to categorize
certain practices as 'skilled' or 'semi-skilled' is of little or no consequence to
our present discussion. Our earlier rejection of ordinary language techniques
was made necessary precisely because an analysis of skill based upon

prevailing opinion was manifestly at odds with a conception based upon more substantive epistemological and ontological considerations. And it is surely *these* considerations which should be central to the educationalist's attempts to explicate notions such as skill. Indeed, a more robust epistemological and ontological account of vocational capability might be the most effective means of countering those who would seek to legitimate social injustices by spurious or disingenuous claims about skills and capabilities. Certainly, such inequalities are not challenged by invoking the orthodox conception of skill, or to put it more precisely, by not having *any* coherent account of vocational capability but simply reiterating the very same aphoristic commonplaces which can be seen often to support such inequities.[55]

Once we have dispensed with the idea that 'social construction' is synonymous with 'social estimation' we can begin to take more seriously the question of how it is possible for vocational capability to be in some important sense a social phenomenon – in other words, we can begin to consider what it is about the learning of skills or capabilities which locates them within the context of those practised by a wider community of practitioners. For reasons which will become clear it will be useful to begin our consideration of this question by looking at it from the perspective of a certain more fundamental theoretical issue.

Rule-governed behaviour and the problem of structure

We will recall that Peter Winch's argument about rule-governed behaviour was part of a critique directed against the idea that the social sciences can progress by the same methods as the natural sciences. Indeed, Winch's argument can be seen as part of a long-standing division in sociological theory between, on the one hand, the positivist approach, which emphasizes the causal effects of 'society' on an individual and his behaviour, and on the other, the phenomenological and interpretative approaches which highlight the reasons and motives an individual might have for acting the way he does. For those who adopt the first approach, even something as deeply personal as suicide is properly to be explained by the correlation of external causes to individual events.[56] In contrast, those who adopt the second approach would tend towards an account of the phenomenon at the level of subjective meaning and it is with this approach, of course, that Winch is to be identified and which to a large extent we have followed here.

But as Anthony Giddens (1993) has noted, neither approach is sufficient. While one posits a manifestly inadequate view of the agent as entirely inert in the face of external social and environmental forces, the other, though succeeding in representing the individual as a purposive actor, nevertheless fails to explain how this 'internal' phenomenon might be related to wider external considerations. To use Giddens' phrasing, we could say that while one is 'strong on structure, but weak on action' the other is 'strong on action, but weak on structure' (see Giddens, 1993, p. 4).

It is possible to draw parallels between this fundamental methodological division and certain features of our present discussion. We might say, for example, that according to one view – the view we rejected earlier – an occupation such as 'engineering' consists in a body of identifiable, regulative rules which constitute an external structural influence on the actions of individual practitioners; the resulting phenomenon being described – in true positivist fashion – in terms of explanatory rules relating to observed regularities. By the same token, it might be said that the view we have developed in opposition to this is one where the agent rather than the structure is foremost; where the agent is conceived of as acting for reasons and where, accordingly, any account of practice must take due account of the agent's own motives, priorities and purposes. Again, while the first view neglects the purposive nature of the agent, it could be said that the second – the position we have adopted here – has insufficient regard for external structural influences and thus lacks the means to locate the actions of the individual in relation to those of the wider community of practitioners. Seen thus, it might be said that the dichotomy of structure and agency is one which runs through our present discussion of vocational capability as rule-governed behaviour.

Now Anthony Giddens (1984) has argued that it is possible to resolve these dichotomous theoretical perspectives by rejecting the traditional dualism of structure and agency in favour of an account which has at its centre neither 'society' nor 'individual' but, rather, the idea of recurrent practices. This, in short, is the central feature of what Giddens calls his 'theory of structuration'.

> The basic domain of the study of the social sciences, according to the theory of structuration, is neither the experience of the individual actor, nor the existence of any form of societal totality, but social practices ordered across space and time. (Giddens, 1984, p. 2)

I want to suggest that Giddens' theory of structuration – expounded in a number of books, beginning with *New Rules of Sociological Method* (1993, first published 1976) and receiving perhaps its most thorough explication in *The Constitution of Society* (1984) – provides a possible solution to the problem of how we might more properly regard the actions of individual actors in relation to those of their fellow practitioners. What makes Giddens' approach particularly valuable is the way in which, by adopting a different conception of structure, he is able to bring the 'subjective' back into the picture without abandoning the idea of social structure. There is space here to give only the briefest account of Giddens' thesis, but it will be useful to consider some of its most important features – namely, the 'duality of structure', the idea of 'recurrent practices' and the conception of 'practical consciousness'.

In contrast to the idea of structure as something which is 'fixed' and which acts (in the Durkheimian sense) as an external constraint upon the actions of individual agents, Giddens argues that structures only exist and have effects insofar as they continue to be produced and reproduced through the practices of individuals; this is what Giddens refers to as the 'duality of structure'.

> As I shall employ it, 'structure' refers to 'structural property', or more exactly, to 'structuring property', structuring properties providing the 'binding' of time and space in social systems. I argue that these properties can be understood as rules and resources, recursively implicated in the reproduction of social systems. Structures exist paradigmatically, as an absent set of differences, temporally 'present' only in their instantiation, in the constituting moments of social systems. (Giddens, 1979, p. 64)

On Giddens's view, 'society' should more properly be thought of as the totality of the structures created by recurrent practices; the apparent 'objectivity' of social reality being, in effect, an unintended consequence of recurrent practices having structuring properties.[57]

As Giddens says,

> Human social activities, like some self-reproducing items in nature, are recursive. That is to say, they are not brought into being by social actors, but continually recreated by them via the very means whereby they express themselves *as* actors. In and through their activities agents reproduce the conditions that make these activities possible. (Original emphasis; Giddens, 1984, p. 2)

Language, for example, has a structure and it is one which can appear very fixed – we do not have to stray far from the conventions of normal speech for a listener to become confused or puzzled. But that structure only exists inasmuch as people continue to practise the conventions which constitute that structure. What is true of language here is true of any skill or capability; hence we might say that the structural qualities of vocational and professional practice derive not from any system of regulative rules, but are rather the unintended consequence of the recursive qualities of the practices themselves. This is something which is entirely in accord with Oakeshott's view that

> We acquire habits of conduct, not by constructing a way of living upon rules or precepts learned by heart and subsequently practised, but by living with people who habitually behave in a certain manner: we acquire habits of conduct in the same way as we acquire our native language. (Oakeshott, 1991, p. 468)

Similarly, according to Giddens,

> practices depend on the habits and forms of life which individuals adopt. Individuals don't just 'use' these in their activity but these life practices constitute what that activity is. (Giddens and Pierson, 1998, pp. 76–7)

Rule-governed behaviour, on this view then, should be thought of as something which is 'secured as a means and an outcome' (Giddens, 1979, p. 88) through recurrent practice. Structure thus exists not just as a constraint on social action but also as a *condition* of social action – hence its 'duality'. While, on the one hand, the notion of agency presumes constraint, on the other, constraint presumes agency. Put another way, while our being an agent is dependent upon our acting in accordance with certain conventions or traditions, the existence of those conventions or traditions is dependent upon our continuing, collectively, to act in that particular way. It is thus that the possibility of both change and constancy of practice are bound up together. We can now begin to see how this 'reciprocity of practices' (*ibid.*, p. 76) can thus give rise to an 'interdependence of action' (*ibid.*) between actors or between collectivities, in other words how the actions of the individual come to be related to those of the occupational group of which he or she is a member. Michael Oakeshott (1991) perhaps captures the essence of this more eloquently when he says that 'A tradition of behaviour is not a fixed and inflexible manner of doing things; it is a flow of sympathy' (p. 59).

Now in order to consolidate his theory of structuration Giddens finds it necessary to elaborate on the notion of the self, and there are two important elements of his account which have a particular resonance with the kind of position we have been developing here. First, Giddens (1984) notes that the recursiveness of practice involves us in a 'specifically reflexive form of knowledgeability' (p. 3) and by 'reflexivity' Giddens means not simply a form of self-consciousness but rather 'the continuous monitoring of action which human beings display and expect others to display' (*ibid.*). We might recall our earlier point about the craftsman continually monitoring each of his moves, all the while determining whether his actions are 'appropriate', 'correct', 'suitable', etc. It is also worth remembering at this juncture how Donald Schön (1996) famously places 'reflection in action' at the centre of his account of professional expertise. Indeed, according to Giddens, part of what it is to be a human being is precisely to be involved in a continual assessment of one's actions in relation to those of others.

We might note that this aspect of reflexivity is also strikingly reminiscent of Heidegger's references to *das Man* (the They) and the notion of *Abständigkeit* (distantiality) (see Heidegger, 1962, pp. 164–5) – although Heidegger sees his task as one of drawing attention to the negative, almost destructive aspects of the phenomenon. According to Heidegger, Dasein always has 'the They' in view, constantly comparing itself with them, trying to achieve their level or perhaps better it – never to do *too* much better or worse but rather to maintain a comfortable distantiality from *das Man*, a level of 'averageness', the consequence of which is a ' "levelling down" (*Einebnung*) of all possibilities of Being' (*ibid.* p. 165). It is thus that we invariably tend to do what *one* does; we perform a task as *one* would normally carry out that task, we adopt the form of behaviour which *one* would normally adopt in the circumstances. Moreover, just as Abercrombie demonstrates that the processes of perception, being profoundly dependent upon certain predispositions or schemata, can be influenced by others, Heidegger too suggests that 'the They' can influence perception through the use of language:

> It is not so much that we see the objects and things but rather that we first talk about them. To put it more precisely: we do not say what we see, but rather the reverse, we see what *one says* about the matter. (Original emphasis; Heidegger, 1992b, p. 56)

It would thus seem that because of our capacity for reflexivity, 'the They' can even affect the way we see the world. We might say that through our involvements in recursive practices the Background which ultimately constitutes our experience itself, reflexively, becomes constituted.

Now it seems to me that this 'reflexive form of knowledgeability', this innate capacity to monitor not only our own actions but also those of others, is of crucial educational significance. Certainly, it would seem that this capacity, one which for Heidegger is a necessary part of Dasein's 'Being-with', is fundamental to our explanation of how it is possible for the acts of any one individual, acting in accordance with his or her own *constituted and constitutive* Background, to be related to the similarly rule-governed behaviour of fellow practitioners. In saying that the Background is both constituted and constitutive we are simply acknowledging what Giddens refers to as the duality of structure. What makes this hypothesis so plausible is the fact that there is such abundant evidence of our use of this form of knowledgeability, of the undeniable influence of 'the They' in all our activities. Yet even though we are clearly conscious of this influence it nevertheless remains tacit, something which though not uncon-scious, nevertheless seems to operate at a level of consciousness below the discursive. This brings us to the second aspect of Giddens' account of the self.

In place of the Freudian triad of ego, super-ego and id, Giddens posits the idea of three different levels of consciousness: discursive consciousness, practical consciousness, and unconscious motives/cognition (see Giddens, 1984, pp. 41–5 and *passim*). The notion of practical consciousness is of central importance in his account, both to the concept of agency and to the concept of structuration. According to Giddens, practical consciousness relates to the kind of knowledge or beliefs that people have about their actions yet cannot express discursively – but this is not because it is submerged (by means of repression) in the unconscious (see *ibid.*, p. 375). As Giddens puts it:

> The choice isn't between what people say about why they act as they do, on the one hand, and some kind of causal force that makes them act as they do, on the other. In between these there is the knowledgeable use of convention in practical consciousness ... (Giddens and Pierson, 1998, p. 84)

What is particularly important about the notion of practical consciousness, as distinct from discursive consciousness, is that it allows us to acknowledge that what people know is not limited to what they can *say* about what they know – something which, as we have seen, is a theme continually recurring in the work of Polanyi, Ryle, Schön and others. To all intents and purposes Giddens's notion of 'practical consciousness' is pretty much at one with the notion of Background as we have employed it here. It constitutes the most basic level of understanding of how the world works – how to 'go on', to use Wittgenstein's famous phrase. Practical consciousness can be seen to account for much of what the agent can be said to know, and yet as Giddens says, it is almost entirely neglected by those who adopt a positivist/objectivist point of view and who assume consciousness to be essentially discursive. But perhaps the most important thing here is that, given its essentially reflexive nature, it is practical consciousness that enables our skills and capabilities to be receptive to structural effects and thus ultimately grounded – irredeemably so – in a social context. If Giddens is correct, then social life is continually produced and reproduced by agents who bring practical consciousness to bear on the world. It is in this sense that we might say our skills and capabilities are 'socially constructed'.

It seems to me that Giddens' notion of structuration theory is broadly consistent with the conception of vocational capability that has been developed here. In our earlier discussion of Background, of schemata, and the kind of understanding indicated by Heidegger's conception of Being-in-the-world, we saw how, in order to become vocationally capable, we must learn to perceive, experience, in effect learn to *be* in a particular 'world' – a world of interconnected meanings inextricably related to certain priorities and purposes. Importantly, such learning takes place not in isolation but in the midst of those who have already learned to experience and cope in this world. The recursive nature of practice gives rise to certain structural effects which impact on the agent by virtue of being a member of a community of practitioners and taking part in common practices. It is our innate capacity to apply a reflexive form of understanding both to our own behaviour and to that of others which enables us ultimately to come to share the priorities, perceptions and capabilities of our fellow practitioners. It is thus that the Background which constitutes our experience itself becomes constituted, for in the process of learning we come to adopt certain schemata – the Background or practical consciousness equips us to recognize things *as* certain things. Things come to matter to us in certain ways and we accordingly come to see features of this 'world' as 'correct', 'appropriate', etc. By virtue of this reflexively created, constituted and constitutive Background we learn to perceive right and wrong ways of doing things – it is predominantly in this sense that our actions are 'rule-governed', not because in acting we refer to some external, formally imposed rules but because our Background has already constituted the world for us in those terms.

Notes

55   Our previous discussion of the orthodox approach to the concept of skill highlighted the divisiveness of many of the analyses and alluded to several such instances, but to take just one example, employing the orthodox approach (I am thinking specifically of Ronald Barnett's 'axis' of 'formal knowledge and physical activity' considered earlier; see Barnett, 1994, p. 56), an occupation might be characterized as requiring skills of a 'physical' kind and thus be summarily deemed more suitable for men than women.

56   For example, Durkheim's classic text, *Suicide* (1963); see also Sainsbury (1955).

57   We might here recall the earlier reference to Berger and Luckmann (1991) concerning the way in which language can be seen to play an important role in the objectification of social reality.

9

The Trouble with Competence-Based
Education and Training

In our earlier consideration of competence-based education and training it
was concluded that the prevailing assumption that CBET is characterized by
'the concept of competence' is mistaken and that the approach is more
properly characterized by its use of statements. Having proposed an
alternative to the orthodox conception of vocational capability, a more
coherent account of what it is to be vocationally capable, we are now in a
position to return to reconsider CBET's methodological strategy in more
detail. It would seem that in the light of what has been discussed, there are a
number of fundamental difficulties with the competence approach which
cannot be remedied by piecemeal modification or by devising 'alternative
models' of competence. As discussed earlier, my intention is to show that
CBET is untenable even from a default position which approximates to
philosophical realism and a correspondence notion of truth, a position which
acknowledges the foundational status of empirical science – in other words,
from a position broadly consistent with the prevailing consensus in modern
Western societies. From this position I want to suggest that CBET, correctly
understood as a 'statement-based approach', can be seen to vacillate between
two erroneous assumptions relating to the semantic status of such statements
and the ontologies to which they are intended to correspond.

**1 The assumption that human capabilities are intrinsic, ontologi-
cally objective features of the world.**
Let us assume it to be non-problematical that objects, people and behaviour
have certain intrinsic features, an underlying physicochemical ontology which
can be described in terms of the brute facts of the natural sciences. However, we
have seen that to regard a person or a performance as competent, or to see an
object as skilfully made, is to add observer-relative features to this basic
ontology. Their existence qua competent performance or skilfully made object
is entirely dependent upon human agreement; in other words, they constitute a
reality which is *socially constructed*. The addition of these observer-relative
features does not add any new material objects to the world because the features
added are *ontologically subjective* (e.g. a performance is competent only insofar as

people regard it as such). Our sense of objectivity derives from such features being *epistemically objective* (i.e. it isn't just my opinion that it is competent).

As Searle (1995) says, 'it is tempting to think of *social objects* as independently existing entities on analogy with the objects studied by the natural sciences' (original emphasis; p.36). To assume that competence can be described by providing an empiricist account of objects and/or behaviour is precisely to make the mistake of thinking that competence is an intrinsic, ontologically objective feature of the world. We have seen that the rules which might be used to describe the regularities of these ontologically objective features of the world, i.e. *explanatory* rules, are not the rules used in the performance of a skill, i.e. those rules which are *constitutive* of that performance. The essential difficulty is that when the competence strategist sets about describing 'competence' with a precision 'approaching that of a science' his or her account inevitably slides into descriptions of objects and behaviours. When this account remains impracticably equivocal the assumed cause is insufficient empirical detail – hence CBET's inherent reductionistic tendency, producing ever more cumbersome inventories of empirical minutiae in the vain hope of providing a less indeterminate account.

In *One Dimensional Man*, Herbert Marcuse (1964) notes how the 'total empiricism in the treatment of concepts' (p. 12) which gives rise to behaviourism in the social sciences has its equivalent in the physical sciences in the shape of 'operationalism'. He cites the following passage from P. W. Bridgman as an example of this 'one-dimensional' way of thinking.

> We evidently know what we mean by length if we can tell what the length of any and every object is, and for the physicist nothing more is required. To find the length of an object, we have to perform certain physical operations. The concept of length is therefore fixed when the operations by which length is measured are fixed: that is, the concept of length involves as much and nothing more than the set of operations by which length is determined. In general, we mean by any concept nothing more than a set of operations; *the concept is synonymous with the corresponding set of operations.* (Original emphasis; Bridgman, 1928, p. 5; cited in Marcuse, 1964, p. 13)

Using the same legislative tone as the linguistic analysts Bridgman (1928) goes on to insist that we should 'no longer permit ourselves to use as tools in our thinking concepts of which we cannot give an adequate account in terms of operations'. As Marcuse (1964) says, by this means the operationalist is able to be rid of 'troublesome concepts' – he or she effectively defines them out of existence. And Marcuse could almost be referring to the competence approach when he says of this way of thinking that it 'serves to coordinate ideas and goals with those extracted by the prevailing system, to enclose them in the system, and to repel those which are irreconcilable with the system' (*ibid.*, pp. 13–14).

In Heideggerian terms we might characterize the competence strategist as mistakenly seeking to represent human capabilities as if they were present-at-hand entities. As Richard Polt points out, this tendency towards a 'metaphysics of presence' has pernicious consequences:

> It dulls us to the depth of experience and restricts us to impoverished ways of thinking and acting. In particular, if we identify Being with presence, we can become obsessed with getting beings to present themselves to us perfectly and in a definitive way – with *re*presenting beings accurately and effectively. (Original emphasis; Polt, 1999, p. 5)

In short, Dasein errs because it regards itself as a thing, as *zuhanden* or more likely *vorhanden*; it tends towards an understanding of its own being in terms of the way it understands the world: 'the way the world is understood is ... reflected back ontologically upon the way in which Dasein itself gets interpreted' (Heidegger, 1962, pp. 36–7). For Heidegger these are inevitable features of the human predicament which ultimately lead us into an erroneous view of ourselves. Our absorption in things in the world leads us to think of Dasein as present-at-hand, a kind of machine or computer whose features can be 'objectively' and accurately represented.

The assumption that competence is something that can be regarded as ontologically objective inevitably causes a shift in the focus of any descriptive statement towards features that *are* ontologically objective, i.e. objects and behaviours. This shift in attention away from the person to more concrete ontologies is antithetical to true educational concerns since the focus will be at some remove from and therefore preclude due consideration of the kinds of abilities which, as we have seen, are more substantively at issue. As we have seen, this 'ontological shift' is implicitly divisive since the degree of shift will vary between occupations in large part according to the extent to which any given occupation happens to lend itself to being described in terms of brute ontologies.

2 The assumption that it is possible for statements to unequivocally, accurately and sufficiently describe ontologically subjective/epistemologically objective features of the world.

Central to Searle's account of socially constructed reality is his conception of intentionality – the capacity of the mind to represent objects or states of affairs in the world. To form the judgement or have the belief that 'S competently performed task T' is to have an intentional state, and statements of outcome can be regarded as attempts to represent or communicate such intentional states. As we have already seen, however, such states are far more complex than might first appear. We have already noted that any intentional state only is the state that it is – 'given its position in a *Network* of other Intentional states and against a *Background* of practices and preintentional assumptions that are neither themselves Intentional states nor are they parts of the conditions of satisfaction of Intentional states' (original emphasis; Searle, 1983, p. 19). Thus in order for me to have the belief that 'S competently performed task T', that belief has to be embedded in a Network of other intentional states. We can only understand that belief within that context.

Now the competence strategist may respond 'very well, we will provide a fuller account by listing these other states'. However, on Searle's view there are a number of reasons why we would find the task impossible.

> First, because much, perhaps most, of the Network is submerged in the unconscious and we don't quite know how to dredge it up. Second, because the states in the Network do not individuate; we don't know, for example, how to count beliefs. But third, if we actually tried to carry out the task we would soon find ourselves formulating a set of propositions which would look fishy if we added them to our list of beliefs in the Network; 'fishy' because they are in a sense too fundamental to qualify as *beliefs*, even as unconscious beliefs. (Original emphasis; *ibid.*, p. 142)

So my intentional state that 'S competently performed task T' only is the state that it is against a Background of non-intentional, non-representational abilities, dispositions, tendencies or forms of 'know-how'. It is particularly appropriate here to recall the important role that the Background plays in enabling linguistic interpretation to take place. If, as Searle says, we consider the sentences 'Sally cut the cake', 'Bill cut the grass' and 'The tailor cut the cloth', we note that while there is no lexical ambiguity in the use of the word 'cut', nevertheless, in each case the verb will determine different conditions of satisfaction. We understand the verb differently in each case even though its literal meaning is constant. If, on being asked to cut the cake, someone attempted to cut it with a lawnmower we would not regard him or her as having done what was asked. But nothing in the semantic content of the sentence indicates the interpretation we should make; there is, as Searle says, 'a *radical* underdetermination' (original emphasis; 1995, p. 131) of what is actually said by the literal meaning of the sentence. Our understanding of it is crucially and inescapably dependent upon our Background abilities relating to what it is to cut cake as opposed to grass or cloth. It could be said that much the same point is made by Heidegger when he says that:

> Any assertion requires a fore-having of whatever has been disclosed ... When an assertion is made, some fore-conception is always implied; but it remains for the most part inconspicuous, because the language already hides in itself a developed way of conceiving. (Heidegger, 1962, p. 199)

Similarly, Bar-Hillel notes that our being able to understand a sentence such as 'The box was in the pen' (intended in the sense of a child finding a toy box in the playpen) is fundamentally dependent upon our knowledge that the relative sizes of pens, in the sense of writing implements, toy boxes, and pens, in the sense of playpens, are such that when someone writes under ordinary circumstances and in something like the given context, 'The box was in the pen' he almost certainly refers to a playpen and most certainly not to a writing pen. (Bar-Hillel, 1964; cited in Dreyfus, 1992, p. 215)

The point here, as Bar-Hillel says, is that 'The number of facts we human beings know is, in a certain very pregnant sense, infinite.' (*ibid.*) This is why, as both Bar-Hillel and Hubert Dreyfus have argued, it is impossible for a computer program to interpret language as a human does: it simply does not possess the Background capabilities that a human being does and is thus unable to be sensitive to these kinds of distinctions in language.

Of course, most of us can and do make sense of statements such as 'Sally cut the cake' because most of us possess, in common, the necessary Background abilities to do so. But many of the Background abilities required to understand statements relating to, say, medical practice, engineering or teaching are far from common. We have seen that the complex, interconnected and pervasive nature of such abilities has a profound educational significance, as do the processes through which, by immersion in the shared culture and collective practices of experts, such abilities are assimilated. But the most immediate consequence of Searle's thesis is that it categorically refutes the idea that it is possible, as the competence strategist assumes it is, for statements of outcome to contain semantically all that is necessary to describe competence.

What is clear is that the competence strategist radically underestimates the extent of the knowledge we bring to the act of interpretation. Even if competence statements were used to describe only the simplest of abilities, the sheer *extent* of knowledge necessary to fix a 'correct' interpretation, knowledge which is not and indeed cannot be contained semantically in the statement itself, is quite astonishing. Our understanding of a 'competence statement' intended to 'communicate' something as apparently straightforward as 'the ability to sit in a chair' would ultimately be dependent upon a vast array of knowledge. Hubert Dreyfus gives a vivid illustration of the scale and extent of what we are dealing with here:

Anyone in our culture understands such things as how to sit on kitchen chairs, swivel chairs, folding chairs; and in arm chairs, rocking chairs, deck chairs, barber's chairs, sedan chairs, dentist's chairs, basket chairs, reclining chairs, wheel chairs, sling chairs, and beanbag chairs – as well as how to get out of them again. This ability presupposes a repertoire of bodily skills which may well be indefinitely large, since there seems to be an indefinitely large variety of chairs and of successful (graceful, comfortable, secure, poised, etc.) ways to sit in them. Moreover, understanding chairs also includes social skills such as being able to sit appropriately (sedately, demurely, naturally, casually, sloppily, provocatively, etc.) at dinners, interviews, desk jobs, lectures, auditions, concerts (intimate enough for there to be chairs rather than seats), and in waiting rooms, living rooms, bedrooms, courts, libraries, and bars (of the sort sporting chairs, not stools). (Dreyfus, 1992, p. 37)

Yet even with this huge range of possibilities, with all their various permutations, we can still say that in each different instance of 'chair use' there is something which *counts as* the correct way of sitting in a chair that distinguishes it from certain other ways of sitting in chairs, and all of these different ways can be correct in different circumstances. Following from our earlier discussion we are now able to say that our reflexive understanding of recursive practices (i.e. of sitting in chairs) enables our Background capacities, our practical consciousness, our perceptual schemata, to become constituted in certain ways – ways which are unavoidably permeated with the priorities and purposes we have come to adopt in the process of assimilating each and every skill.[58] If anything, the extent to which our practices are value-laden is understated in Dreyfus's inventory of chair use. Even with something as simple as sitting in a chair the influence of 'the They' is pervasive: we sit in a chair as *one* does and in order to do this we have to be sensitive to an incredibly diverse range of equipment and scenarios; we have to adopt certain ways of seeing and understanding the world and certain things must come to matter to us – it is thus that we come to see things as correct or appropriate, etc.

The important thing here is that our judgement as to whether an instance of chair use is correct or appropriate is certainly not a matter of personal preference or opinion, but neither is it derived from a structure of regulative rules relating to how one should or shouldn't sit in chairs. Rather, the recursive nature of our practices creates structural effects which are produced and reproduced each time we take part in such practices – hence there *really is* something which counts as correct or appropriate for each particular context or circumstance, but crucially this is not something which can be contained semantically within a 'statement of competence'.

Of course, when faced with the complaint that his 'statement of competence' is vague or equivocal, the competence strategist falls back on his other assumption – that competent performances, skilfully made artefacts, etc. are ontologically objective features of the world – and thus proceeds to give an account couched in terms of the explanatory rules which describe the phenomenon. To be fanciful for a moment we can imagine that he might set about describing with great precision the kinds of chairs we might sit in, perhaps cataloguing their various shapes and dimensions. In order to describe the correct way of sitting he might amass certain empirical data which, after subjected to suitable statistical analysis, could provide a precise specification of the coordinates relating to the positioning of the human body in the chair. But what the competence strategist fails to recognize is that no matter how much detail is included in such an account it cannot represent what it is that *to us* counts as sitting correctly – in short, he fails to recognize the distinction between explanatory and constitutive rules. Gilbert Jessup's (1991) proclamation that competence statements 'must accurately state their intent' with a precision 'approaching that of a science' (p. 134) is a clear indication of the failure to recognize this distinction. Intuitively, the competence strategist might sometimes correctly adopt the *form* of a constitutive rule[59] but when this is seen to be equivocal, he mistakenly treats it as if it were an *explanatory* rule, i.e. one which *describes* ontologically objective features of objects or behaviours in the manner of the natural sciences – rather than the rule which is *constitutive* of the competent performance. But as both Polanyi and Oakeshott recognized, the rule which *describes* a performance is not the rule *used* in the performance. The rule we are interested in is the one the skilled performer uses to make appropriate judgements of identity – the rule which, in Peter Winch's (1965) words, will determine 'what is to count as "doing the same kind of thing" in relation to that kind of activity' (p. 87).

Of course, the constitutive rule – as an expression of what we have referred to as the 'constituted and constitutive Background' – cannot be articulated in the precise terms of explanatory rules. It is, as we have said, infinitely more difficult to express what it is for the cyclist that constitutes the correct 'feel' or what it is for him or her that constitutes the 'appropriate' positioning of the cycle, than it is to describe empirical data relating to the cyclist's performance. Winch can be seen to acknowledge this fundamental distinction when he notes that while some things can be determined by experimental means, others cannot. As he says, we can settle experimentally the question of how many degrees one would have to reduce the temperature of water by for it to freeze, but the question 'How many grains of wheat does one have to add together before one has a heap?' (*ibid.*, p. 73) cannot be answered by experimental means. We might say that what makes the second question different from the first is that the notion of a 'heap' is essentially a *constitutive* matter – it is a matter of what it is to us that *counts as* a heap. It is the difficulty, if not sheer impossibility, of expressing the constitutive rule which leads the competence strategist to resort to an account of explanatory rules. In this respect the approach adopted by the competence strategist may remind us of the story of the drunk who lost his keys in the dark but insisted on looking for them under the streetlight where he was able to see.[60]

Now that we have identified the two erroneous assumptions underlying the competence approach it is clear that one of the things that has tended to render CBET impervious to criticism is precisely its tendency to oscillate between these two mistaken assumptions, these two different ways of interpreting competence statements: offering at one moment an account which has the appropriate value-laden constitutive structure but which is unable to contain semantically what is required, and at the next resorting to empirical descriptions of objects or behaviours which allow for an inordinate amount of detail, but nevertheless fail to represent what it is that *for us* 'counts as' a competent performance. This shift in meaning between the constitutive (value-laden) and the explanatory (literal) might be seen as part of a more fundamental dynamism which, as Paul Standish (1991) has argued, is implicit in the use of competence statements. Drawing on the work of Roland Barthes, Standish argues that this dynamism is

> constituted by the elusive and shifting centre of meaning: as we focus on the literal, meaning shifts to the metalanguage, and vice-versa. Meaning shifts, Barthes suggests, like the gate of a turnstile. Its ambiguity is essential to its dynamism. As we 'press against' the literal sense, it gives way and the framework of value comes into view. As we press against these values, they give way as the literal meaning is restored. Like the drop of mercury in a puzzle, the meaning runs away from us when we think we may have contained it. (Standish, 1991, p. 178)

Standish demonstrates how by vacillating between these two levels of meaning – between the literal, common-sense level (articulated, we might say, in terms of explanatory rules) and that which operates at the level of metalanguage (constitutive and value-laden) – the competence strategist is effectively able to evade crucial questions about the extent and nature of the values implied by these statements:

> When we try to focus on either the literal meaning or the framework of value, the turnstile principle will come into play. As we are reassured of the coherence of the statements, the framework of value will gain its strength. As we try to confront this, we will feel impelled to concede the common sense credibility of the statements. (*Ibid.*, p. 180)

Again, if we were to take a Heideggerian perspective we might say that the entire CBET project is based upon a fundamental misunderstanding of how we interpret the world and statements about the world. For the competence strategist, interpretation is the means by which descriptive statements are made to fit the world: interpretation, it is assumed, comes to an end when we have succeeded in constructing a system of perfectly precise assertions which accurately represent the world. But this kind of absolutist project, as Heidegger showed all too well, is ill conceived and can succeed only in producing a petrifaction of concepts – something which, as we have seen, was a failing of the ordinary language philosophers.

> The life of actual language consists in multiplicity of meaning. To relegate the animated vigorous word to the immobility of a univocal, mechanically programmed sequence of signs would mean the death of language and the petrifaction and devastation of Dasein. (Heidegger, 1979, p. 144)

For Heidegger, our engagement with and understanding of the world cannot be reduced to a set of propositions because understanding is necessarily prior to our being able to formulate propositions. Moreover, any single object or instance of behaviour is inextricably entwined in involvements with other entities and other features of the world and this has to be understood by both speaker and listener – otherwise they could not make, hear, or understand assertions. So interpretation is of necessity an ongoing process whereby our fore-conceptions are continually modified in the light of what we learn. In this sense we might say that those who are responsible for defining a 'standard', those who presume to assess to that 'standard' and those who aspire to act to that 'standard', necessarily bring to the act of interpretation their own continuously modified fore-conceptions. We get an illustration of this in an experiment conducted by Abercrombie. She asked medical students to read a short paragraph on anatomy in which the terms 'average' and 'normal' were used. The students were then asked to write down what it was they understood these terms to mean.

> At the beginning of the discussions the students usually agreed that the meaning of the passage was clear, but they soon disagreed when they tried to define more precisely what they thought the author meant. They found that each was talking about what *he* meant by average and normal, and this was not the same as what the others meant. (Original emphasis; Abercrombie, 1989, p. 93)

The point here is that words, assertions and statements do not contain concrete meanings independent of the world which can then be assessed as to whether they correspond with the world; assertions, as Heidegger would say, are not a kind of 'free-floating' source of truth.

> Assertion is not a free-floating kind of behaviour which, in its own right, might be capable of disclosing entities in general in a primary way. (Heidegger, 1962, p. 199)

Moreover, we always stand to lose something in the act of asserting:

> Whenever a phenomenological concept is drawn from primordial sources, there is a possibility that it may degenerate if communicated in the form of an assertion. It gets understood in an empty way and is thus passed on, losing its indigenous character, and becoming a free-floating thesis. (*Ibid.*, pp. 60–1)

Indeed, competence statements might even be regarded as a form of what Heidegger calls 'chatter' (*Rede*), in other words the reiteration of statements that have become detached from the original context of ideas and perceptions in which they were first created. We can become addicted to chatter; we uproot statements from their original context and treat them as if they were semantically self-contained, free-floating judgements in their own right. As Michael Inwood (1997) puts it, chatter '"tranquillizes" us into thinking that matters are entirely settled and disinclines us to look further.' (p. 49). And this is precisely what we see with the use of competence statements; uprooted from whatever origins or context they might initially have had, they are repeated as jargon and passed around, as though their meaning was agreed upon and obvious.

But underlying this general disorientation about the role and status of such statements is a more fundamental ontological confusion, a confusion about *what* it is they are intended to describe: attempting at one moment to describe attributes, capabilities, capacities centred in the person, and in the next shifting the focus of the description to features ontologically at some remove from the person – to behaviours, objects, artefacts and the like. To say that statements describe 'outcomes' does nothing to avoid this ambiguity or the ontological shift in the focus of attention. Similarly, to speak of *learning* outcomes leaves unanswered the question of whether such statements are intended to describe what is learned, or merely the concomitant outward effects of what is learned.

The inference of competence

There are those who, obliged to acknowledge the distinction between knowledgeable states and the outward, contingent manifestations of those states, will adopt an approach which allows them to concede this distinction while retaining CBET's essential methodology, the use of statements. Conceding that it is problematic to describe or gather evidence of competence directly, the strategy adopted is purportedly one of *inferring* competence from evidence of the things that *can* be described. On this view, behaviour is seen as an 'outcome' from which competence is then inferred (see Wolf, 1989).[61]

> competence is inferred from performance, rather than being directly observed. While performance of tasks is directly observable, abilities or capabilities that underlie the performance are necessarily inferred. (Hager and Beckett, 1995, p. 3)

What makes this prima facie plausible is the fact that we obviously *do* make such inferences. Whenever we predicate the mental attributes of others we clearly base our judgements on the evidence available to us; we can only see how that person behaves and make inferences from that behaviour. This, as we saw earlier, is what makes Gilbert Ryle's argument compelling. The essential difficulty with it is that it leaves us incapable of explaining how, faced with instances of identical behaviour, we are able to differentiate those which result from skill from those which result from, say, luck or accident. Ryle's solution, as the following passage illustrates, was to introduce the notion of 'dispositions':

> a skill is not an act. It is therefore neither a witnessable nor an unwitnessable act. To recognise that a performance is an exercise of skill is indeed to appreciate it in the light of a factor which could not be separately recorded by a camera. But the reason why the skill exercised in a performance cannot be separately recorded by a camera is not that it is an occult or ghostly happening, but that it is not a happening at all. It is a disposition, or a complex of dispositions ... (Ryle, 1949, p. 33)

On Ryle's view, then, we are able to distinguish between the tripping and tumbling of a skilful clown and the 'visibly similar trippings and tumblings of a clumsy man' because the clown has a *disposition* to behave in a particular way. Significantly, this implies that our judging a performance to be skilful is dependent upon on our having a *sufficiency* of evidence, in other words accumulated evidence of repeat performances – a requirement usually made explicit in competence-based assessment procedures.

Yet this simply won't do, neither as an account of how we make such judgements, nor as a way of preventing the slide into behaviourism. The crucial point missed by Ryle is that it is not the clown's dispositions but, rather, the dispositions of his audience that are vital here. It is how the *spectator* is disposed to see the performance – the spectator's schemata, his background understanding – which determines whether the clown's skilfulness is recognized and differentiated from merely accidental or clumsy behaviour. It is the spectator who is predisposed by past experience of, say, the kind of things that happen in circus tents and the sort of appearance that clowns tend to have. And it is the spectator who is predisposed to interpret what he sees according to the context in which he perceives it: subconsciously picking up clues from the context of the performance, perhaps subtle nuances in the clown's behaviour before he began to fall about, the reactions of other performers, and of the other spectators, etc. Of course, the clown's dispositions are significant too: it is necessary that there is some correspondence between the clown's idea of what a clown is and does and that of the audience; and a good performer might also have an eye to the kind of contextual clues by which he might predispose his audience to respond in the way he wants. But the clown's dispositions are quite literally meaningless except within the wider context of the dispositions of those he seeks to entertain.

So, with due deference to Ryle, we can say that a skill *is* a witnessable act but it is not witnessable in any sense that would satisfy a positivist. A skill is not something that can be witnessed by an 'objective', detached observer but only by someone disposed to see the world in a particular way. If we adopt

Ryle's view of the agent as a disengaged, passive spectator – a direct corollary of his logical positivist leanings (see Rorty, 1980) – then behaviourist consequences inevitably follow. But we avoid such consequences if we reject this view in favour of the view of human agency that has been developed earlier here, whereby the agent is predisposed to perceive the world in terms of a background of constituted and constitutive understandings. Such an agent perceives an instance of behaviour not as a discrete, isolated phenomenon but as part of a wider scheme of things, something that has meaning by virtue of the understandings and processes of inference and judgement brought to the act of perception.

Now in light of this we can get a clearer idea of what is meant when it is said that competence can be 'inferred from performance'. For the competence strategist, competence is 'inferred' when there is sufficient evidence of someone being able to do X, Y and Z, where X, Y and Z are performances that have been identified and specified in advance. Put more precisely, someone who is able to do X, Y and Z is *assumed* to be competent. Accordingly, competence is *not* inferred but taken as equivalent to the ability to do X, Y and Z. The difficulty is that this leaves the competence strategist in exactly the same position as Ryle, unable to differentiate between instances in which identical behaviours result from very different capabilities.

The crucial point here is that it is one thing to say that competence must be inferred from the evidence; it is quite another to say that competence is equivalent to certain evidence presenting itself. To properly infer competence it is necessary to be able to draw on the fullest range of evidence rather than being restricted to pre-specified performance criteria. This point is brought home by what I have referred to elsewhere as the 'Right/Wrong Scenario'[62] in which it is imagined that someone being assessed is able to give the requisite answer or perform in exactly the way required but with every answer or performance adds something by way of extra information or additional behaviour that betrays some profound misunderstanding. Perhaps, on being asked the name of the current prime minister the person would reply 'Gordon Brown – leader of the Conservatives', or perhaps, on being required to make appropriate electrical connections to a motor starter, would perform the task perfectly but then do something inexplicably inappropriate, throwing doubt on whether the person really understood what he or she was doing. Importantly, whether the performance is deemed 'correct' or 'incorrect' in this kind of situation depends on what *kind* of assessment is being employed. On one view, the CBET view, the requisite criteria have been met and the performance merits a tick in the appropriate box. On the other hand, there is good reason to suspect that the person does not properly understand the matter at hand. The distinction hinges on whether the responses prompted by the test are regarded as *ends* in themselves, or as the *means* by which inferences are to be made. There is no middle ground here; either the performance is judged solely against predetermined criteria or the assessor is at liberty to make inferences from any evidence which presents itself. Instinctively, we will always adopt the latter approach whenever it is imperative to make the best estimation of a person's abilities or knowledge. Yet the competence approach commits us to the former. It might be thought that CBET could be rehabilitated by extending the range of criteria or making them more detailed. However, this would be to miss the point, which is that however many criteria are set it is still logically possible that the Right/Wrong Scenario could obtain.

None of this is to diminish the important role practical tests can play in the estimation of a person's occupational competence. It is simply to say that success in such tests should properly be regarded, along with all other relevant evidence, as the *means* to determining competence, rather than such success being regarded as *equivalent* to competence. The reason we instinctively base our judgements on the widest range of evidence is because it allows the best possible estimation of a person's competence, knowledge, thoughts, attitudes, etc. And it is not only educators who are required to infer person-centred attributes or states of mind from evidence in this way. In a criminal court, for example, the prosecution must show not merely that a defendant committed the criminal act (*actus reus*) but also that he had criminal intent, a guilty mind (*mens rea*); evidence that he left the premises of a shop without paying for goods is not sufficient for he may have done so by accident. It has to be shown beyond reasonable doubt that he *intended* to take the goods without paying for them. Of the two components of a crime one is represented by the facts of what happened, while the other must be *inferred* from the totality of evidence available. The *mens rea* is certainly not merely inferred from the *actus reus*. Of course, it would be impossible to specify in advance all the states of affairs which a court might admit as evidence that the defendant either did or did not intend to commit theft. Interestingly, some minor offences are prosecuted in the first instance on the basis of the *actus reus* only: parking tickets, for example, are issued regardless of the driver's reasons, intentions or legitimate excuses. But it is significant that even here there is nearly always the opportunity for appeal, the opportunity for the court to hear *all* relevant evidence and to make *inferences* from that evidence. It is a sobering thought that if criminal prosecutions proceeded in the manner of competence assessments the defendant's guilt would be decided solely on the basis of the *actus reus*.

But there is a more pertinent reason to compare the procedures employed in competence-based assessment with those employed in courts of law. The UK has a number of regulative requirements under health and safety law which make it a criminal offence for a person to do certain kinds of work unless it can be shown that he or she is competent by virtue of having sufficient technical knowledge and experience.[63] But the approach used by the courts to make judgements about competence stands in contradistinction to the methods employed by CBET. As we have seen, CBET is concerned solely with the fact of whether a person did or did not perform a given task. For the competence strategist, that is what competence *is*. In the courts, the question of worker competence most often arises in the event of a death or serious injury at work. If courts were to adopt CBET's approach, they would have no option but to conclude that the worker was not competent by virtue of that fact. The approach taken, however, is to assess competence *notwithstanding* the fact of someone's performance on a given occasion. The worker may have been, say, careless or absent-minded and thus failed to carry out the task correctly *despite* being competent. Similarly, evidence to the effect that the task had been performed successfully on previous occasions would be unlikely to satisfy the court as to someone's competence – particularly where the level of danger was substantial. Rather, the court's attention would be focused on what the person had received by way of training and experience, whether that person had been provided with all the information needed to do the job safely, and so on and so forth. CBET, of course, proudly proclaims its purposeful disregard of such 'inputs' – for CBET, competence is determined solely on the basis of performance evidence *regardless* of what someone may or may not have received by way of training, the length of time in the job, the extent of experience, etc. Clearly, the law recognizes something that the competence strategist fails to see: that the substantive extent of a person's competence may be very different from that indicated by any de facto performance, that competence cannot be presumed from the fact of such performances but must be inferred by making use of *all* available and relevant evidence. Indeed, this is precisely how we judge the attributes or abilities of persons in the course of our everyday lives. As we saw in our consideration of Abercrombie's notion of schemata, the processes of inference and judgement we use can be prone to error. The simple fact is, however, that these are the processes which allow us to make the best possible estimation of the attributes and capabilities of other people.

It might be said, then, that the bureaucratization of education and the demand for precise specifications compounds two mistakes that are of devastating consequence for the educational enterprise. The first is to deflect attention away from the learner and his or her capabilities towards ontologies at some remove from the person. The second is to preclude from the business of assessment the very processes of inference and judgement that are so vital for making the best estimation of a person's capabilities. To the extent that educators and assessors succeed in their efforts they do so in spite of rather than because of these arrangements. Their success serves to conceal what is perhaps the real catastrophe of so-called competence-based education and training: the sheer waste of effort and resources as educators struggle to compensate for the inadequacies of official arrangements by engaging in a tacit, parallel enterprise – all the while being compelled to contort and misrepresent their efforts in order to pay lip-service to official procedures.

Notes

58 There is ample evidence of the extent to which even these quite mundane practices can be seen to be inextricably bound up with the values and priorities we have. We might, for example, think of how we are able to deduce a great deal about a person's attitudes or dispositions by 'reading their body language' (e.g. the way they sit in a chair), and conversely, we know how to give the impression of having certain attitudes or dispositions by adopting certain behavioural traits. Moreover, it is well known that a person's dispositions can be modified by predetermining the nature of the practices open to him or her, as for instance when seating arrangements in the business meeting, interview or classroom are purposefully configured to achieve, or avoid, certain effects on attitude, self-esteem, relations of power, etc.

59 The competence strategists' use of performance criteria (X counts as Y) and range statements (in context C) might be said to follow the structure of constitutive rules.

60 I think it is Peter Winch who uses this analogy in a not dissimilar context.

61 Of course, the whole idea of 'inputs' and 'outputs' here is of questionable value. One problem in referring to a person's actions as an 'outcome' is that he or she might equally be regarded as an 'input' as, for example, when we make inferences about what a person is likely to be able to do *as a consequence* of having undergone certain experiences. As Hubert Dreyfus (1992) notes in a not too dissimilar context: 'The whole I/O model makes no sense here. There is no reason to suppose that the human world can be analysed into independent elements, and even if it could, one would not know whether to consider these elements the input or the output of the human mind.' (p. 266)

62 I develop the implications of the 'Right/Wrong Scenario' in more detail in a yet to be published paper 'Two Concepts of Assessment'.

63 For example, Regulation 16 of the Electricity at Work Regulations requires anyone carrying out electrical work to be 'competent to prevent danger and injury' (HSE, 1989, p. 34).

10

Rethinking Vocational and Professional Education

This study began by examining a number of inter-related assumptions concerning those 'concepts' most closely related to VET, i.e. skill and training, it being suggested that despite their prevalence in the literature, it was difficult to derive a convincing or coherent account of the vocational from this orthodoxy. We examined the ordinary language methodology upon which it was claimed analyses of these concepts were based and determined that this methodology consisted in large part of spurious linguistic reasoning which was unable to support the claims being made about these concepts. Since this conception of the vocational was conceived primarily in order to protect liberal education from vocationalizing tendencies this clearly has important implications for how we understand the relationship between the vocational and the liberal. But before considering how this relationship might be understood in light of the account of capability that has been developed here it is appropriate at this point to reassess the claims of the orthodoxy and consider some implications of this reassessment for vocational and professional education provision generally.

It will be remembered that according to the orthodoxy one feature that marks off concepts such as skill and training from the wider educational enterprise is the idea that these notions are always related to specific or definite ends; it is in this sense that the vocational is said to be characterized by a sort of confinement or narrowness of focus. Now in one fairly trivial sense this is certainly true. It is usually the case that the vocational curriculum is directed at some specific area such as nursing, construction or engineering. Yet this will not serve as a distinguishing feature of the vocational, for the academic, too, is characterized by just this kind of specialization, particularly at the higher levels. Perhaps it is the capacity to narrow the focus to specific curricula aims which distinguishes the vocational; within engineering, for example, we could narrow the focus down to electrical engineering, then maintenance of electrical machines, and so on down to something as specific as 'testing electrical generators'. But again, we can see that the same is true of any other curriculum. The school curriculum, for example, could be focused specifically upon the arts, literature, the plays of Shakespeare, and so on down to the lines of John of Gaunt in Act I of *King Richard the Second*. It would seem, then, that the claim that the vocational is characterized by a narrowness of focus cannot be a claim about the *curriculum*.

Rather, what seems to be being suggested is that vocational *learning* is something which can be specific in the sense that it is possible for it to be detached from any wider context without detriment to that learning – in other words, that it is possible for one specific element, as it were, to be assimilated in isolation. Indeed, precisely this assumption is central to competence and skills-based approaches. Thus Richard Pring concedes that the 'advantage of the concept of skill ... is that it is quite specific' (1995, p. 153). In other words, it suggests the existence of discrete capacities such as might be procured individually and in isolation from any wider programme of learning. On this reading, then, what seems to be suggested is that it is possible to learn specifically about 'testing electrical generators' in a way that one could not learn specifically 'the lines of John of Gaunt in Act I of *King Richard the Second*' because for the latter to be truly educational it must form part of a richer and wider understanding. It would seem that this is what is meant when it is said that the vocational is characterized by a 'narrowness of focus' – or at least it seems to be the only intelligible interpretation we can make of this claim.

Yet the idea that vocational capabilities can be assimilated in isolation from any wider understanding is one which is unequivocally refuted by the notion of vocational capability that has been developed here. We have seen that an understanding of even the simplest tool is inextricably related to some wider understanding of the 'world' in which the user wishes to operate and to that person's wider purposes and goals. Of course there *is* a sense in which it is possible to learn to do a task in isolation, just as it is possible to learn lines of Shakespeare by rote and with no real appreciation of their meaning. But just as there is a world of difference between being able to understand Shakespeare's text within a historical and cultural context and simply being able to parrot the lines, so too is there quite literally a world of difference between being able to operate within, as Heidegger would say, a 'totality of equipment' (1962, p. 97), within a world of engineering meanings, protocols and systems, and simply being able to execute a task with no understanding of its wider implications. To fail to grasp this difference is to risk a disservice to both kinds of student – it risks impoverishing the life of one and endangering the life of the other. To assume that it is possible for learning to occur in discrete fragments isolated from any wider context is as damaging to vocational education as it is to any other kind of education. As Peter Ashworth (1992) has rightly put it, any form of skill or knowledge is part of a person's 'lived world' and cannot be regarded as an 'isolated capacity' (p. 14).

Certainly, the account of vocational capability that has been developed here is such as to categorically refute the assumption that the vocational is characterized by a 'lack of cognitive implications' (Chambers, 1984, p. 24).

We have seen that to be vocationally capable is very much about developing the understandings, conceptions and even perceptions appropriate to the world in which one is to operate. Enough has already been said here to counter the orthodox claim that it is appropriate to associate training with behaviourist learning principles, and similarly we can emphatically refute the suggestion that a person's view of the world is not transformed by undergoing training or possessing skills. Our examination of vocational capability has revealed that VET is far from 'inert' in this or any other sense, for to be skilled, competent or capable is precisely to come to adopt certain purposes and priorities; things must come to *matter* in a particular way – even our facility to perceive that particular world, quite literally *see* things, is dependent upon our adopting a certain interested stance. It is thus that being involved in work activities, as R. F. Dearden recognized, 'modifies the worker in all sorts of ways; in his skills and sensitivities, in his knowledge and attitudes, and in his self-concept' (1991, p. 93).

Each and every one of these assumptions can be seen to underpin competence-based education and training in one way or another. But there is one assumption within the orthodoxy upon which the entire competence approach is built: the assumption that the vocational can be specified accurately and unequivocally in the form of statements, that it can be 'tied down to specifiable rules' (Peters, 1973, p. 16). This assumption is effectively the central tenet of CBET's methodology. As we have seen, however, it is an assumption which derives from a whole range of confusions – about the semantic viability of so-called competence statements, about the ontological status of human capabilities, and not least, about the kinds of rules that operate in relation to rule-governed behaviour. Suffice it to say that this assumption is comprehensively and conclusively repudiated by the account of vocational capability that has been developed here.

However, perhaps the most pervasive and persistent feature of the orthodoxy is the assumption that there is a meaningful epistemological distinction to be made between knowing how and knowing that. The use of this distinction to characterize and thus distance the vocational and the liberal was easily rebuffed by the skills/competence lobby. As Gilbert Jessup (1991) was quick to remonstrate, 'My head does not have two separate compartments to receive education and training' (p. 4). Yet the distinction persists widely in thinking about curriculum design and assessment, and is reproduced in the distinction made in CBET between 'performance' and 'knowledge and understanding'. Yet we have seen the mistake in taking this kind of distinction to denote two epistemologically distinct categories of knowledge, the distinction more properly being seen as indicating the evidential conditions of our claims about the knowledgeable states of others. One important consequence of coming to see the 'knowing how–knowing that' dichotomy thus is that it frees us of the compulsion to reduce all knowing to either one or the other of these manifestations. Not only can we come to see, with Ryle (1949), the folly of regarding the mind's 'defining property' as its 'capacity to attain knowledge of truths' (p. 26) and with Heidegger acknowledge the essential derivativeness of theory, but just as importantly, we can also come to recognize the folly of emphasizing practice at the expense of theory – the kind of 'crude empiricism' which, as Richard Smith (1987) says, 'stresses the importance of the learner getting out and learning in "the real world" (and where) Academic understanding is denigrated in comparison with "learning by doing"' (p. 37). When we come to see the dichotomy as indicative of the profound limitations placed upon our attempts to articulate what it is that is known, we begin to appreciate the crucial importance of both practice *and* theory – understood, not as forms of knowledge, but as forms of *provision*. If, as has been argued here, to become vocationally capable is about gaining certain understandings of how a particular world works, then it is clear that *theory* – the opportunity to *think* about that world and get the measure of its values and priorities – has an important part to play in learning even the most practical of skills.

Indeed, another benefit of escaping the constraints of this dichotomy – by which account learning is inevitably truncated, prematurely curtailed at the point where it becomes impracticable to specify any further facts, behaviours or objects – is that we begin to recognize the sheer *extent* of the learning that must take place. We begin to get a clearer understanding of what is required for occupations which may require conspicuously little by way of either physical deftness or propositional knowledge. The difficulty, however, given the profoundly tacit nature of the understandings at issue, is that we are inevitably at a loss to describe the kind of capacities upon which language itself ultimately is dependent upon.

Of course, this raises vital questions about curriculum design, for it might reasonably be asked how it is possible to say anything at all about what we aim to achieve if our substantive educational ends are inexpressible. Indeed, this is why the dichotomies of 'knowing how and knowing that' and 'theory and practice' will always be implicated in our attempts to delineate the educational enterprise - the former properly indicating the *consequent* conditions of knowledge and the latter denoting the *antecedent* conditions (Lum, 2007). The point here is that in our attempts to describe the understandings substantively at issue we have no option but to resort to descriptions of either the antecedent or consequent conditions of understanding – to put it crudely, either the inputs or the outputs of knowing.

To give an account in terms of the consequent conditions is, as we have seen, inevitably to underestimate the nature and extent of both the understandings required and the processes necessary to cultivate those understandings. The only remedy, it would seem, is to centre our descriptions, instead, on the antecedent conditions of knowledge, on the educational processes and interventions most likely to cultivate those understandings. Of course, the difficulty with a curriculum thus conceived is that it is at constant risk of losing sight of its intended ends and thus becoming encumbered with the merely autochthonous or irrelevant. The means of protecting against this eventuality centres on the use of *inference*: first, in inferring substantive educational ends (the understandings which are in themselves inexpressible) from the requisite *consequent* conditions; and second, in inferring the most feasible antecedent conditions, i.e. the educational processes and interventions most likely to cultivate those understandings (see Lum, 2003).[64]

To conceive of curriculum design thus has several broad implications. First, since the antecedent conditions of knowing can be articulated in the clearest of terms we can dismiss the often implicit assumption that tacit ends necessarily entail indeterminate means and the relinquishment of account-ability. Second, it indicates that the means employed to evaluate the efforts of educators must similarly be construed less in terms of the empirically verifiable and more in terms of inference-based judgement. Third, it shows that the process of realizing explicit curricular content from tacit ends cannot be simply one of deduction but must be grounded in the educator's own understandings of what it is to be capable. And since this is manifestly an *educational* task it is clear that the possession of a skill or a capability will most often be a necessary but not a sufficient qualification for determining how that skill or capability should be taught – something which, in the context of the present vogue for 'workplace learning', stands to be overlooked.

What is clear is that in ridding ourselves of the orthodoxy we are able to envisage a far richer conception of vocational and professional education than that which currently predominates. But also clear is the fact that in rejecting these assumptions important questions arise about the relationship between a vocational education and a liberal or academic education. It is to these questions that we now turn.

Rethinking the vocational–academic divide

It might be thought that in rejecting the orthodox conceptions of skill and training – the very concepts explicated by philosophers with the sole purpose of distancing the liberal and academic education from vocational ends – we have abandoned the sole defence against vocationalizing tendencies within general and higher education. Certainly we have refuted the claim that there is an epistemological or cognitive distinction to be made between the vocational and the academic. However, as we shall see, it turns out that the conception of vocational and professional capability developed here provides a far more effective aegis against such tendencies than the orthodoxy ever did. The tactic of defending liberal education by portraying the vocational in epistemologically impoverished terms ultimately can be seen to have backfired on liberal philosophers of education due to the failure to substantiate the claim that the vocational and the liberal are characterized by two different kinds of knowledge. This claim was manifestly implausible and summarily dismissed by the competence/skills lobby. In the apparent absence of any coherent distinction between the vocational and the liberal, all that remained for the competence/skills lobby was to apply the very same epistemologically impoverished notions of skill and competence to the entire educational enterprise. It is ironic, then, that there is a sense in which the long-standing liberal denigration of vocational capability can be seen to have indirectly supported the spread of competence-based and skills-based approaches into general and higher education.[65]

While it is not the main purpose of this study to construct a defence of general or academic education against vocationalizing tendencies it would appear that the conception of vocational capability that has been developed here has important implications for how we conceive of the relationship between the vocational and the academic and in turn, for the sort of case that might be presented against the current trend towards a competence or skills-based curriculum in schools and universities.

It is well known that there is presently a certain kind of anxiety in higher education. Commentators such as Alasdair MacIntyre (1990) and Allan Bloom (1987) have famously drawn attention to the fact that modernity has left the educational enterprise without a clear sense of direction or a raison d'être; in short, it is claimed that the modern university possesses no coherent idea of what should be taught or how what is taught can be justified. Here is not the place to enter into this debate except to say that much seems to hang on what we are prepared to accept as 'justification' and that vocational education, or rather vocational 'ends', appears to constitute an important touchstone for what is to count as 'justified'. In a useful paper on this issue Susan Mendus makes the following observation:

> Of course, university departments which offer vocational or technological courses do justify themselves by reference to the national need for people pursuing those vocations or possessing those technological skills. But this defence is unavailable to pure science, to the humanities, or to the social sciences. (Mendus, 1992, p. 173)

This remark, made almost in passing, would find few dissenters. It is generally taken for granted that vocational education is undoubtedly justified by virtue of the ends to which it is related and that a defence of the non-vocational must therefore be achieved by stressing the value of *other* ends, for example culture, citizenship, and so on. Although I would certainly not wish to detract from the importance of ends of this kind, I think it is important to recognize that there is another kind of defence which can be employed against those who suggest that the non-vocational in higher education stands in need of justification.

The claim that priority should automatically be afforded to certain kinds of education because certain kinds of ends have been given priority is one which requires closer attention. The fact that it normally goes unchallenged probably arises from the fact that on one reading it has the appearance of a truism: 'it is desirable that people should be trained for certain occupations hence training people for those occupations is something that is desirable'. Certainly, if there is an acknowledged need in society for medical care then courses in medicine are going to provide for that need more adequately than courses in palaeontology. But closer scrutiny indicates that this claim may entail certain questionable assumptions. For even allowing that certain ends are justified by virtue of their being publicly sanctioned, to thus infer that vocational education is automatically and exclusively justified is to assume first, that vocational education is non-problematically related to those ends, and second, that non-vocational, liberal, general education is *not* related to those ends. Seen thus, the matter is no longer one of competing ends, but rather an educational question about precisely what kind of knowledge is required and how that knowledge is best assimilated. It seems to me that in the light of what has been said here about the nature of vocational capability there may be good reasons to cast doubt on both of these assumptions. Indeed, when we subject this issue to closer scrutiny we will see that much of what the liberal portrays as a crisis of 'justification' is essentially a problem of his or her own making.

Let us first of all consider the way in which vocational education is related to utilitarian or instrumental ends. It is only to be expected that such ends be foremost in the minds of those in industry and commerce – employers, managers, accountants, and so on. We should be neither surprised nor particularly concerned that their priorities are couched in terms of outputs, performances, artefacts, production figures or bottom lines on balance sheets. But what we need to be clear about is that an account made in these terms is not an *educational* account. Throughout this study we have seen the difficulties encountered when it is assumed that descriptions of things and behaviours are equivalent to a description of what it is to be skilled, capable or competent. The crucial thing is that there is a basic ontological distinction to be made between these ends and those human capabilities which, although causally related to such ends, cannot be sufficiently specified by them. The distinction is somewhat blurred by the fact that in our attempts to provide an account of those capabilities we will invariably make reference to those more concrete features of the world to which those capabilities are teleologically related. Nevertheless, the essential point here is that an account of the former is not equivalent to an account of the latter, and to miss this distinction is to fundamentally misunderstand the nature of the educational enterprise.

One manifestation of this misunderstanding is the widespread puzzlement that is often evident when questions arise about the precise nature of the capabilities required. For instance, Finn (1990) observes that employers are often 'extremely ambiguous' if not 'contradictory' or 'confused' (p. 48) about their VET needs, with one think-tank reporting that 'There are quite serious difficulties about interpreting what the needs of industry are' (Central Policy Review Staff, 1980, cited in Finn, 1990, p. 48). Clearly, this is not because industry is unable to articulate what it requires by way of 'outputs, performances, artefacts, production figures or bottom lines on balance sheets'; rather, it is because there is a basic difference between descriptions of these things and an account of the human capabilities which will enable such things to be attained.

Now it seems to me that our acknowledging this distinction has several important implications. Not least it points up what has been the central theme of this study: the inadequacy of the orthodox/CBET conception of vocational capability and the importance of having a philosophically more rigorous explanation of what it is to be vocationally skilled or capable. However, a further implication is that it seems to indicate that much of the clamour for vocational and economic relevance in general and higher education may be more correctly perceived as a failure to grasp this basic ontological distinction, and that what we generally characterize as 'vocationalism' might often be more properly thought of as an implicit or even unconscious demand for an account of the educational enterprise couched exclusively in terms of objectivist/positivist descriptions of objects, performances, behaviours, etc. In other words, wrapped up in 'vocationalist' demands for an educational enterprise which is 'relevant' are certain deep-seated assumptions about what *counts* as an appropriate description of that enterprise. For the vocationalist, a 'relevant' curriculum is one which is couched in the positivistic language of instrumental ends; he or she is not prepared to accept or even contemplate an account expressed in any other terms than the descriptions of objects and behaviours which constitute those ends. The vocationalist simply fails to see that descriptions of such ends do not equate to descriptions of those capabilities which will attain those ends and that it is with the latter, as educators, we are primarily concerned.

This kind of ontological myopia is problematic for two reasons. First, as we have seen, vocational provision is likely to be impoverished to the extent that its specification is conceived of in terms of the ontologically objective. This is precisely why the competence approach in being overtly based on descriptions of objects and behaviours 'cannot provide the necessary *educational* foundation' (original emphasis; Hyland, 1994, p. 84) for vocational capability. But what is more to the point here, the second consequence of failing to recognize the distinction between instrumental ends and the human capabilities necessary to attain those ends is that much of what *does* contribute to the formation of those capabilities and *is* of educational value will not be recognized as such. As Broudy (1962) has rightly observed, 'the vocationalist usually does not realise how much general education ... does contribute to employability' (p. 260). We might say that the vocationalist's failure to recognize the distinction between instrumental ends and the capabilities which will attain such ends leads to a radical underestimation of the role which general or 'non-vocational' education has in the development of vocational capability. It would seem that one consequence of our acknowledging the epistemological and ontological complexity of vocational capability is that it points to the important role of a general or liberal education in providing for such capabilities.

It seems to me that this has profound implications for how we might conceive the relationship between the vocational and the liberal. For what it seems to suggest is that the value of a liberal education may indeed consist, as the liberals intuitively recognized, in the fact of its detachment from instrumental ends – in its specifically *not* being predominantly constituted by reference to such ends. But what is being suggested here, in marked contrast to the liberal position, is that such detachment has an inherent value *even where ultimately we want to give priority to those ends*. We might say that the value of such detachment lies in the fact that it precludes our making the same kind of mistake and radically underestimating the extent of what is required. It enables us to attend more fully to the kind of Background capabilities that have been discussed at length in this study, and thus ultimately provide more effectively, albeit indirectly, for the instrumental ends. As Michael Oakeshott (1989) recognized, a liberal education provides the opportunity to 'disentangle oneself from the here and now of current happenings and engagements, to detach oneself from the urgencies of the local and the contemporary' (p. 39). It is in thus being released from concentrating on those contingent features of the world that we are able to attend more properly to the capabilities which ultimately enable us to deal with that world. This is not to suggest that this could ever replace a specifically vocational education; it is simply to say that this would seem to constitute an invaluable and essential component of what is required for a comprehensive vocational preparation.

Dewey (1966) can be seen to make much same point when he acknowledges that for any vocational activity to be conducive to learning it must be 'pursued under conditions where the realization of the activity rather than merely the external product is the aim' (p. 309). To focus education specifically on predetermined instrumental ends is to produce at best routine, 'machine-like' capabilities which succeed only in producing 'distaste, aversion and carelessness' (*ibid.*, p. 310). Dewey's insight is to recognize the importance of focusing the educational process on persons and their understandings – rather than on the concrete manifestations of these understandings – even when learning is through occupations and its content is specifically vocational. In other words, there is a sense in which we should detach ourselves from ultimate instrumental ends in order to best serve those ends. It is in this sense that a liberal education detached from instrumental ends can contribute to a comprehensive vocational preparation.

All this, of course, runs counter to the long-standing tradition running from Kant to Peters that certain forms of knowledge are of intrinsic rather than extrinsic worth.[66] Indeed, we have seen that the concept of a liberal education was purposefully and 'perversely' associated with a 'lack of utility' (Edel, 1985, p. 313) and with the 'theoretical rather than practical or useful' (Pring, 1995, p. 78). It is hardly surprising, therefore, that whenever the political and economic mood is such as to give overriding priority to the practical or useful, general/academic education appears to lose its raison d'être and finds itself without the means to resist 'the inroads of vocationalism' (*ibid.*, p. 194). For those who have convinced themselves of the lack of extrinsic worth or utility of such an education the only option is to reluctantly concede to 'closing the gap' (*ibid.*) between the liberal and the vocational, hoping that demands for the 'useful' can be placated while desperately hanging on to some last vestiges of a 'useless' liberal curriculum.

But there is neither theoretical nor historical substance to the claim that a liberal education is of no extrinsic worth or vocational relevance. To begin with, there are certainly grounds to refute Peters' 'intrinsic value' condition of education for, as Dearden (1986) reminds us, some types of education (e.g. consumer, medical, management) have 'further aims written all over them' (p. 78). But perhaps more to the point here is the important fact that 'education has *always* in practice had a vocational dimension, even when it pretended it had not' (original emphasis; Walsh, 1993, p. 105). As Broudy puts it:

> the liberal arts curriculum became firmly entrenched in our culture partly because it did have a vocational value. Latin, for example, was a vocational prerequisite for the statesman, the clergyman, and indeed, for all the learned professions in the Middle Ages. Because the lesser vocations did not at that time require formal presentation, we are too prone to argue that the training they now do require is 'merely' vocational. (Broudy, 1962, p. 261)

Dewey, too, recognized that historically 'education has been much more vocational in fact than in name' (1966, p. 311). It was not just schooling for the masses which had a vocational element; education for the upper classes was also, as Dewey says, 'to a considerable extent ... essentially vocational' (*ibid.*, p. 312). It provided a preparation for those who would be involved in government, or social or economic affairs. But it also constituted a preparation for the other 'callings' of the upper classes: the 'display, the adornment or the person, the kind of social companionship and entertainment which give prestige, and the spending of money' (*ibid.*). Similarly, the 'literary intellectuals' condemned by C. P. Snow were clearly equipped with capabilities which were eminently useful given the social and cultural context in which they were required to operate. Higher education can be seen to play an important role in providing for a vast range of capabilities and yet generally remains in a state of self-deception as to its own usefulness:

The literary training which indirectly fits for authorship, whether of books, newspaper editorials, or magazine articles, is especially subject to this superstition: many a teacher and author writes and argues in behalf of a cultural and humane education against the encroachments of a specialized practical education, without recognizing that his own education, which he calls liberal, has been mainly training for his own particular calling. He has simply got into the habit of regarding his own business as essentially cultural and of overlooking the cultural possibilities of other employments. (Dewey, 1966, p. 313)

In similar vein, Bernard Williams militated against what he called the 'leather blotter from Harrods' conception of the arts and humanities; that is, 'something to give people when no *useful* gift can be found, no more than a species of conspicuous wealth' (original emphasis; cited in Warnock, 1989, p. 34). As Welton (1916) rightly pointed out, to study literature with a view to earning a living from it is just as utilitarian as learning woodwork in order to become a carpenter. Indeed, 'it is precisely its *general and fundamental utility* that provides part of the justification of a liberal general education' (original emphasis; Bailey, 1984, p. 28). Even where it does not provide any pecuniary advantage there is, nevertheless, as Mary Warnock has remarked, a basic sense in which *any* education must have some utility:

All education, at whatever level, is in one sense utilitarian, in that it is undertaken not for its own sake here and now, but for the sake of the future. The *outcome* of education must be shown to be good, whatever its subject matter. So it is essential that we should abandon the common view that the sciences are useful, looking to the future, and the humanities useless, looking only to the past, or to the pleasures and enjoyment of the education-process itself. (Original emphasis; Warnock, 1989, p. 32)

All this is entirely consistent with Michael Oakeshott's (1973) suggestion that 'all we can be said to know constitutes a manifold of different "abilities", different amounts of knowledge being represented in different degrees of ability ...' (p. 163). But the crucially important point to be derived from all this is that we should be prepared to reappraise the way in which the vocational is assumed to have a monopoly on knowledge which is 'useful' and thus 'justified'. As Mary Warnock herself says 'we should defend the humanities on a wider front, and thus extend still more widely the concept of the 'useful' in education' (1989, p. 35).

The idea that it is possible to assimilate knowledge without any extrinsic purpose is not only questionable in terms of its feasibility but also highly suspect in its logic. As A. N. Whitehead succinctly put it:

The insistence in the Platonic culture on disinterested intellectual appreciation is a psychological error. Action and our implication in the transition of events amid the inevitable bond of cause to effect are fundamental. An education which strives to divorce intellectual or aesthetic life from these fundamental facts carries with it the decadence of civilisation. (Whitehead, 1962, p. 73)

Once we are free of the assumption that a liberal education should or even could be entirely divorced from extrinsic ends we can begin to take seriously the idea that much of a liberal education *as traditionally conceived* contributes far more to vocational capability than is generally acknowledged. With T. M. Greene (1953) we can begin by recognizing the important sense in which a liberal or general education is a prerequisite to any vocational preparation, not just because it provides such things as 'literacy and numeracy skills', but because it provides what is necessary to become a person, or more precisely, a person able to make sense of the world. Not only does such an education foster a far richer personal life, but also the wherewithal to develop a profession or a vocation. Indeed, elsewhere Greene suggests that the liberal and the vocational

> should be conceived of neither as hostile rivals nor as mutually exclusive enterprises but, on the contrary, as two essential and complementary aspects of the total preparation of the individual for his total life. (Greene, 1955, p. 118)

Similarly, A. N. Whitehead has argued that

> The antithesis between a technical and a liberal education is fallacious. There can be no adequate technical education which is not liberal, and no liberal education which is not technical: that is, no education which does not impart both technique and intellectual vision. (Whitehead, 1962, p. 74)

Phenix (1958) suggested that there is a sense in which *whatever* contributes to our vocational effectiveness, however indirectly, might be regarded as vocational – hence in one sense *all* education is vocational to the extent that it enable us to become more completely human. And, as Dewey (1966) was at pains to point out, to the extent that a person develops in one single area of activity to the exclusion of others he is a 'less developed human being ... a kind of monstrosity' (p. 307). It is in this sense that a person's vocational involvement will be impoverished if it is not supported and enriched by his wider experience; since his capabilities are ultimately dependent upon the 'alertness and sympathy of his interests', an exclusive emphasis upon technique or method will tend to be 'at the expense of meaning' (*ibid.*, p. 308). Accordingly, Dewey tells us, it is not the business of education to foster this tendency, but rather to safeguard against it, so that the scientific inquirer shall not be merely the scientist, the teacher merely the pedagogue, the clergyman merely one who wears the cloth, and so on. (*Ibid.*)

Of course, this may be one good reason for protecting liberal education from the encroachment of vocational aims, but it is not the only one. We have seen how liberal philosophers have long been keen to characterize the vocational as 'inert', as being value-neutral, as having no impact on a person's general outlook or world view. Yet it turns out that in maintaining this deception they would seem to have missed the most vital justification for defending liberal education against vocational tendencies. We have seen that vocational capability is first and foremost about coming to make sense of a particular 'world', a sphere of meanings and involvements inextricably related to particular purposes, goals and priorities. To become vocationally capable we must come to adopt, in common with our fellow practitioners, a certain interested stance; in other words, certain things must come to *matter* to us. In short, the whole business of vocational education is shot through with values. The important question, however, is *whose interests* are served by those values. I would suggest that what distinguishes a vocational from a liberal education is primarily that a vocational education requires the learner to assimilate values which are directed at the interests of *others*: employers, customers, clients, patients, and so on. *Their* interests are served by virtue of certain things coming to matter to *him*. This is not to say it is their values he adopts, for the values he adopts will be those held in common by the community of his fellow practitioners. He will certainly have an interest in assimilating those values insofar as he is likely to profit from doing so, but this is not to say that those values are directed at *his* interests. Certainly, if he has a vocation rather than merely an occupation he will take the interests of others to heart, which is to say that their interests become important to him. But still they are not his interests; he merely has an interest in serving others' interests.

In contrast, with a liberal education it is the *learner's* interests that are directly served.[67] And to the extent that such values, once assimilated by the learner, come to be indistinguishable from his interests, then such values differ from their vocational counterparts by virtue of being an end in themselves rather than merely a means to an end. This, I would suggest, is the reason why a vocational education can never be a substitute for a liberal education; ultimately, the effect of such a substitution is to deprive the learner of an education which serves his interests.

Sometimes it is the indeterminate nature of the capabilities required which highlights the importance of a liberal or general education to vocational capability. As Husen (1974) suggests, given the difficulty of predicting what specific vocational attainments will be needed in future, it is general education which, paradoxically, might be thought of as 'the best kind of vocational training' (p. 201). Similarly, Argyris and Schön (1974) have argued that because the kinds of skills and capabilities required will change through time, it follows that 'the foundation for future professional competence seems to be the capacity to learn how to learn' (p. 157).

Yet caution is needed here on two counts. First, it would be a mistake to think that this somehow calls for some generic 'learn how to learn skill'; what has been said already should be sufficient to dismiss the feasibility of such a proposition. Second, it would be a mistake to infer from this that general education is of value only where the nature of vocational activities change – this would be to imply that for those whose tasks ostensibly remain static such an education is of negligible vocational worth. We would inevitably fall into the trap of distinguishing between occupations according to whether the nature of the work changes, and invariably the line would again be drawn between the professions – where the use of judgement is more explicit – and the crafts, where judgement tends to remain tacit (note how, above, Argyris and Schön refer specifically to *professional* competence). The important thing here is that we recognize that the capacity to respond to change is the very *essence* of what it is to be skilled, competent or capable; we might recall here how the craftsman, with every cut of the tool, is faced with changed circumstances which have to be assessed and a decision made. To be skilled or competent is precisely to have the capacity to make judgements, to interpret the world in particular ways and tailor our responses according to the circumstances in which we find ourselves – *this is what skill is*. Moreover, as Mary Warnock says,

> amid fashionable jargon of 'problem-solving', (it is easy) to forget that the form in which a problem is set could be otherwise. There might be different ways to describe phenomena, different responses to the familiar and the given. The past need *not* be a guide to the future; the immediate and the present is always capable of being reinterpreted. (Original emphasis; Warnock, 1989, p. 3)

Mathew Arnold (1868) similarly recognized the importance of a general education in ensuring that future workers have the 'aptitude for finding their way out of a difficulty by thought and reason' (p. xx). Seen thus, we can begin to see that a general education is not an 'optional extra', something to be added to our skills if we are required to be flexible in some way – rather, our being skilled or capable consists in no small part of *precisely* the kind of capacities which a liberal education can provide. Even the capacity for imagination can be as fundamental to our occupational involvements as our cultural ones.

> It is the possibility of envisaging a future different from either past or present that lies at the heart of the human imagination. And, without

imagination, we should neither be able to succeed as industrialists, nor understand our own environment, ecological, social or political. It must be the expansion of imagination which is the first demand of the universities. (Warnock, 1989, p. 3)

It should be clear then, that what is being suggested here is to be contrasted with the tendency to 'vocationalize' general education by applying competence or skills-based techniques aimed at precise, discrete, useful 'skills' described in terms of the ontologically objective. What may be obtained from a liberal/general education is not to be confused with some notion of core or generic 'skills' – supposedly 'transferable' across occupations and contexts, and which purport to 'enhance learner flexibility, adaptability and autonomy' (Employment Department, 1993, p. 9). Rather, what is at issue here are the kinds of complex understandings and capacities we have considered at length in this study, the kind of fundamental understandings which will allow us to make sense of the world at large, and eventually the more specific world of a particular vocational role. The claim that the competence/skills approach is non-problematically related to instrumental ends is, as we have seen, a deception which leads us inevitably to underestimate the extent and complexity of the capabilities required in order to attain such ends. Adler (1982) makes the important point that schooling which is *truly* vocational should provide the most basic capabilities which are common to *all* work. Certainly, the competence/skills approach falls short of what Dewey refers to as 'an education which acknowledges the full intellectual and social meaning of a vocation' (1996, p. 318).

In addition, we can see that what is proposed here is also in stark contrast to the position adopted by some liberal philosophers of education who, in order to distance education from instrumental ends, systematically mis-represent both the vocational *and* the liberal: attempting to persuade us of the epistemological and cognitive vacuity of the one, and the lack of utility of the other. It is a direct consequence of this that general and higher education find themselves in a crisis of justification. Of course, there are many other important ways in which they might be justified, but what I have suggested here is that once we have a more coherent conception of vocational capability and once we have dispelled the myth that a liberal or a 'non-vocational' higher education does not contribute to such capabilities, then much of the perceived problem of justification evaporates. John Stuart Mill captured the essence of the matter in the following passage:

men are men before they are lawyers and if you make them capable and sensible men, they will make themselves capable and sensible lawyers ... what professional men should carry away with them from University is not professional knowledge, but that which should direct the use of their professional knowledge, and bring the light of general culture to illuminate the technicalities of a special pursuit. (1867, inaugural address; cited in Pring, 1995, p. 184)

* * *

I have said that this study was driven by two preoccupations. First, by a conviction that prevailing accounts of vocational capability are inadequate and philosophically incoherent. Second, by a concern that these theoretical shortcomings have resulted in a failure to formulate a coherent critical response to the spread of competence and skills-based strategies throughout education. In offering an alternative theoretical conception I have tried to show how many of the prevailing theoretical assumptions about skill and training are to the detriment of both vocational education and the wider educational enterprise. In particular, our attention has been drawn to the serious inadequacies of competence or skills-based strategies in education, which through sheer philosophical artlessness stand to greatly impoverish education at all levels.

Moreover, we are now able to see why these assumptions have proved so intractable: for they are held in common both by those who remain intent on bolstering the social and cultural prejudices of our age, and by those whose anti-philosophic tendencies prevent them from comprehending the intensely complex nature of vocational capability. Indeed, if this study has one single overarching motif it is surely this: that questions about the nature of skill, competence and capability are first and foremost *philosophical* questions and to assume otherwise is inevitably to underestimate the metaphysical complexity of human action.

Notes

[64] Elsewhere (Lum, 2003), I have referred to this process as a 'double inferential leap' (p. 12), the term 'leap' being used to indicate the precarious nature of this process.

[65] Again, I should emphasize that it is certainly not being suggested that the competence/skills movement was at any time directly influenced by liberal theorizing. Rather, the influence was indirect by virtue of liberals being unable to respond effectively against those who echoed the very same misconceived assumptions about the vocational. The only defence open to the liberals was to continue to reiterate the manifestly untenable claim that the vocational and the liberal are characterized by two fundamentally different kinds of knowledge.

[66] On this point see Harris (1979).

[67] This is not to deny, of course, that such an education may serve other ends – for example social, cultural – *indirectly*.

References

Abercrombie, M. L. J. (1989) *The Anatomy of Judgement*. London: Free Association Books.

Adler, M. (1982) *The Paideia Proposal: An Educational Manifesto*. New York: Collier Books.

Aiken, H. D. (1966) 'Analytical philosophy and educational development', in G. Barnett (ed.) *Philosophy and Educational Development*. London: Harrap & Co.

Ainley, P. (1993) *Class and Skill: Changing Divisions of Knowledge*. London: Cassell.

Ainley, P. and Corney, M. (1990) *Training for the Future*. London: Cassell.

Akinpelu, J. A. (1981) *An Introduction to the Philosophy of Education*. London: Macmillan Press.

Argyris, C. and Schön, D. A. (1974) *Theory in Practice: Increasing Professional Effectiveness*. San Fransisco: Jossey-Bass.

Aristotle (1952) *The Politics* (ed. E. Barker). Oxford: Clarendon Press.

Aristotle (1975) *Ethica Nicomachea* (ed. D. Ross). London: Oxford University Press.

Arnold, M. (1868) *Schools and Universities on the Continent*. London: Macmillan.

Arnold, M. (1882) 'Literature and science', in R. H. Super (ed.) (1974) *The Complete Prose Works of Matthew Arnold*, vol. x. Ann Arbor: University of Michigan Press.

Ashby, E. (1958) *Technology and the Academics: An Essay on Technology and the Universities*. London: Macmillan.

Ashworth, P. (1990) 'Is "competence" good enough?', *NATFHE Journal*, 15, (6), 24–5.

Ashworth, P. (1992) 'Being competent and having "competencies"', *Journal of Further and Higher Education*, 16, (3), 8–17.

Ashworth, P. and Saxton, J. (1990) 'On competence', *Journal of Further and Higher Education*, 14, (2), 1–25.

Atkinson, R. F. (1972) 'Indoctrination and moral education', in I. A. Snook (ed.) *Concepts of Indoctrination: Philosophical Essays*. London: Routledge & Kegan Paul.

Attewell, P. (1990) 'What is skill?', *Work and Occupations*, 17, (4), 422–48.

Austin, J. L. (1962) *How to Do Things with Words*. London: Oxford University Press.

Austin, J. L. (1970) *Philosophical Papers*. London: Oxford University Press.

Bailey, C. (1984) *Beyond the Present and the Particular*. London: Routledge & Kegan Paul.

Bantock, G. H. (1963) *Education in an Industrial Society*. London: Faber and Faber.

Bar-Hillel, Y. (1960) 'The present status of automatic translation of language', in F. L. Alt (ed.) *Advances in Computers*. New York: Academic Press.

Barnett, R. (1994) *The Limits of Competence: Knowledge, Higher Education and Society*. Buckingham: Society for Research into Higher Education/Open University.

Barrow, R. (1981) *The Philosophy of Schooling*. Sussex: Harvester Press.

Bartram, D. (1990) 'An appraisal of the case for adaptive assessment of knowledge and understanding in the delivery of competence-based qualifications', in H. Black and A. Wolf (eds) *op. cit.*

Bereiter, C. (1972) 'Schools without education', *Harvard Educational Review*, 42, (3), 390–413.

Berger, P. and Luckmann, T. (1991) *The Social Construction of Reality*. London: Penguin.

Bernstein, R. J. (1983) *Beyond Objectivism and Relativism: Science, Hermeneutics and Praxis*. Philadelphia: University of Pennsylvania Press.

Bigge, M. L. (1982) *Educational Philosophies for Teachers*. Colombus, OH: Merrill Publishing.

Black, M. (1973) 'Rules and routines', in R. S. Peters (ed.) *The Concept of Education*. London: Routledge & Kegan Paul.

Blackmore, J. (1992) 'The gendering of skill and vocationalism in twentieth century Australian education', *Journal of Education Policy*, 7, (4), 351–77.

Blake, N., Smeyers, P., Smith, R. and Standish, P. (1998) *Thinking Again: Education after Postmodernism*. London: Bergin & Garvey.

Blake, N., Smith, R. and Standish, P. (1998) *The Universities We Need: Higher Education after Dearing*. London: Kogan Page.

Bleth, M. (1965) *Education as a Discipline: A Study of the Role of Models in Thinking*. Boston: Allyn & Bacon.

Bloom, A. (1987) *The Closing of the American Mind*. New York: Simon and Schuster.

Bridges, D. (1996) 'Competence-based education and training: progress or villainy?', *Journal of Philosophy of Education*, 30, (3), 361–76.

Bridges, D. (1997) 'Philosophy and educational research: a reconsideration of epistemological boundaries', *Cambridge Journal of Education*, 27, (2), 177–89.

Bridgman, P. W. (1928) *The Logic of Modern Physics*. New York: Macmillan.

Broudy, H. S. (1962) 'Implications of classical realism for philosophy of education', in H. W. Burns and C. J. Brauner (eds) *Philosophy of Education*. New York: Ronald Press.

Broudy, H.S., Smith, B.O. and Burnett, J. (1964) *Democracy and Excellence in American Secondary Education*. Chicago: Rand McNally.

Broudy, H. S. (1988) *The Uses of Schooling.* London: Routledge.

Brown, L. (1985) *Justice, Morality and Education: A New Focus in Ethics in Education.* London: Macmillan Press.

Bull, H. (1985) 'The use of behavioral objectives, a moral issue?', *Journal of Further and Higher Education,* 9, (3), 74–80.

Burke, J. (1989) 'The implementation of NVQs', in J. Burke (ed.) *op. cit.*

Burke, J. (ed.) (1995) *Outcomes, Learning and the Curriculum.* London: Falmer Press.

Campbell, M. (2000) *Learning Pays and Learning Works.* Sudbury: National Advisory Council for Education and Training Targets (NACETT).

Carr, D. (1993) 'Questions of competence', *British Journal of Educational Studies,* 31, (3), 253–71.

Cato, D. (1987) 'Getting clearer about 'Getting Clearer': R.S. Peters and second-order conceptual analysis', *Journal of Philosophy of Education,* 21, (1), 25–36.

Chambers, J. H. (1984) *The Achievement of Education.* New York: Harper & Row.

Cockburn, C. (1983) *Brothers: Male Dominance and Technological Change.* London: Pluto Press.

Collin, F. (1997) *Social Reality.* London: Routledge.

Collini, S. (1964) 'Introductory essay', in C. P. Snow (1964) *op. cit.*

Collins, M. (1991) *Adult Education as Vocation.* London: Routledge.

Copleston, F. (1956) *Contemporary Philosophy: Studies of Logical Positivism and Existentialism.* London: Burns and Oates.

Corfield, K. (1991) 'The education-industry mismatch', in G. Esland (ed.), *Education, Training and Employment.* Vol. 1. Wokingham: Addison-Wesley/Open University.

Cotgrove, S. F. (1958) *Technical Education and Social Change.* London: Allen & Unwin.

Damasio, A. R. (1996) *Descartes' Error: Emotion, Reason and the Human Brain.* London: Macmillan.

Daveney, T. F. (1973) 'Education – a moral concept', in G. Langford and D. J. O'Connor (eds) *New Essays in the Philosophy of Education.* London: Routledge & Kegan Paul.

Dawkins, R. (1999) *Unweaving the Rainbow.* London: Penguin Books.

Dearden, R. F. (1984) *Theory and Practice in Education.* London: Routledge and Kegan Paul.

Dearden, R. F. (1991) 'Education and training', in G. Esland (ed.), *Education, Training and Employment.* Vol. 2. Wokingham: Addison-Wesley/Open University.

Dearden, R. F. (1990) 'Education and training', in Esland (ed.) *op. cit.*

Debling, G. (1989) 'The Employment Department/Training Agency Standards Programme and NVQs: implications for education and training', in J. Burke (ed.) *op. cit.*

Descartes, R. (1890) *Discourse on Method* (trans. J. Veitch). Edinburgh and London: Blackwood and Sons.

Dewey, J. (1929) *Experience and Nature*. London: Open Court Publishing Company.

Dewey, J. (1966) *Democracy and Education*. New York: Free Press.

Dreyfus, H. L. (1992) *What Computers Still Can't Do: A Critique of Artificial Reason*. Cambridge, MA: MIT Press.

Dreyfus, H. L. and Dreyfus, S. E. (1986) *Mind over Machine: The Power of Human Intuition and Expertise in the Era of the Computer*. Oxford: Basil Blackwell.

Ducasse, C. J. (1958) 'What can philosophy contribute to educational theory?', in J. Park (ed.) *Selected Readings in the Philosophy of Education*. London: Macmillan.

Durkheim, E. (1963) *Suicide: A Sociological Study*. London: Routledge.

Edel, A. (1973) 'Analytical philosophy of education at the crossroads', in J. F. Doyle (ed.) *Educational Judgements*. Henley: Routledge & Kegan Paul.

Edel, A. (1985) *Interpreting Education*. New Brunswick, NJ: Transaction Books.

Edwards, R. (1991) 'Winners and losers: the education and training of adults', in P. Raggatt and L. Unwin (eds) *Change and Intervention: Vocational Education and Training*. London: Falmer Press.

Employment Department (1993) *Development of Transferable Skills in Learners*, Research and Development Report No 18. Sheffield: Employment Department.

Enslin, P. (1985) 'Are Hirst and Peters liberal philosophers of education?', *Journal of Philosophy of Education*, 19, (2), 211–22.

Eraut, M. (1985) 'Knowledge creation and knowledge use in professional contexts', *Studies in Higher Education*, 10, (2), 117–33.

Eraut, M. (1989) 'Initial teacher training and the NVQ model', in J. Burke (ed.) *op. cit.*

Eraut, M. (1994) *Developing Professional Knowledge and Competence*. London: Falmer Press.

Finn, D. (1990) 'The great debate on education: Youth Employment and the MSC', in G. Esland (ed.) *Education, Training and Employment*. Vol. 2. Wokingham: Addison-Wesley/Open University.

Fuller, T. (ed.) (1989) *The Voice of Liberal Learning: Michael Oakeshott on Education*. New Haven, CT: Yale University Press.

Gellner, E. (1959) *Words and Things*. London: Victor Gollancz.

Giddens, A. (1979) *Central Problems in Social Theory: Action, Structure and Contradiction in Social Analysis*. Basingstoke and London: Macmillan Press.

Giddens, A. (1984) *The Constitution of Society*. Cambridge: Polity Press.

Giddens, A. (1993) *New Rules of Sociological Method: A Positive Critique of Interpretative Sociologies*. Cambridge: Polity Press.

Giddens, A. and Pierson, C. (1998) *Conversations with Anthony Giddens: Making Sense of Modernity*. Cambridge: Polity Press.

Greene, M. (1973) *Teacher as Stranger*. Belmont, CA: Wadsworth Publishing.

Greene, T. M. (1953) *Liberal Education Reconsidered*. Cambridge, MA: Harvard University Press.

Greene, T. M. (1955) 'A liberal Christian idealist philosophy of education', in N. B. Henry (ed.) *Modern Philosophies and Education*. Chicago: National Society for the Study of Education/University of Chicago Press.

Gribble, J. (1969) *Introduction to Philosophy of Education*. Boston: Allyn & Bacon.

Guy, R. (1991) 'Serving the needs of industry', in P. Raggatt and L. Unwin (eds) *Change and Intervention: Vocational Education and Training*. London: Falmer Press.

Hacking, I. (1997) Review Symposium on John R Searle, The Construction of Social Reality, *History of the Human Sciences*, 10, (4), 83–92.

Hacking, I. (1999) *The Social Construction of What?* Cambridge, MA: Harvard University Press.

Hager, P. (1999) 'Know-How and Workplace Practical Judgement', paper presented at the conference of The Philosophy of Education Society of Great Britain, Oxford, April 1999.

Hager, P. and Beckett, D. (1995) 'Philosophical underpinnings of the integrated conception of competence', *Educational Philosophy and Theory*, 27, (1), 1–24.

Hall, H. (1993) 'Intentionality and world: division I of Being and Time', in C. Guignon (ed.) *The Cambridge Companion to Heidegger*. Cambridge: Cambridge University Press.

Halliday, J. (1990) *Markets, Managers and Theory in Education*. London: Falmer Press.

Halliday, J. (1996) 'Empiricism in vocational education and training', *Educational Philosophy and Theory*, 28, (1), 40–56.

Hamm, C. M. (1989) *Philosophical Issues in Education: An Introduction*. London: Falmer Press.

Harris, K. (1979) *Education and Knowledge: The Structured Misrepresentation of Reality*. London: Routledge & Kegan Paul.

Harris, K. (1980) 'Philosophers of education: detached spectators or political practitioners?', *Educational Philosophy and Theory*, 12, (1), 19–35.

Hart, H. L. A. (1961) *The Concept of Law*. Oxford: Oxford University Press.

Hartland-Swann, J. (1956) 'The logical status of 'knowing that', *Analysis*, 16, (5), 111–115.

Harvey, D. (1990) *The Condition of Postmodernity*. Oxford: Blackwell.

Hayes, D. (1996) 'Wasted youth', in D. Hayes (ed.) *Debating Education: Issues for the New Millennium?* Canterbury: Department of Education, Canterbury Christ Church College.

Heidegger, M. (1962) *Being and Time*. Oxford: Basil Blackwell.

Heidegger, M. (1979) *Nietzsche, i. The Will to Power as Art*. New York: Harper & Row.

Heidegger, M. (1982) *The Basic Problems of Phenomenology*. Bloomington and Indianapolis: Indiana University Press.

Heidegger, M. (1992a) *The Metaphysical Foundations of Logic*. Bloomington and Indianapolis: Indiana University Press.

Heidegger, M. (1992b) *History of the Concept of Time*. Bloomington and Indianapolis: Indiana University Press.

Heidegger, M. (1993a) 'The origin of the work of art', in D. F. Krell (ed.) *Martin Heidegger: Basic Writings*. London: Routledge.

Heidegger, M. (1993b) 'What calls for thinking?', in D. F. Krell (ed.) *Martin Heidegger: Basic Writings*. London: Routledge.

Henderson, K. B. (1961) 'Uses of subject matter', in B. Smith and R. Ennis (eds) *Language and Concepts in Education*. Chicago: Rand McNally.

Hirst, P. H. and Peters, R. S. (1970) *The Logic of Education*. London: Routledge & Kegan Paul.

Hodkinson, P. (1991) 'NCVQ and the 16–19 curriculum', *British Journal of Education and Work*, 4, (3), 25–38.

Hodkinson, P. (1992) 'Alternative models of competence in vocational education and training', *Journal of Further and Higher Education*, 16, (2), 30–9.

HSE (1989) *Memorandum of Guidance on the Electricity at Work Regulations 1989*. London: HMSO.

Husen, T. (1974) *The Learning Society*. London: Methuen.

Huxley, T. H. (1880) *Science and Education: Essays*. London: Macmillan.

Hyland, T. (1990) 'Education, vocationalism and competence', *Forum*, 33, (1), 18–19.

Hyland, T. (1991a) 'Knowledge, performance and competence-based assessment', *Educa*, 118, 7.

Hyland, T. (1991b) 'Taking care of business: vocationalism, competence and the enterprise culture', *Educational Studies*, 17, (1), 77–87.

Hyland, T. (1991c) 'Vocational studies that won't work', *The Times Educational Supplement*, 20 September.

Hyland, T. (1992) 'Moral Vocationalism', *Journal of Moral Education*, 21, (2), 139–150.

Hyland, T. (1993a) 'Competence, knowledge and education', *Journal of Philosophy of Education*, 27, (1), 57–68.

Hyland, T. (1993b) 'Professional development and competence-based education', *Educational Studies*, 19, (1), 123–32.

Hyland, T. (1994) *Competence, Education and NVQs: Dissenting Perspectives*. London: Cassell.

Hyland, T. (1997) 'Reconsidering competence', *Journal of Philosophy of Education*, 31, (3), 491–503.

IEE (1997) *Requirements for Electrical Installations: IEE Wiring Regulations Sixteenth Edition* (BS 7671 AMD. 2). London: Institution of Electrical Engineers.

Inwood, M. (1997) *Heidegger*. Oxford: Oxford University Press.

Inwood, M. (1999) *A Heidegger Dictionary*. Oxford: Blackwell.

Jackson, N. (1991) *The Politics of Skill*. Geelong, Victoria: Deakin University Press.

Jarvis, V. and Prais, S. J. (1991) 'Two nations of shopkeepers: training for retailing in France and Britain', in G. Esland (ed.) *Education, Training and Employment.* Vol. 1. Wokingham: Addison-Wesley/Open University.

Jessup, G. (1991) *Outcomes: NVQs and the Emerging Model of Education and Training.* London: Falmer Press.

Jonathan, R. (1985) 'Education, philosophy of education and context', *Journal of Philosophy of Education,* 19 (1), 13–25.

Kleinig, J. (1982) *Philosophical Issues in Education.* London: Croom Helm.

Langford, G. (1973) 'The concept of education', in G. Langford and D. J. O'Connor (eds) *New Essays in the Philosophy of Education.* London: Routledge & Kegan Paul.

Lum, G. B. (2003) 'Towards a richer conception of vocational preparation', *Journal of Philosophy of Education,* 37, (1), 1–15.

Lum, G. B. (2007) 'The myth of the golden mean', in J. Drummond and P. Standish (eds) *The Philosophy of Nurse Education.* London: Palgrave Macmillan.

Lyons, W. (1980) *Gilbert Ryle: An Introduction to His Philosophy.* Sussex: Harvester Press.

MacIntyre, A. (1971) *Against the Self-Images of the Age: Essays on Ideology and Philosophy.* London: Duckworth.

MacIntyre, A. (1973) 'The idea of a social science', in A. Ryan (ed.) *The Philosophy of Social Explanation.* Oxford: Oxford University Press.

MacIntyre, A. (1981) *After Virtue.* London: Duckworth.

MacIntyre, A. (1990) *Three Rival Versions of Moral Enquiry.* London: Duckworth.

Maclure, S. (1991) *Missing Links: The Challenge to Further Education.* London: Policy Studies Institute.

Magee, B. (1973) *Modern British Philosophy.* St Albans: Paladin.

Magee, B. (1998) *Confessions of a Philosopher.* London: Phoenix.

Mansfield, B. (1990) 'Knowledge, evidence and assessment', in H. Black and A. Wolf (eds) *op. cit.*

Marcuse, H. (1964) *One Dimensional Man.* London: Routledge & Kegan Paul.

Marres, R. (1989) *In Defence of Mentalism: A Critical Review of the Philosophy of Mind.* Amsterdam: Rodopi.

Marshall, K. (1991) 'NVQs: an assessment of the "outcomes" approach to education and training', *Journal of Further and Higher Education,* 15, (3), 56–64.

Maskell, D. (1999) 'Education, education, education: or, What has Jane Austen to teach Tony Blunkett?', *Journal of Philosophy of Education,* 33, (2),157–74.

Mathews, D. (1995) 'Outcomes in management', in Burke, J. (ed.) *Outcomes, Learning and the Curriculum.* London: Falmer Press.

Matthews, M. (1980) *The Marxist Theory of Schooling.* Henley: Routledge & Kegan Paul.

McAleavey, G. and McAleer, J. (1991) 'Competency-based training', *British Journal of In-Service Education,* 17, (1), 19–23.

Mendus, S. (1992) 'All the king's horses and all the king's men', *Journal of Philosophy of Education*, 26, (2), 173–82.

Merleau-Ponty, M. (1962) *Phenomenology of Perception* (trans. C. Smith). London: Routledge.

Mill, J. S. (1876) *A System of Logic*. New York: Harper & Brothers.

Mitchell, L. (1989) 'The definition of standards and their assessment', in J. Burke (ed.) *op. cit.*

Moore, G. E. (1925) 'A defence of common sense', in J. H. Muirhead (ed.) *Contemporary British Philosophy*, vol. 2. London: Allen & Unwin.

Moran, D. (1991) 'The role of knowledge in competence-based measurement', *Educa*, 115, 8–9.

Moss, J. (1981) 'Limiting competency based education', *Studies in Curriculum Research*, 19, (1), 14–18.

Mundle, C. W. K. (1979) *A Critique of Linguistic Philosophy*. London: Glover & Blair.

Nagel, T. (1986) *The View from Nowhere*. Oxford: Oxford University Press.

NCVQ (1991) *Criteria for National Vocational Qualifications*. London: National Council for Vocational Qualifications.

Norman, G. R. (1985) 'Defining competence: a methodological review', in V. U. Neufeld and G. R. Norman (eds) *Assessing Clinical Competence*. New York: Stringer.

Norris, N. (1991) 'The trouble with competence', *Cambridge Journal of Education*, 21, (3), 331–41.

Oakeshott, M. (1973) 'Learning and teaching', in R. S. Peters (ed.) *The Concept of Education*. London: Routledge & Kegan Paul.

Oakeshott, M. (1989) 'A place of learning', in T. Fuller (ed.) *op. cit.*

Oakeshott, M. (1991) *Rationalism in Politics and Other Essays*. Indianapolis: Liberty Press.

O'Leary, J. (1999) 'Let failing pupils learn a trade', *The Times*, 6 October.

O'Reilly, D. (1989) 'On being an educational fantasy engineer: incoherence, "the individual", and independent study', in S. W. Weil and I. McGill (eds) *Making Sense of Experiential Learning*. Milton Keynes: Society for Research into Higher Education/Open University Press.

O'Reilly, N. (1996) 'Skills myths', *Personnel Today*, 16 July, 23–6.

Passmore, J. (1988) *Recent Philosophers*. London: Duckworth.

Peters, R. S. (1964) *Education as Initiation*. London: University of London Institute of Education/Evans Brothers Ltd.

Peters, R. S. (1966) *Ethics and Education*. London: Allen & Unwin.

Peters, R. S. (1973) 'What is an educational process?', in R. S. Peters (ed.) *The Concept of Education*. London: Routledge & Kegan Paul.

Peters, R. S. (1977) *Education and the Education of Teachers*. London: Routledge & Kegan Paul.

Peters, R. S. (1980) *Authority, responsibility and education*. London: Allen & Unwin.

Phenix, P. H. (1958) *Philosophy of Education*. New York: Henry Holt & Co.

Phillips, A. and Taylor, B. (1980) 'Sex and skill: notes towards a feminist economics', *Feminist Review*, 6, 79–88.

Platts, M. (1979) *Ways of Meaning*. London: Routledge & Kegan Paul.

Polanyi, M. (1962) *Personal Knowledge: Towards a Post-Critical Philosophy*. London: Routledge and Kegan Paul.

Polanyi, M. (1983) *The Tacit Dimension*. Gloucester, MA: Peter Smith.

Polanyi, M. and Prosch, H. (1975) *Meaning*. Chicago and London: University of Chicago Press.

Polt, R. (1999) *Heidegger*. London: UCL Press.

Poole, J. (1999) 'Woodhead must go, says Blair', *Independent on Sunday*, 10 October.

Popper, K. (1959) *The Logic of Scientific Discovery*. London: Hutchinson.

Popper, K. (1978) *Conjectures and Refutations: The Growth of Scientific Knowledge*. London: Routledge and Kegan Paul.

Popper, K. and Eccles, J. C. (1986) *The Self and Its Brain*. London: Routledge.

Prauss, G. (1999) *Knowing and Doing in Heidegger's Being and Time* (trans. G. Steiner and J. S. Turner). New York: Humanity Books.

Pring, R. (1976) *Knowledge and Schooling*. London: Open Books.

Pring, R. (1995) *Closing the Gap*. London: Hodder and Stoughton.

Quine, W. V. (1960) *Word and Object*. New York and London: John Wiley & Sons.

Quine, W.V. (1969) 'Epistemology Naturalised', in W.V. Quine, *Ontological Relativity and Other Essays*. New York and London: Columbia University Press.

Quinton, A. (1973) *The Nature of Things*. London: Routledge & Kegan Paul.

Rawls, J. (1967) 'Two concepts of rules', in P. Foot (ed.) *Theories of Ethics*. Oxford: Oxford University Press.

Roderick, G. W. and Stephens, M. D. (1972) *Scientific and Technical Education in Nineteenth Century England*. Newton Abbot: David & Charles.

Roland, J. (1958) 'On "knowing how" and "knowing that"', *Philosophical Review*, 67, (3), 379–388.

Roland Martin, J. (1961) 'On the reduction of "knowing that" to "knowing how"', in B. O. Smith and R. H. Ennis (eds) *Language and Concepts in Education*. Chicago: Rand McNally.

Rorty, R. (1980) *Philosophy and the Mirror of Nature*. Oxford: Blackwell.

Rumelhart, D. E. (1980) 'Schemata: the building blocks of cognition', in R. Spiro, B. C. Bruce and W. F. Brewer (eds) *Theoretical Issues in Reading Comprehension*. Hillsdale, NJ: Lawrence Erlbaum.

Russell, B. (1967) *The Problems of Philosophy*. London: Allen & Unwin.

Ryle, G. (1949) *The Concept of Mind*. London: Hutchinson.

Ryle, G. (1971) 'Systematically misleading expressions', in *Collected Papers: Vol. 2. Collected Essays 1929–1968*. London: Hutchinson.

Ryle, G. (1972) 'Can virtue be taught?', in R. F. Dearden, P. H. Hirst and R. S. Peters (eds) *Education and Reason*. London: Routledge & Kegan Paul.

Sacks, O. (1986) *The Man Who Mistook His Wife for a Hat*. London: Picador.

Sainsbury, P. (1955) *Suicide in London*. London: Chapman & Hall.

Schofield, H. (1972) *The Philosophy of Education: An Introduction*. London: George Allen & Unwin.

Schön, D. (1987) *Educating the Reflective Practitioner: Towards a New Design for Teaching and Learning in the Professions*. San Francisco: Jossey-Bass.

Schön, D. (1996) *The Reflective Practitioner*. Aldershot: Ashgate Publishing.

Schopenhauer, A. (1969) *The World as Will and Representation*. New York: Dover.

Scruton, R. (1982) *From Descartes to Wittgenstein: A Short History of Modern Philosophy*. London: Routledge & Kegan Paul.

Scruton, R. (1997) *Modern Philosophy*. London: Arrow Books.

Searle, J. R. (1969) *Speech Acts*. London: Cambridge University Press.

Searle, J. R. (1983) *Intentionality: An Essay in the Philosophy of Mind*. Cambridge: Cambridge University Press.

Searle, J. R. (1995) *The Construction of Social Reality*. London: Penguin Press.

Silver, H. and Brennan, J. (1988) *A Liberal Vocationalism*. London: Methuen.

Smith, A. (1996) 'Do not hanker after the days of Plato and Aristotle', *The Times Educational Supplement*, FE Focus, 1, 1st November.

Smith, R. (1987) 'Learning from experience', *Journal of Philosophy of Education*, 21, (1), 37–46.

Smithers, A. (1993) *All Our Futures*. London: Channel 4.

Snow, C. P. (1956) 'The two cultures', *New Statesman*, 6 October.

Snow, C. P. (1960) 'The "two cultures" controversy: afterthoughts', *Encounter*, February, 64–8.

Snow, C. P. (1964) *The Two Cultures: A Second Look*. Cambridge: Cambridge University Press.

Standish, P. (1991) 'Educational discourse: meaning and mythology', *Journal of Philosophy of Education*, 25, (2), 171–82.

Standish, P. (1997) 'Heidegger and the technology of further education', *Journal of Philosophy of Education*, 31, (3), 439–59.

Straughan, R. and Wilson, J. (1987) *Philosophers on Education*. London: Macmillan.

Taylor, C. (1993) 'Engaged agency and background in Heidegger', in C. Guignon (ed.) *The Cambridge Companion to Heidegger*. Cambridge: Cambridge University Press.

Taylor, C. (1997) *Philosophical Arguments*. Cambridge, MA/London: Harvard University Press.

TES (1997) 'Wake-up call', *The Times Educational Supplement*, 20 June.

Tomlinson, P. (1996) *Understanding Mentoring*. Buckingham: Open University Press.

UDACE (1989) *Understanding Competence*. Leicester: Unit for the Development of Adult Continuing Education.

Vesey, G. (1973) 'Conditioning and learning', in R. S. Peters (ed.) *The Concept of Education*. London: Routledge & Kegan Paul.

Waismann, F. (1951) 'Verifiability', in A. G. N. Flew (ed.) *Logic and Language*, First Series. Oxford: Blackwell.

Walsh, P. (1963) *Education and Meaning: Philosophy in Practice*. London: Cassell.

Warnock, M. (1989) *Universities: Knowing Our Minds*. London: Chatto & Windus.

Weinstock, A. (1976) 'I blame the teachers', *The Times Educational Supplement*, 23 January.

Weldon, T. D. (1953) *The Vocabulary of Politics*. London: Penguin.

Welton, J. (1916) *What Do We Mean by Education?* London: Macmillan.

Whitehead, A. N. (1962) *The Aims of Education and Other Essays*. London: Ernest Benn.

Wickham, A. (1985) 'Gender divisions, training and the state', in R. Dale (ed.) *Education, Training and Employment: Towards a New Vocationalism?* Oxford: Pergamon Press/Open University.

Wiener, M. (1981) *English Culture and the Decline of the Industrial Spirit 1850–1980*. Cambridge: Cambridge University Press.

Wilkinson, R. H. (1970) 'The gentleman ideal and the maintenance of a political elite', in P. W. Musgrave (ed.) *Sociology, History and Education*. London: Methuen.

Williams, D. I. (1994) 'Is competence enough?' *Educational Child Psychology*, 11, (1), 6–8.

Wilson, J. (1972) *Philosophy and Educational Research*. Slough: National Foundation for Educational Research.

Wilson, J. (1979) *Preface to the Philosophy of Education*. London: Routledge & Kegan Paul.

Winch, P. (1965) *The Idea of a Social Science and Its Relation to Philosophy*. London: Routledge and Kegan Paul.

Wittgenstein, L. (1967) *Zettel*. Oxford: Basil Blackwell.

Wittgenstein, L. (1968) *Philosophical Investigations*. Oxford: Blackwell.

Wittgenstein, L. (1978) *Tractatus Logico-Philosophicus*. London: Routledge and Kegan Paul.

Wolf, A. (1989) 'Can competence and knowledge mix?', in J. Burke (ed.) *op. cit.*

Wood, R. and Power, C. (1987) 'Aspects of the competence-performance distinction: educational, psychological and measurement issues', *Journal of Curriculum Studies*, 19, 409–24.

Woods, R. G. and Barrow, R. (1975) *An Introduction to the Philosophy of Education*. London: Methuen.

Zimmerman, M. E. (1990) *Heidegger's Confrontation with Modernity*. Bloomington and Indianapolis: Indiana University Press.

Index